The Smartest Kid in the Bronx

World Selected Prose

Latin Heritage Foundation

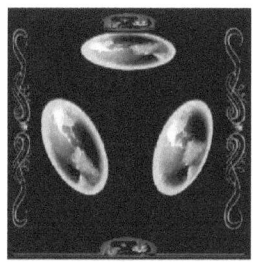

Latin Heritage Foundation

The Smartest Kid in the Bronx, World Selected Prose.

First edition.

Publisher: Gualdo Hidalgo.

Editor: Mariela M. Bonachea.

A Latin Heritage Foundation Edition.

Manufactured in United States of America.

For information, write:
ISBN: 978-0615558417

Latin Heritage Foundation.
8 Nunn Avenue, Washington, NJ 07882
United States of America
www.latinhf.com

Don Scheer
Boynton Beach, Florida, United States

DON SCHEER is a retired civil servant who has worked at American Embassies in Southeast Asia as well as the White House under President Jimmy Carter. He has a Master Degree in medical sociology from the University of North Carolina, Chapel Hill. Scholarly as a young man, he now longs to climb trees and always orders extra sprinkles on his ice cream. In 2010 Mr. Scheer earned an award from Twisted-Tails, a respected international short story publisher. This award is presented to authors who write a "thought-provoking or mind-grabbing ending. "In May of 2011 the Writer's

Network of South Florida presented Mr. Scheer with a first place award for his short play, "The Diagnosis." The play was created from his original short story featured in the late Tim Russert's anthology, Wisdom of Our Fathers, published by Random House. "The Diagnosis" received high praise on several major television news and talk shows.

One journalist's reaction:

"I guess maybe my favorite story in the book (Wisdom of Our Fathers) is "The Diagnosis." It makes you laugh out loud and cry out loud."

Another journalist concluded, "It's the small moments that make the big difference." This is the writing style that Mr. Scheer brings to the reader.

Mr. Scheer's ability to craft comic exchanges among his characters and employ engrossing plots that contain surprising tidbits underscores his skill as a fiction writer of note.

Other Awards: First Place for Prose in both 2006 and 2007 for the Sylvia Wolens Writing Competition.

The Smartest Kid in the Bronx
By Don Scheer

When I was a teenager back in the Bronx in the early 1950s, one of my neighborhood friends was Burton Mickenburg. He grew up in the building alongside mine, played the same sports, went to the same schools, did the same things we all did. Maybe he was a little more serious than the rest of us, but that might have been because his dad died when Burt was ten years old and his mother struggled financially raising him and his baby sister, Sandra.

His mom worked in a dress store on 170th Street, and Burt always had a part time job in Bollinger's grocery store stacking shelves and delivering groceries. He was a good student, and his homework was always handed in on time.

One day there was an announcement over the public address system in our high school for six students to report immediately to the principal's office. I heard Burt's name, and then I heard mine, so I hurried off to Mr. Brody's office.

I was the last one to reach the principal's office; five other boys, including Burt, were sitting outside of Mr. Brody's office, all wondering out loud why they had been summoned over the PA system.

Mr. Brody, smiling, welcomed us into his office and introduced us to a Mr. Bernardi, who was from Bell Laboratories in New Jersey. Mr. Brody told us that Mr. Bernardi had an interesting offer to make to us, so he turned the meeting over to him.

Mr. Bernardi told us a bit about Bell Labs, that it was the research organization of AT&T and that it had lots of important scientists working for it, some of whom had won the Nobel Prize. He added that Bell Labs held more U.S. Patents than any company in the history of the U.S. Patent Office.

Then he got down to why we were there. He said that our teachers and Mr. Brody considered us – the six of us – to be really bright fine boys who were extremely good in mathematics, and Bell Labs was always interested in young people who might have promising futures in mathematics and physics. Mr. Bernardi said he'd like to give us a short examination – not longer than 30 minutes – to test our ability to reason in mathematics. He would pay us $25 simply to take the exam. Also, he said if we did particularly well, Bell Labs might offer us a part time position while we were still in high school.

As Mr. Bernardi spoke, Mr. Brody, whose bald head was nodding, said, "It's quite an honor to be chosen, boys. I'd recommend you all take this examination. You have nothing to lose and you will receive $25 when you hand in your paper."

One of the boys, who I didn't know, asked Mr. Bernardi if he'd still get the $25 if he didn't do well in the test. Mr. Bernardi said, "Absolutely, everyone gets the $25."

So we all said "yes." The test was to be given Thursday right after the final period.

When Mr. Bernardi handed out the test papers, my heart sank. There were six questions and I didn't have any idea how to begin. I read and reread the questions. They might as well have been in Swahili. I was lost. I looked over at the other boys and they appeared equally confused, except for Burt who was calmly going through the questions as though this test was just like any other geometry or trigonometry exam.

Ten minutes into the exam two of the boys got up and handed in blank papers. One of the boys apologized to Mr. Bernardi, saying, "Sorry, sir, this test is beyond me. I haven't a clue how to answer these questions." Mr. Bernardi smiled and handed each boy an envelope containing a check. Then the two other boys in the group handed in their papers – also blank – got their checks and left.

Only Burt and I remained. I looked over at Burt thinking what the hell is he writing? Surely he can't make any sense out of this test. It must be some joke, some exercise in group behavior, a clever prank being played upon us.

Finally, I inserted my name in the upper right hand corner of the test sheet as called for and wrote, "Dear Mr. Bernardi, My training in mathematics always involved working with numbers and these questions have no numbers. I am out of my realm. Sorry." And I also handed in a blank paper and left the room, holding a Bell Labs envelope containing a $25 check.

I was walking out of the building when Burt caught up to me. "Wait up," he said, smiling. "Did you get all the answers?"

"Burt, forget the answers. I never got the questions. Was that test for real or what?"

"What do you mean?" he asked. "I thought it was well put together."

"Well put together? You must be kidding. And by the way, what the hell is Avogadro's number, that phrase I could at least read. I believe it was question number four?"

"Avogadro's number is used to measure molecular density," Burt said. "You know, it's a constant. All you have to remember is 6.02×10^{23}, which represents the number of atoms in a gram atom."

"Oh. Thanks, Burt. That clears that up. Where did you learn that? I don't recall ever being taught anything at Taft High School about Avogadro's number."

"I don't know. I must have read it somewhere," said Burt. "I read a lot."

Two weeks later I bumped into Burt in the school cafeteria and he told me, "I guess I did okay on that Bell Labs test. They offered me a part time job. They're sending a car to pick me up at 2:00 p.m. tomorrow. Mr. Brody's letting me leave school an hour early every Monday, Wednesday and Friday. The Bell Labs driver will take me to Murray Hill, New Jersey, where I'm supposed to spend two hours talking to other young guys; then we have an early supper and they drive me home. The best part is they're paying me $500 a month. My mom is so happy, but I have to leave my job at the grocery store."

I knew then that Burt was not like the rest of the boys in our neighborhood. He was the smartest kid in the Bronx.

* * *

I didn't see much of Burt after that except for a couple of times when I saw him climb into the rear of a blue Oldsmobile sedan with a Bell Labs logo on its door.

Then one day in our gym class Burt came over to me and said he'd been offered a scholarship to Columbia University in the fall, and he'd be leaving Taft after his junior year.

"You mean you're not going to graduate?" I asked.

"Yeah. Mr. Brody said I won't need a high school diploma. The degree from Columbia will let prospective employers know I could've gotten the high school diploma but didn't really need it."

"Don't you feel funny going to college? You're only sixteen."

"I did when I first got the offer, but Bell Labs is raising my salary to $1,000 a month as soon as I get to Columbia. I couldn't turn it down. That raise in pay will let my mom cut her hours at the dress store down to part time, or she might quit completely, so it's a good thing."

We shook hands. I wished Burt luck and told him to keep in touch. "If you get stuck trying to solve a long division problem, let me know, Burt. I'll give you all the help you need. We both smiled and said goodbye. I was going to miss Burt.

Three years passed. I was enrolled in a pre-med program at New York University, the uptown branch in the Bronx, and saw Burt only a couple of times on the street. He was always carrying a stack of books and in a hurry to get someplace. We just waved at each other.

But one day I was on a bus on the Grand Concourse riding to Fordham Road and my old friend Burt got on at Mount Eden Avenue. We had time to talk.

He told me he'd be graduating Columbia in two weeks and was considering doing something out of the ordinary.

"What do you mean, out of the ordinary?"

"Well, the Columbia folks want me to continue on in graduate school, enter the M.A. /Ph.D. program, maybe end up in the world of academia. Bell Labs has offered me a full time job after I graduate or a part time job if I stay on in Columbia's graduate program. But do you know what I want to do?"

"I give up. Run away and join the circus?"

"Almost," smiled Burt. "I want to join the Army. I'd like to become a private first class and be told what to do. I don't want to think or read a damn book. I'd love to go overseas, shine my boots, drive a jeep, maybe go to a bar and get drunk. I really need to get away from this grind. And I need to have a girlfriend. You know, I hate to admit it but I've never kissed a girl. Never really kissed a girl. There're two girls in my calculus class at

Columbia. One is a lesbian and other looks like William Bendix with boobs. My life is a mess."

"Gosh, Burt, I know just how you feel. I hate my classes at NYU. I'm not learning anything. I'm just memorizing textbooks and spewing it back at exam times. I'm doing well in my classes, but I'm not getting an education. Maybe I'll join the Army with you. We're going to be drafted soon any-way."

"Oh, wow," said Burt. "Am I happy to hear you say that? Look, all of us have to go to the Army. All the guys we know have been drafted or soon *will* be drafted. It's part of our birthright. But I say let's not wait for them to draft us.

"There's a little known regulation which I discovered that allows us to enlist for two years. Usually you enlist for three years, but there is this regulation that permits a two-year enlistment in the Regular Army program, and if you enlist with a friend, they'll allow you to enroll in their buddy plan."

"What's the buddy plan?"

"The buddy plan means you and a buddy stay together for two years. Wherever they send one of us, the other gets to go."

"No kidding. I love it. I finish my junior year at NYU in two weeks. Let's join up right after that. I'll finish college right after the Army. Let's do it."

By the time Burt and I had reached Fordham Road we had worked out our future for the next two years. If was off to the Army for us.

My parents, of course, objected strenuously, and my college counselor at NYU objected even more strenuously, but my mind was set. I wanted to be a Private First Class and peel potatoes. No real responsibilities.

Burt was able to appease his mother since Bell Labs agreed to pay him $500 a month while he was in the Army if he agreed to work for them for at least a year – on a part time or full time basis – right after Burt's Army career was over. He had to sign a contract with them.

So on February 23, 1953, Burt Mickenburg and I, carrying only the barest of toiletry supplies and two pairs of underwear, traveled to Whitehall Street in lower Manhattan and joined the Army for two years under the buddy plan. We arrived at the Recruitment Center at 8:00 a.m. That night we slept in our barracks at Fort Dix, New Jersey. We were in the Army and happy as could be. Away from books and tests.

Of course, the first thing the Army did was give us and all the other new recruits a battery of tests that lasted for three days straight.

"Here we go again," said Burt. "We just can't get away from people picking our brains."

On the fourth day in the Army at our early morning formation on the Company Street outside of our barracks, the Sergeant announced, "Private

Burton Mickenburg, report to the Commanding Officer. On the double."

I saw Burt running into the Administrative Offices while the other recruits and I were marched off to the mess hall.

Before breakfast was over, Burt joined us and told me, "Would you believe it? They think I cheated on the tests! Seems like I got a perfect grade, and that has never happened before in the history of Fort Dix, so I'm going to have to take the tests all over again – this time while I'm being guarded by two guys with M-1 rifles."

Three days later Burt was packing his toiletries and underwear plus Army-issued stuff into his duffle bag. "I'm leaving," he said. "The makeup exams turned out like the first ones. They're sending me to Cryptology School in Washington."

"What about me?" I asked. "What about our buddy plan?"

"I asked the C.O. about that, and he told me if there is a national security issue involved, they can break the agreement, and apparently this is a national security issue, so bye, bye, buddy plan. The best laid plans and all that."

We shook hands, promised to keep in touch, and Burt was off in the C.O.'s staff car with a driver heading to Washington, D.C.

I loved the Army. It was just what I needed at the time. But they couldn't figure out what to do with me. They made all sorts of offers to me because my test scores were pretty good: Officer's Training School, helicopter pilot training, Army Intelligence School, etc., but all the offers had the same catch – I would have to extend my Army tour for an additional year – from two to three years – and I wouldn't agree to that.

So first they sent me to Fort Sam Houston in Texas to become a medic, and then they transferred me to Friedberg, Germany where I became a speechwriter for a Colonel who was in charge of German-GI relations in Germany. We toured dozens of Army posts around Germany in his jeep while he gave speeches which I wrote. When the Colonel retired, I became battalion clerk to a tank outfit, and then a medic assigned to the U.S. Army Competitive Shooting Team, and we traveled around Europe attending various competitions.

When I only had six months remaining in the Army, they sent to Oberammergau in Bavaria to an eight week Army Intelligence School where they pressured me almost daily to extend my tour of duty for an additional year in order to complete another, more intensive intelligence course after this one was over. But I held firm: Two years was it for me.

As I looked at the schedule for the eight-week course I was pleased to see that one of the sessions – on cryptology – was to be given by a guest lecturer, Sergeant Burton Mickenburg, who I later learned was visiting the area on hush-hush business for Washington but had agreed to give a brief lecture while he was in Oberammergau.

When Burt arrived in the classroom, he was surprised to see me smiling. We embraced and couldn't stop talking, but the class had to be given so we agreed to meet after his lecture was over. I was surprised how gaunt and tired he looked. He was not quite twenty years old but looked like a man twice his age. He had dark rings under his eyes and his once curly black hair was thinning. His lecture was excellent, filled with detailed information and lots of humor. He wrote a real code on the blackboard, which was Russian in origin, and then went through six basic steps that all decoders used to solve this type of code. It was a giant puzzle. Fascinating stuff and he presented it so well.

After the class we went to a snack bar at the Post and talked about the Bronx and Mr. Brody and Taft High School. But I could see that he was troubled and I asked him straight out how his life was going.

He told me the Army was working him to death. "I'm busier than ever," he said. "It seems like every problem code the Army gets ends up on my desk. They're really pushing me. I'm exhausted."

"How about women? Any time for females in your life?" I asked.

"No time. No females. It's pathetic. I'm the oldest virgin in the Army."

I really felt bad for Burt, so I changed the subject. "Have you decided what you're going to do when you get out? We only have six months left in the Army."

"Yes," he smiled. "I have, and you'll never believe what I'm going to do. I've accepted a job in Frankfurt, Germany with a U.S. firm selling new cars to GIs. I'll be going from base to base throughout Europe selling new cars to GIs who are about to rotate back to the States. Their new cars will be waiting for them stateside."

"All that education and mathematical ability and you're going to sell cars? Makes no sense to me, "I said.

"Makes a lot of sense to me. I'll get a little apartment in Frankfurt. I'll be making good money. I'll be able to send my mom some money every month and I'll be able to meets lots of young women. There are many German and Swiss girls working for the company. I can have some dates, maybe do some serious kissing, maybe even, you know. God, I can't wait. I've negotiated an arrangement with Bell Labs to work with them after my year with the car business is over. It's all set. And, oh yes, the car firm is loaning me a new Thunderbird for a year as I toodle around Europe. I've chosen one that's bubblegum pink. That has to be a fraulein magnet, right?"

We talked for another couple of hours and then Burt had to leave. We promised once again to keep in touch, buy each other egg creams if we ever got back to the Bronx and go to the Paradise Movie Theater.

I was very sad to see him leave. He was a genuinely nice guy who deser-ved some happiness which I hoped he would get. I pictured him driving his bubblegum pink T-Bird alongside the Rhine River, and I smiled.

* * *

I never saw Burt again, but every time I spoke to one of my friends from the Bronx I asked where Burt was. It was a great mystery. No one knew Burt's whereabouts.

A few nights ago while surfing the net I saw an advertisement which offered to track down high school buddies and friends from the old neighborhood, so I logged on and typed in the information that I knew about Burton Mickenburg. I thought if I could locate him I'd learn he won the Nobel Prize or was Dean of some prestigious university, perhaps in Europe.

It didn't take long to find him. There was a short blurb that said he attended Taft High School in the Bronx, New York, graduated from Columbia University, and fulfilled his military obligation with the Army from February 23, 1953 to February 16, 1955, and was killed instantly in a car accident on the Autobahn ten miles north of Frankfurt on March 3, 1955.

My hope was that some wonderful, pretty young woman kissed Burt with passionate love and tenderness before my old friend was gone.

Drumsticks
By Don Scheer

*L*ike Ensign Pulver in *Mr. Roberts* who served on a U.S. Navy cargo vessel for almost two years while totally eluding the ship's captain, I spent at least half of my four years at Taft High School in the Bronx away from the school, cutting classes. Beginning in my sophomore year in 1950, I showed up at school each morning, made lots of noise so the teachers would notice me, went to a class or two and then simply walked out of the main doors around 10:30 a.m. and stayed out until close to 3:00 p.m., at which time I returned to make a lot more noise.

Friends gave me homework assignments and let me know when crucial exams were given. I got through by studying my sister's detailed class notes from two years before. It worked perfectly. My teachers were either fooled by my actions or, more likely, didn't give a hoot. I graduated near the head of my class. My close friends voted me, "the student most likely to disappear."

I was not alone. I played hooky with a large contingent of fellow slackers. We hung out together in various apartments, went to the movies, cafeterias and restaurants, ballgames, and public parks. We played poker and blackjack and fine-turned our knowledge of shooting craps. At fifteen minutes to 3:00, we graciously held open the side door of Taft High School for each other so we could rejoin the student body.

My closest buddy during those non-school days was Bernie Newman, who could recite from memory the entire text of T.S. Eliot's *The Waste Land* and Oscar Wilde's *Ballad of Reading Gaol*. While reciting, he would accompany himself by playing the drums, using two stubby wooden drumsticks and a small black and white square of linoleum.

"You have to understand the rhythm," he'd say. "T.S. Eliot is a pompous fake Englishman born in America's Midwest, but he has the soul of Charlie Parker. Wilde was simply kissed by the gods. You can't write stuff like, 'each man kills the thing he loves, by each let this be heard, some do it with a bitter look, some with a flattering word.' No, this stuff can't be written. It's a gift that God pours into your heart. You simply take dictation from God."

And Bernie would stop reciting and let his drumsticks tap out several lines of Wilde's poem. "It's the rhythm. Do you feel the rhythm?"

Then he would put his drumsticks and linoleum square into the back pocket of his jeans and say, "It's time to eat."

Bernie and I spent most of our restaurant time in Bucknoff's Delicatessen on 170th Street across from Taft High School, between Morris and Grant Avenues. We always ordered the same lunch: two corned beef sandwiches on rye, two bottles of Dr. Brown's cream soda, and two side orders of baked beans.

We ordered from Julius, the only daytime waiter at Bucknoff's Delicatessen. He was like a living compass, but he didn't face the north. Julius always faced the kitchen. You gave your order to the back of his head, and you had to do it quickly, because Julius couldn't exist for long outside of Bucknoff's kitchen. It was like there was a powerful unseen wind chasing Julius. You learned to give him your order promptly, but invariably before you completed it, Julius was blown back into the kitchen.

He returned quickly with the corned beef sandwiches and the cream sodas, but was never able to produce the sides of baked beans on the first trip. Julius would clunk the sandwiches onto the Formica tabletop and say, "Not to worry, the beans are coming," and he'd fly back into the kitchen.

When he reappeared, he returned to our table leaning over close to Bernie and me, conspiratorially saying, "The beans are coming."

We never knew why those beans took so long to come. Behind the counter we could see a hundred neatly stacked green mini-cans of Heinz Vegetarian Baked Beans. How long could it take to heat those beans?

After Julius made his second announcement, Bernie would say, "The American colonists had Paul Revere to tell them the British were coming. We have Julius telling us the beans are coming." Then Bernie would take out his drumsticks and tap out the rhythm of the beans on the formica tabletop. "They're coming. The beans are coming."

On the third trip from the kitchen, Julius would return triumphantly carrying the two small dishes of beans. "They're here," he'd say with a broad smile. And they were delicious.

For Bernie and me those beans became an important milestone in our lives. They came to represent anticipation and goodness. Sometimes you had to wait in life, but if you were patient, goodness would come. Julius taught us that.

Years later when Bernie and I entered adulthood, married our wives and had children, and Bernie moved to California, we talked over the telephone. Business problems and marital difficulties were discussed and sometimes these were tough problems not easily resolved. But either Bernie or I would stop the gloomy conversations cold by saying, "Don't worry, the beans are coming," and we'd laugh because we knew this was true. Good times always come, and they will be delicious.

When we weren't at Bucknoff's, much of our time was spent at the movies. While we enjoyed watching top flight films featuring Hollywood's leading stars, it was the B film icons we really admired. Brian Donlevy was our hands-down favorite. He usually played tough-guy fast-talking roles. Bernie and I watched him not for his acting ability, but because we discovered that Brian Donlevy had no neck to speak of. His handsome head sat directly on his beefy body. He was quite neckless. We learned from his earliest films that when Donlevy needed to turn his head, he had to move his entire body because of his missing neck.

Bernie and I would sit in the balcony with our fellow hooky players and point out to our buddies when a Brian Donlevy full-body turn was imminent. Donlevy never disappointed. In a barroom scene while in a spirited argument with other toughs, Donlevy would spot his nemesis at the other end of the bar walking towards him. His cronies would all turn their heads as though watching a tennis match, but not Donlevy, who readied himself to make a full-body turn to face his foe.

Bernie would provide the narration. "Watch carefully," he'd say loudly. "Note the eye movement; he's seconds away from a full-body turn. See, he's shifting his feet; he's getting ready for the full turn. It's coming. One, two, three, bango, there it is – the Donlevy full-body turn," and the balcony filled with hooky players would erupt in loud applause. God bless Brian Donlevy; he gave us such pleasure – a fine neckless actor.

Our favorite female actress was far and away Maria Ouspenkaya, a tiny wrinkled old lady who played every scene with a thick Russian accent. To me she was a voice-double to the lady who sold pickles in the appetizing store near my apartment. In fact, Maria Ouspenkaya sounded like lots of older folks who lived in the Bronx of my youth.

If there were a need for a gypsy lady in a Hollywood film from the late 1930s through to the early '50s, Maria Ouspenkaya would get the part. She was the ultimate gypsy. Her most important role was the gypsy woman named Maleva in the classic film *The Wolf Man*, starring Lon Chaney.

To Bernie and me Ouspenkaya and Chaney acted out the greatest single scene in movie history. No other scene comes close. It is set in a forest where Chaney is looking up at the rising full moon and running from tree to tree, for he knows he's about to turn into the dreaded wolf man. He's running because he wants to be as far from people as possible so when he is transformed into a wolf, he won't kill anyone. Deep down he's really a very decent fellow named Lawrence Talbot, son of an English Lord who was played by Claude Raines, and not a blood-thirsty beast who tears people to shreds.

But try as he may to get away from people, he runs smack into a gypsy campsite deep in the woods, and he is spotted by Maleva (played by Ouspenkaya). She approaches Chaney who is starting to sprout chunks of heavy facial hair as his nose lengthens into a muzzle.

Maria is without fear, for she knows all the hidden secrets of the netherworld. She puts her wrinkled hand on Chaney's, which is quickly becoming a hirsute paw, and she says, "Don't vorry, mein son; all vill be vell."

And Chaney answers, "I appreciate the kind words, but look at the moon. I will soon become a wolf, and I will kill. Please, gypsy lady, I beg of you, use your gypsy powers to kill me before I kill some innocent person. I want to die. I need to break the hideous cycle of beastly violence. You must kill me. Please kill me."

And then the moon rises to its full height. Maria Ouspenkaya responds to Chaney, who is now 98 percent wolf with buttons bursting from his English cotton poplin tailored shirt, and she utters the greatest non-sequitor in movie history. In response to Chaney's plea to be killed, Maria assures him, "Don't vorry, mein son. Your secret is safe!"

Chaney, of course, doesn't give a rat's ass about his secret; he just wants to die. He doesn't want to do harm, but he has no other choice, for he is now fully transformed into a werewolf. He runs away from Maria, searching for his next victim as Maria meanders back to her gypsy wagon.

Bernie and I never forgot that scene in the forest. To us it was the total embodiment of the world's absurdity, and when, as middle-aged men we communicated by phone, neither of us ever said goodbye to the other. One of us would interrupt the other's conversation abruptly by saying, "Don't vorry, mein son. Your secret is safe!" And we just hung up the phone. Nothing more needed to be said.

I hadn't spoken to Bernie for three months when I received a call from Fiona, his wife. I had never received a call from Fiona, so I quickly realized something serious had happened to Bernie. But I wasn't prepared for the news of his death.

"He was diagnosed only a month ago," she said in her English accent. "And the prognosis was excellent. His doctors felt he could beat this thing – this Hodgkin's' Lymphoma, but he just got worse. Yesterday morning he died. We're having a bit of a service for him on Saturday morning, and we'd love for you to join us and say a few words. I know you two haven't seen each other in a while, but Bernie adored you. Sometimes, I think, he felt closer to you than to me and the kids."

"Fiona," I interrupted. "This is a total shock to me, and I'm afraid I'm not taking this well. Give me some time to absorb what you've said and I'll call you later. Of course I'll come to the service and say some words.

Please forgive me, but I'll talk to you later. I'm terribly sorry. Bye."

At the Unitarian Church in Santa Barbara, California, there were more than two hundred people present for the memorial service. My first reaction upon entering the church was that I was at the wrong place. I had just walked through the church grounds which were beautifully landscaped with row after row of vibrant flowers and a long narrow koi pond meandering among the flower beds, the deep golds and reds of the large fish contrasting with the dazzling purples, whites, reds and blues of the flowers.

The church interior had pews and walls tastefully covered in maroon and light grey fabrics. This didn't look like a place Bernie would want to hang out. We were clearly a long way from the Bronx.

I spotted Fiona and her two lanky teenage sons, Ned and Michael, who introduced me to the Unitarian minister, Reverend Chuck Davis, looking as if he had just come in from a brisk morning workout in the California surf. Everything was sparkling clean and orderly.

When I asked Reverend Chuck where the remains were, he pointed to a small chapel and told me Bernie's urn was on the altar if I wanted to pay my respects.

"Urn? Was Bernie cremated?"

"Oh, yes," replied Reverend Chuck. "We followed Bernie's wishes."

Then I saw Bernie's first wife, Phyllis, and her two adult daughters, Jen and Beth. Phyllis threw her arms around me and said, "Would you believe this place? It's Bernie's last practical joke to the world. I doubt if he was ever in this church."

"Being cremated doesn't sound like much of a joke. Did Bernie agree to all this?"

"He did it for Fiona, I'm sure. Cremation is the cheapest way to go, and I think they were having money problems towards the end." Fiona was a Unitarian.

Before the service began, I was led to a seat on the stage in a place of ho-nor with two other fellows who were also eulogizing Bernie. Reverend Chuck raised his hands and the soft playing of a guitar and a harp ceased.

The first speaker was Bernie's business partner in their advertising firm. He spoke about Bernie's business ethics and his civic activities of coaching a Little League baseball team sponsored by the firm.

The second gentleman was Mr. James Reel, the CEO of a large regional chain of supermarkets. Mr. Reel said he was proud of the fact that his supermarket chain was Bernie's first account, which grew to be Bernie's firm's largest account. He praised Bernie for creating the jingle which the supermarket chain had retained for a dozen years: The jingle went, "For a wow of a deal, get your produce at Reel."

"Produce was the first item we used in the jingle, recalled Mr. Reel.

"But it was so successful it was used with dozens of other products over the years, from yogurt to pork chops. Bernie was the composer of that jingle, and we're very proud of it."

Mr. Reel then said in a solemn voice, "For a wow of deal, get your produce at Reel. Wonderful. We thank you, Bernie." And Mr. Reel sat down.

Next Reverend Chuck said a few words, and it was obvious to me that Phyllis was right: Bernie had never been inside of this church and probably never had met the good Reverend. Reverend Chuck spoke in general terms about Bernie's faith in the Lord, his love for his family, his kindness to friends and neighbors, and his decency. I was certain this was Reverend Chuck's standard "one speech fits all deaths," because his words could have been about anyone. Bernie was a lot of things, but he was not just anyone. He was a distinct soul, and Reverend Chuck clearly never knew him.

When it was my turn, I said, "I've been blessed by having many friends, some of whom go back a long way, some as far back as when I was a small boy growing up in the Bronx. I still have many of these friends. We call each other and try to get together at reunions and parties, as often as we can. I even meet once a year with my first girlfriend, who's now a grandmother in Tampa. Old friends are important to me, and Bernie was the most cherished friend I ever had, because quite simply, he was my best friend.

"I've lived a long time and have known lots of people, but when I look back and I'm honest, really honest with myself, I have to say there are only a handful of people in my life with whom I was ever really close, and I'm including family members. Very few people. There are only a few, with whom after a long absence you reconnect, and within seconds you feel that closeness, that human bonding. It's a rare thing. I had that with Bernie.

"But let me not depress you, for Bernie was not a person who depressed anyone. Let me tell you about Bernie's teen years." I then told everyone about Bernie and me and Bucknoff's Delicatessen and how we waited for the beans to come. And I told them about Brian Donlevy, the actor who had no neck. I concluded with a discussion about the wolf man and Maria Ouspenkaya.

The mourners smiled and some laughed, and I was pleased because I wanted these people to know that Bernie was a unique human being, someone more than just a good father, husband and neighbor. Someone more than the guy who wrote, "For a wow of a deal buy your produce at Reel." And as I described to the mourners the Bernie I had known, they responded with smiles and laughter. I noticed that Phyllis, Bernie's first wife, was wee-ping quietly. She was looking at me, smiling, but the tears were slowly dripping from her eyes. The people around her laughed at my descriptions of Bernie as a teenager, but Phyllis' emotion increased, and she began to sob.

She pulled out some tissues to wipe the tears from her eyes and cover her mouth so that people would not hear her sobs, but they increased and soon were echoed by her two daughters who sat beside her. Jen and Beth made no attempt to stifle their emotions - because they had their own rec-ollections about their dad. And then other women whom I did not know were sobbing, and throughout the beautifully appointed maroon and grey upholstered church, there was a flood of tears which become contagious; even many of the men had tear-filled eyes. The congregation was touched by Bernie's death and they were crying, not only because Bernie was gone, but also because they were thinking of their own mortality.

As I quickly glanced back at Reverend Chuck and saw that he, also, was misting up, I decided it was time to end my eulogy. I concluded with: "What did Bernie's life mean to me? Without Bernie I probably never would have known that Brian Donlevy had no neck. I might never have known that there is a distinct rhythm in language, that even a delicatessen waiter understands anticipation, and that even something as commonplace as baked beans can take on importance in one's life. Bernie taught me to listen carefully to words and conversations and to see life's absurdities, to understand that conversations between gypsies and wolf men go on all the time in real life in everyday situations, and that often people don't really listen to each other.

"In brief, Bernie taught me more about life than all my teachers had – he taught me to open my eyes, my ears and my heart. He helped me to understand, and I'll always be thankful to him for that gift.

"Thank you, Fiona, and thank you, Bernie's children, for letting me share just a little of the love I have in my heart for Bernie."

After I said goodbye to Fiona and her two sons, and to Phyllis and her two daughters, and to dozens of people who pumped my hand whom I didn't know but who said they were moved by my words, I walked back to my car to return to the airport. Fiona ran after me.

"I almost forgot to give you this letter," as she handed me a small en-velope. "Bernie wrote it to you three days before he died. He put it into an envelope himself. I have no idea what he said, but he told me to give it to you. I think he knew he had only a short while left. Anyway, here's the letter."

"I'll read it on the plane, Fiona. Bye and God bless."

Once the plane took off, I fell into a deep doze and completely forgot a-bout Bernie's letter. I awoke when dinner was served, remembering vague-ly that I needed to do something, but I couldn't remember what. It was after a second cup of coffee that I remembered Bernie's letter in the breast pocket of my jacket.

Opening it was like hearing Bernie's voice once again. "Hey, good buddy," he wrote. "Sorry I went and died on you. Wherever I'm headed I sure hope they have good egg salad sandwiches. It'll be a bitch to spend eternity without good egg salad."

But that's not why I'm writing this letter. I need a favor from you, and you're the only one who could pull off this crazy Bronx caper.

Remember my old apartment at 1320 Sherman Avenue, Apartment 3C? Stupid question. You and I logged zillions of hours at that place during our Taft High School hooky days. Anyway, before I quit Taft soon after my 16th birthday and ran away to marry Phyllis, I told my mother and older brother, Seymour, what I was going to do. Seymour said, "Good. Now I can have the bedroom to myself for a while. "And Mom, God rest her soul, was really relieved, because she was about to marry a fat guy named Murray, and she wasn't sure about starting a new marriage knowing that I, a juvenile delinquent who played the drums, would be hanging around. So my unexpected departure was a clear way out for Mom.

Anyway, Mom said, "If that's what you want, I give you my blessing." She was free and clear, because Seymour had already announced he was going to get his own place on his 18th birthday which was fast approaching.

The plot thickens. My mother, after giving me her blessing, tells me she needs me to replaster a large hole in the wall in my bedroom, because one day I threw an African spear that I bought for God-knows-why and threw it at the bedroom wall right over the steam radiator. The spear tore out a large chunk of plaster from the wall. My mom was concerned that unless that hole got fixed, she wouldn't get her $45 security deposit back from the landlord; so I agreed to do a spackle job on the wall and then finish with some paint we had left over from our last paint job.

While preparing the jagged gash for spackling, I got a brilliant idea. I thought to myself, 'This spackling job is a momentous time in my life.' You know, Donnie boy, I was always a dramatic putz of a kid. I said to myself, 'Before spackling this hole, I should take my cigar box filled with kid stuff and shove it into that hole in the wall as a way of putting my childhood to rest and getting myself ready for a new life with Phyllis, etc.'

So I did it; I widened the hole first, put in the cigar box, and covered it with spackle. Then I painted it, and it was perfect. You couldn't tell at all that some fool had flung an African spear into the wall. Mom got her $45 security deposit back and remarried. I got rid of my childhood and married Phyllis, and Seymour got his own place.

Well, guess what? I haven't thought about that cigar box in 50 years until last week. I'm daydreaming as I'm lying here dying, and suddenly it hits me. Do you know what I put into that cigar box? Well, I'll tell you: one rubber band ball, two French postcards with naked ladies (remember, this was 1952 when naked ladies were at a premium), three incredible marbles, one of which was the best aggie in the Bronx, my precious drumsticks and a square of linoleum, and nine, repeat nine, rookie baseball cards of Mickey Mantle, my idol.

You remember how crazy I was about Mickey? My uncle Saul told me once I looked like the Mick, what with my blonde hair, and I went nuts just to be considered to look like my favorite person in the whole world. Well, those cards are now worth $50,000+ for each of them, or a total of $450,000, maybe more. If they still exist. Hell, if the *building* still exists! I haven't been back to the Bronx in 25 years, but I hear lots of the old buildings are no longer there.

That's where you come in. You are perfect for this job. I need you to find out: 1) if the building is there, and 2) if yes, somehow get into that apartment, demolish the wall over the steam radiator, and retrieve the cigar box. Only you with your insane Bronx background could pull this off. My two sons are California kids and would be eaten alive walking around the Bronx today, no less demolishing somebody's wall looking for a cigar box.

Now, listen carefully. If you can pull this caper off and recover the box and the baseball cards, sell them and give $25,000 to Fiona, $25,000 to Phyllis, and split what's left ($400,000 or more) among my four kids. I hate to admit it, but I'm not leaving much to my family, other than some debts. My insurance policy has been borrowed against, and I've got a second mortgage on my house. I'm dying broke, so if that cigar box caper happens, it'll be the only real legacy I can leave.

What do *you* get out of this, good buddy? I hereby bequeath to you: two French postcards, three marbles (one of which is a great aggie), my rubber band ball, and my drumsticks and linoleum. That's not a bad haul for you, you rich bastard.

Anyway, do it.

I love you, Donnie boy. I really do.

Bernie

P.S. Let me know how it turns out.

I suppose a normal person's reaction would have been, "Are you crazy? You want me to get into some stranger's apartment and tear down one of his walls looking for a cigar box that was buried some 50 years before?"

But like someone once said, "If you're a high school graduate with at least a C average from a New York school, you could easily run NASA or be the Governor of Nebraska," and I was a top student graduate from Taft High School, even though I played hooky for a couple of those high school years. This caper is doable, so doable.

By the time my plane landed in Atlanta, I had concocted several plans to get into apartment 3C at 1320 Sherman Avenue, if the building was still standing. All of my plans were based upon subterfuge: I'd tell whomever answered the door that I was a building inspector, and I needed to check one of the load bearing walls in the apartment for its structural strength, or I'd tell them I was from Con Edison and I needed to drill into a certain wall to get to a certain circuit, etc., or that I was from the Water Department and needed to blah, blah, blah.

Each scam had an appropriate uniform and helpers and fake IDs and lots of cash to reimburse the occupants for their inconvenience and on and on. I got home after midnight without choosing which ruse I would employ. *When I get up tomorrow*, I told myself, *I'll make the choice and then put together all the details of the chosen plan.*

In the clear light of morning, I told myself, *Get real. This isn't some Hollywood movie. I'm liable to get arrested here or worse. People aren't stupid and gullible enough to buy some cockamamie story.* I decided I needed some professional guidance, so I called Steve Matthews in Hoboken, New Jersey.

Steve was an extraordinary private investigator who had worked for me years ago. A football player during his college days at William & Mary, he now stood six feet four inches tall and weighed over 350 pounds, most of which was muscle. Despite his size, he was soft-spoken, unusually polite, and had a boyish grin that belied the fact that he was no one with whom you wanted to tussle. He was always immaculately dressed in hand tailored suits.

I had employed him in two separate circumstances where I was attempting to collect debts from former business associates. I had gone the legal routes in both cases, and had valid court judgments, but was never able to secure a cent from either party until Steve paid each of them a personal visit. Since I was concerned that Steve might use overzealous methods in attempting to obtain payment, I had him tape each encounter to assure me that no illegal pressure would be placed upon these two gentlemen. Quite the contrary, Steve was most polite in his request that each settle his debt with me. In each case I received full payment by bank checks via Federal Express within 48 hours after Steve's visits.

"How did you do it?" I asked him. "Why did these guys pay up when all my lawyers and court actions got me nowhere? I've listened to the tapes and still can't figure out why they paid."

"Oh, I simply stopped smiling when I said goodbye to each of these fellas, and I stared at them just briefly without saying anything. That usually works."

Steve was expensive but highly effective. Other people I knew who had used him in divorce actions and in complicated business situations couldn't sing his praises loudly enough. So I thought I'd call him and see if the Bernie situation was something he felt comfortable doing.

I reached him at 9:00 a.m. at his office in Hoboken and gave him the details. I told him everything except the exact wall in the apartment and the contents of the cigar box. I figured he didn't need to know either. Steve told me the Bernie caper was a piece of cake. "I'd love to do it," he added.

At 3:00 p.m. he called me back to tell me 1320 Sherman Avenue, apartment 3C still existed and was rented by a Mr. Felix Gutierrez, originally from Belize, who was married to Rosa and had three young children. "They've been renting the apartment for four years," he said, "and always pay their rent on time. Felix drives a cab. While only the Gutierrez family is on the lease, it seems lots of people live there along with them, perhaps as many as a dozen men, women and children. They may be extended family, but I'm not certain. Anyway, here's how the deal will go down if you want to move ahead.

"To keep everything legal and to run things smoothly, we'll need two New York off-duty policemen in full uniform. They'll require $100 an hour and a minimum of three hours for each. I'd use two fellows I've used before. Very capable and big guys, about my size. One is fluent in Spanish.

The superintendent of the building is Nelson Sanchez, who must be in on the deal, and he'll get $250 so he won't cause any problems. To get into the wall I'll need two guys, one skilled and one helper. They will cost you $500 just to show up. They assure me they can complete the job in fewer than 45 minutes and will leave the premises spotless. To do the complete job, they'll need another $500 or a total of $1,000 for everything. If they do nothing, they will still get $500.

We'll also need to pay Mr. and Mrs. Gutierrez $250 for their inconvenience. Plus, my fee is $2,500 to oversee and guarantee the outcome is a success. So the whole exercise is as follows:

2 cops @ $300 each	$ 600
1 superintendent @	250
2 construction guys @	1,000 Max
Tenants	250
My fee	2,500
Total	$ 4,600

"If the construction guys do nothing, the cost is only $4,100. I promise you a very smooth, trouble-free operation with no complications. We can do this Saturday morning. Arrive at 10:00 a.m. and be out of there well before lunchtime. What do you think?"

"I'm concerned about the cops," I replied. "Are they going to be asking questions about the contents of the cigar box?"

"Definitely not," Steve answered. "The only way you'll have problems with the cops is if Jimmy Hoffa falls out of that wall."

"Let's do it, then," I said. "I'll fly into La Guardia on Friday evening. Pick me up and take me to my hotel, and I'll buy you a great dinner."

"Deal. Call me with details."

Early Saturday morning Steve and I had breakfast at my hotel in Manhattan, then headed up to the Bronx. It was just a little after 9:00 a.m. when we reached the old neighborhood. I had not been back to this area for many years, and memories were behind every stoop and parked car as Steve drove slowly up the Grand Concourse and turned right onto 170th Street.

"Do you mind cruising around a bit?" I asked Steve. "We're early, and I'd love to revisit some of my old haunts."

When we drove past the shop that used to be Bucknoff's Delicatessen, I asked Steve to stop. The place was now a Bodega and hadn't yet opened for the day. I peered into the front windows, half expecting to see a stack of green cans of Heinz baked beans when I gasped out loud.

Steve heard me and ran to my side. "What's wrong?" he asked. "What did you see?"

I was too stunned to answer. I just managed to point to the window. Finally I said, "It's my father. I saw my father."

Steve peered into the window and laughed. "You see your father and I see my father. What we're looking at is our reflections in the glass!"

"Oh my God," I gasped as I approached the front glass once again. "You're right! The old man looking back at me is myself. Scared the hell out of me!" We both got back into the car, and Steve drove slowly around the neighborhood. We didn't talk. A few minutes before 10:00 a.m. we double parked the car in front of 1320 Sherman Avenue.

Two huge uniformed policemen were waiting for us at the building entrance and greeted Steve warmly. They shook my hand. "Expecting any trouble?" I asked them.

"No way," said one of the cops. "These folks are just happy they aren't being arrested. They're probably guilty of something. It'll be a real smooth operation."

Then Nelson, the superintendent, joined us.

"We're going up to talk to the tenants and pave the way," said Steve. "I suggest you wait here for the two construction guys and join us when they arrive. See you soon." They left.

A crowd of kids had gathered in the courtyard, and when the policemen left, one of the kids, no older than 10 or 11, approached me. "Hey, yellow pops," the boy said to me. "What's going on?"

"Yellow pops? Why do you call me yellow pops?"

"Because you got on a yellow sweater, man, and your hair is white like a poppa."

"Okay, makes sense. And who are you?"

"I'm Luis and I live in this building. What's going down?"

"Nothing big, Luis. We're just looking for something. It's just a normal visit, nothing very important. We'll be out of here soon."

The construction guys arrived; I introduced myself and we entered the building. I was pleased to see the same lobby that I was so familiar with when I was a boy. We turned right and walked up the familiar stairs. There was never an elevator in this building. Even the steps looked the same. I was back in the early 1950s as I climbed the stairs. All was the same, except for the smell of the place.

"This place used to smell like kasha and fried onions when I was a kid," I said. "But it smells different now. I can't place the smell, though. You guys know what this odor is?"

"Sure do," said the head construction guy. "You're smelling black beans and rice and someone's cooking plantains. There ain't no kasha here, whatever the hell kasha is."

At the third floor landing, I saw Bernie's old apartment door – 3C. The door was open. One of the police officers was talking to the superintendent and another man whom I assumed was the tenant, Mr. Gutierrez. They were all smiling. Then the cop said to me, "Steve said you'll tell us which wall is the right one. He said you didn't tell him which one it is."

"Right," I said. "Follow me." I walked past the kitchen on the left, where a woman was washing dishes. Two small children, a boy and a girl, sat on the kitchen floor coloring with crayons.

Bernie's bedroom with the cigar box should have been on the left, but the door into that room was no longer there. Instead, I followed the long foyer directly into a large dormitory-type room which had several partitions dividing many rows of bunk beds. Steve and the other policeman smiled at me as I walked through that room and made a left into another dormitory area. I kept walking, growing more and more disoriented. I was in the right apartment, but except for the kitchen, nothing else was right.

Nelson, the superintendent, caught up with me and said, "You look confused, man. How long has it been since you was here?"

"It was forty years ago. What happened?" I asked.

"Well, I've only been here four years, and since then every apartment in the building has been renovated and remodeled. The building used to have big old rooms, but the landlord chopped them up and divided the big rooms and then subdivided what was left. Lots of the old walls were knocked down and new walls put up. This apartment was fully renovated about three years ago."

That was not good news. I continued my walk and got to the area where the steam radiator and Bernie's spackle job should have been. The radiator was gone and so was the wall.

"Sorry, Bernie, I tried," I said out loud. Then I told Steve the mission was over. "Let's pay everyone and get out of here. The cigar box is long gone."

I gave a roll of bills to Steve to make the payoffs. "I have your money in a separate envelope, Steve. After you pay everyone, I'll meet you at the car."

"Okay," Steve replied. "Sorry it didn't work out."

In the courtyard Luis said, "Hey, yellow pops, that was quick, man. Find what you needed?"

"No, Luis, someone got there before me." I was about to walk to the car when I spotted a black and white square of linoleum in front of Luis, who was seated on the small stoop in front of the building. Then I saw two stubby wooden drumsticks. Bernie's drumsticks. I stopped and asked Luis, "Hey, where'd you get those drumsticks?"

"I found them in a big dumpster that was right here," Luis pointed to the side of the courtyard, "when the construction guys did a lot of work three, four years ago." Luis continued, "There was a pile of junk they threw into the dumpster. I found these." He pointed to the linoleum and wooden drumsticks. "They were tied with a rubberband. I love them. I can play anything on my drums, man."

"Did you find anything else? Like a cigar box with stuff in it?"

"No, man, just the sticks. Lots of plaster and wood and painted walls, nothing else. Want to hear me play something?"

"Yeah," I said. "Play, 'The beans are coming, the beans are coming".

Luis laughed. "You crazy, yellow pops. What kind of song is that?"

"My kind of song," I said. "Here's a dollar. Let's see if you can play it."

Luis took the dollar, put it in his pocket, and tapped out, "The beans are coming, the beans are coming."

"Sounds good," I said. "Sounds real good."

And then Luis changed the beat and lengthened the tune.

"What are you playing now, Luis?" I asked.

"I'm playing. 'The black beans and rice are coming, the black beans and rice are coming.' Do you hear the rhythm, yellow pops?"

THE END

Twinkle, Twinkle
By Don Scheer

Lots of people don't realize it, but when one becomes almost deaf, sounds not only diminish but also appear randomly where none exist.

There are lots of popping noises as though champagne is being uncorked in a distant room; phones ring, but there's no one calling. Taps on doors are not taps at all, and once I heard a mournful soft cry which appeared and suddenly evaporated.

It's as though the brain – after so many years of sound processing – begins to create its own sounds to stay in practice, just as it invents itching on limbs which have been amputated.

When the haunting, unreal sounds began to appear to me, at first I was alarmed, but I slowly adjusted. I've become used to the phenomenon and have gone on with my life, eagerly awaiting the next subtle geriatric malfunction.

One day, a soft mechanical sound like that of a music box echoed in my condominium: "Twinkle, twinkle little star. How I wonder what you are."

I was not concerned. It wasn't an unpleasant sound, and it was certainly better than a popping, ringing or tapping, so I ignored it. It appeared again and then daily at least once, but on some days I'd hear it two or three times.

At some point I realized I could count on the twinkling sound every morning about 7:00 a.m. I thought: "*This is not my brain playing tricks with a child's ditty. Maybe it truly exists.*" It was then that I decided to systematically seek out its origin.

The next morning at 7:00 a.m., as I was brushing my teeth, I heard the catchy song begin, "Twinkle, twinkle, little star." All of my senses went on alert. I quickly left my bathroom, my mouth afoam with toothpaste, my toothbrush high in the air like a divining rod seeking the exact location of the sound.

I placed my good ear on the clock radio in my bedroom. Only *silence*, but in the distance I could hear, "How I wonder what you are." I carefully checked all my TV sets, the VCR, the DVD, and even a cell phone which my daughter had recently bought for me, but I had never used. *Nothing.* All the suspect electronics were silent. Yet, if I froze my body and listened carefully, I could hear the twinkle melody softly playing – teasing me and daring me to find it.

Frantically I ran to open the door of my condo to look for an ice cream truck or some runaway calliope, but there was only a gardener trimming a hedge. He looked at me and smiled and then shook his head. I guess I looked a bit odd since I wasn't wearing clothes, and my mouth was still frothing with toothpaste. I closed the door. I couldn't locate the sound outside. I even looked suspiciously at my two red oranda goldfish in their tank – to see if somehow they were the perpetrators, but they seemed to be swimming silently as usual.

Nevertheless, I could still hear that insidious melody. I began to fear that I would become afflicted like the German composer, Robert Schumann, who eventually went insane because he was unable to get a simple recurring musical phrase out of his mind.

I went back to brushing my teeth, then gargled with mouthwash and left the bathroom. I listened carefully. The melody slowly ceased as oddly as it began.

After attending to my daily grooming, I got dressed and left my apartment to search for antique treasures among the stalls filled with piles of trash at the Lake Worth Flea Market. My intent was to scour the marketplace hoping to find either a rare copy of the Declaration of Independence behind an old picture frame, that stunning but tarnished Faberge egg in a box of old door knobs, or a Tang Dynasty horse on a table standing grandly amongst worthless bric-a-brac. After an hour of careful searching, I found nothing and decided to pick up some tomatoes and soap on the way to my car.

When I approached her stand, the old lady who had previously sold me soap and other toiletry supplies, greeted me with her friendly smile. As I loaded up on soap, shaving cream and toothpaste, the woman asked. "Do you like those cute little tubes of toothpaste?"

"Yes," I told her. "I like them because they stand up on the counter by themselves and dispense the toothpaste cleanly onto the brush."

She said, "I like them, too. I give them to my four-year-old granddaughter because she likes the cartoon characters on the tube, and she likes the song they sing which keeps her brushing her teeth longer than she normally would."

"Song?" I asked with a puzzled look. "What song?"

"This song," she answered, flipping open the broad cap of one of the tubes.

A tiny music box inside the cap proudly played:

"Twinkle, twinkle, little star ..."

El Loro Es Verde
By Don Scheer

*J*eremy Stockton's high school Spanish teacher, Mr. Horowitz, who insisted on being called Señor Horowitz, began all of his classes by having a student read a paragraph in Spanish in front of the class. This day it was Jeremy's turn to bumble through a paragraph.

Jeremy's reading was brutal. Señor Horowitz interrupted him at every third word. He raced to the end of the paragraph with Señor Horowitz in hot pursuit, correcting word after word of his pronunciation.

"*Habla despacio, por favor*, slowly please," Señor Horowitz pleaded as Jeremy sweated and stumbled toward the completion of his reading.

The last sentence was near, and Jeremy suddenly grew confident because he knew he could pronounce the last four words without a mishap. They were a phonetic gift, easy on the tongue. He became calm and self-assured and finished strongly in a clear voice, "*El loro es verde,*" which he knew meant, "The parrot is green."

He delivered those last four words in an exaggerated Spanish accent. Fearing he had overdone it, he stood silently in front of the room, waiting to be accused of not taking the reading seriously.

Instead, Señor Horowitz looked at him the way Professor Henry Higgins had looked at Eliza Doolittle. He asked Jeremy to repeat the last four words to the class.

Jeremy was into it now. A halo formed around his head. He slowly narrowed his eyes to look like Ricardo Montalbon and said distinctly in a booming voice, "*El loro es verde.*"

"Bravo." shouted Señor Horowitz. "That is perfect Castilian Spanish, spoken like a true native. Very good, Jeremy, *muy bueno.*"

Later that day and for days afterward, when Jeremy passed his Spanish language classmates in the hallways, they gave him the thumbs up sign and shouted, "*El loro es verde.*"

Perhaps because there were so few positive high school experiences in Jeremy's life, he remembered the *el loro es verde* moment and tried to seek out situations where he could use that phrase to regain his instant of glory. He thought that surely he would have many occasions to repeat his parrot triumph and was always ready to clear his throat and offer those four simple words. But the years passed, and the moment failed to materialize.

In the Army he did his basic training in San Antonio, Texas, and on a weekend pass went with several of his buddies to Piedras Negras, a sleazy Mexican border town where they went from cantina to cantina drinking tequila. No matter how dull his senses became, he was ever alert to the possibility of a parrot moment. It never came.

Then the Army transferred Jeremy from Texas to Germany. On the boat to Bremerhaven, he met a young soldier who had grown up in Argentina. Jeremy told him the green parrot story. He laughed and sympathized with Jeremy's concern for not having been able to repeat the phrase in a real life situation.

The soldier offered an alternative phrase that he said might be more useful, and he made Jeremy repeat it over and over so that the words were fixed into his memory: "*Yo quiero las señoritas con grande chichas,*" which roughly translated to, "I want young women with big breasts." The soldier assured him that the next time he entered a cantina, the *chichas* sentence would stand him in greater stead than the green parrot phrase. Jeremy thanked him and repeated his newly learned phrase to the soldier many times on that long boat ride to Germany.

After the Army, Jeremy married, and he and his bride spent their honeymoon in Spain. Naturally, he tucked away the *grande chichas* phrase during his honeymoon, but he still looked hopefully for a parrot opportunity. He and his wife toured all of the major cities of Spain, but his opportunity never materialized.

The world turned over many times. Jeremy traveled widely, met hundreds of people from many countries, including countries where Spanish was the official language. He took his children to Parrot Jungle in Miami where there were lots of green parrots and lots of people who spoke Spanish, but the gods never saw fit to align all of life's forces to place him in a situation where he could again say, "*El loro es verde.*"

When Jeremy was poised between middle age and what comes next, he began to realize that the parrot incident had ceased to be simply a humorous one. It was a metaphor for words and events that should have been said and experienced. His marriage disintegrated, and he often thought of kisses that should have been taken and loves that were never realized, of hugs not given and conversations never spoken.

He began to berate himself for not making the opportunity of the parrot happen, since now so many people spoke Spanish and parrots were commonplace pets. *I must have missed the opportunity,* he thought, *just like I missed so much of life.*

Just when all the joy of the Señor Horowitz moment had gone out of his life and he realized that the parrot triumph would never be relived, the gods interceded.

Two old friends of his who also had recently divorced convinced him to take a full week's vacation in San Juan, Puerto Rico, where they would fish, swim, gamble, do some serious drinking, and chase *señoritas* into the wee hours of each morning. They arrived at their hotel late on a Sunday morning, and after checking into their respective rooms, met for a lavish brunch on the hotel's terrace.

The décor of the crowded Terrace Dining Room immediately put them into a festive vacation mood. The walls, chairs, tables were covered with fabrics filled with tropical birds and fish in bright cheerful colors. Even the waiters and waitresses wore azure shirts covered with exotic fish and birds. In the center of the restaurant stood a giant aviary – a cage with no bars, just several large tree limbs on which sat a dozen macaws in blazing colors of blue, yellow and scarlet. A cobalt blue giant hyacinth macaw sat at the center of the flock, and just to the side of them sat a small green parrot, less than half the size of the smallest blue and yellow macaw.

Jeremy smiled when he saw the parrot. *A green parrot,* he told himself, *and I'm in Puerto Rico.* His pulse quickened as Señor Horowitz's face appeared before him.

Jeremy's reverie was interrupted when a waitress came to take the beverage order. He noticed her name tag read "Maggie" and her accent was distinctly Midwestern. He asked her if she was Puerto Rican.

She smiled and said, "No, I'm from Michigan. I'm working here for the summer to improve my Spanish." Then she asked Jeremy if he wanted orange juice.

Before he could answer, there was an enormous crash. A few tables away a busboy had dropped a large steel tray of porcelain dishes, cups, and steel warming containers onto the ceramic tile floor. The noise was overwhelming. In unison, all of the startled birds left their perches and flew wildly a-bout the restaurant – into walls, onto tables, into the faces of several guests. The parrot lighted on the buffet table near a stack of French toast.

The upset *maitre domo* jumped on a chair in the center of the restaurant and shouted orders to his staff to recapture the macaws. He pointed to various servers, specifying which bird to capture. Then he yelled in English, "Maggie, get the parrot."

Maggie hesitated, looked confused, and shouted back in English, "What color is the parrot?"

Jeremy couldn't believe what he'd heard. The perfect cue was his. There it was, down through four decades of time, a blessing, a chance to relive a moment of his carefree youth. He got to his feet and nervously banged a spoon harshly on the glass tabletop and said loudly, " *Señoritas y señores.*"

The *maitre domo*'s mouth dropped open. All of the diners and staff and Jeremy's two friends stared at him. The macaws stared at him, and the little green parrot cocked its head in anticipation.

Jeremy narrowed his eyes and said clearly in a booming voice, "*Yo quiero las señoritas con grande chichas!*"

And he promptly sat down, knowing that something was still wrong with his life.

THE END

Carlos O. Gómez, Jr.
Oceanside, CA. United States

Carlos O. Gomez, Jr. was born in Delicias, Chihuahua, Mexico in 1976. He emigrated to the U.S. with his family at the age of six. He grew up in San Jose, California, and graduated from Yerba Buena High School in 1994. Mr. Gomez earned an A.A. degree from San Jose City College in 1996, and transferred to UC Santa Barbara where he completed a Bachelor's of Science degree in Biological Sciences in the year 2000. In 2001, he finished his teaching credential (science) at UCSB and a Masters of Education. Feeling he needed to give back to his community, he taught high school in East San Jose, helping to establish a Charter High School for three years, and also for the East Side Union High School District. He completed a second Master degree in Administration and Leadership from San Jose State University in 2004 and moved to Southern California to begin his career as a High School Administrator. He is currently an Assistant Principal at the largest high school in San Diego County, Rancho Buena Vista High. He considers the need to cultivate and develop bi-literacy in Latino students as the single biggest challenge facing educators today.

Immigrant Me
By Carlos O. Gómez, Jr.

I had not seen the ocean before I visited Santa Cruz in '84. It was a Friday in mid April. The morning when we set out from San Jose had been gloomy and gray; a persistent fog, the type that burns off in the afternoon, had smothered the South Bay overnight. Beyond our valley, the bus ride to our destination was difficult, uphill on the treacherous Highway 17. As we climbed over the mountain, the switchbacks made me queasy. I suffer from car sickness, and if it weren't for the distracting chatter and excitement around me, I would have puked.

The bus hummed along, slowing in shifts between gears. We stared in awe at the tall redwoods and forest outside our windows. I imagined an amazing scene: seeing a deer along the road, feeding on the brush. If I discovered the animal and pointed it out before anyone else, I'd be the hero of the journey early on. Most of us had never seen a deer, or been outside our neighborhoods.

The bus ride through Scotts Valley as we neared Santa Cruz was like being in another planet. Large rustic-looking homes sat on tracts of green lawns with enough running room for me and my friends to play soccer. At the apartment complex where I lived, the grass was dead and we played on the street.

We came onto Ocean Street from Highway 17. We were finally in Santa Cruz. I looked at the strange sights before me, quaint shops, everyone wearing long shorts and sandals. The beach town, with its slender avenues, was coming alive. I was overwhelmed by the Americana: small U.S. flags hanging on windows and doors, surfers walking with their boards, and skaters doing tricks on street corners. My Mexican existence got shocked. I no longer felt the comfort of my world. The familiar grounds of my *barrio* and school, all I'd ever known, cowered in the back of my mind. On Beach Street we got our first glimpse of the beach. I'd seen desert sand back in Chihuahua, but this sand had an irregular blue boundary that retreated and re-emerged, life giving, not callous.

As we neared the parking lot of the beach boardwalk, you could hear screaming across the street, rising and falling away, the sounds of the roller coaster. We parked, and stood up eagerly on our cramped legs before Mrs. Garcia, our teacher, temporarily popped our balloons. "Stay in your seat," she said, "I have to tell you the park rules…"

Mrs. Garcia was a second mother to us. She was still young, perhaps early thirties, short, dark brown skin, with typical Latina curves, full breasts and hips. There weren't many dark brown people where I'd grown up in Chihuahua: Meoqui, a small town forty-five minutes south of the state capital. The *pueblo* was named after General Pedro Meoqui, who died in battle fighting the French in 1865. Most of the people of Meoqui were fair complexioned. So was I. I'd been called a little *güerito* — a blond, fair skinned person — all of my life.

Being fair-skinned and blond had given me identity and a sense of superiority among my friends back in Mexico. '*Que güerito esta su hijo, señora,*' adults would tell my mother, patting my head, making me feel special. It was like a gift from God, for I could pass for a white kid when in need. The need materialized in Ciudad Juarez, summer of '83. I was six at the time.

'When we get across, I want you and your sister to start playing like skipping, throwing rocks, whatever,' had said the Coyote on whose shoulders I sat as we crossed a canal of the Rio Grande. 'Should be very easy for the two of you *güeritos*,' he'd said, a little further along, huffing and puffing, water up to his knees.

I was competitive by nature. This too was a godsend. The games in class were timed: quickest to complete the addition worksheet got a star. 'I'm finished!' was our call of victory. So sweet to scream it out, please the teacher, and rub it in the face of the other kids. I won many math battles in class. Outside, the boys battled each other: fastest to the wall starting at the swings, best at Four Square, and other games. The lean kids like Jorge, Pedro, and me always beat everyone else at sports.

Things were different in America. Brown-skinned Mexicans like Jorge and Pedro were in the majority. They made fun of *güeros* like me. They called me names like "whiteboy" and "gringo." Then there was Lucas, a Mexican-American, who spoke few Spanish words. Jorge and Pedro called him a name I'd never heard before, "pocho." Lucas was pudgy, pot-bellied, had droopy cheeks, and always bit his bottom lip when nervous. He was li-ke our mascot.

The four of us hated being separated. "Do you speak Spanish?" the teacher asked out-loud every day after lunch, prompting the class. Since Lucas didn't, he had to follow the aide with the one or two black and white kids in the class. They belonged to the, "*Un Poco Nada Más,*" or "Just A Little" group. Jorge, Pedro, myself, the rest of the newcomers, were placed in the, "*¡Si, Cómo No!*" or "Yes, Of Course!" group. The teacher worked

with us on improving our elementary level Spanish. Bilingual Education was in its
heyday.

We got off the bus in Santa Cruz, and breathed the clean air. The smell of beach air and seaweed was distinctive, just like San Jose smog and the dumpster smells of my apartment complex. I wore shorts, sandals, and a t-shirt, as we were told to do in the Spanish letter sent to our families. The sun was out, good thing too. Santa Cruz was cooler than I'd thought it would be. Jorge, Pedro, Lucas, and I walked up the hill into the park, planning how we would spend our day. We'd heard about the arcade and some of the rides from Mrs. Garcia.

We walked onto the boardwalk and quickly noticed we weren't alone. Multiple schools from the South Bay had chosen the same day to have a fieldtrip. We stood still for a few seconds, getting our bearings. Everywhere, kids ran to the rides, cackling in English. 'Let's go to Loggers Revenge!' one white kid had yelled to his friend.

Jorge, our unelected leader, strongest and most aggressive, good with the girls, decided what we should do first. "To the arcade!" he said. Playing video games was the least scary thing to do. We were new to the park. We had no idea what it took to get on a ride, where to get food, or even where to find the arcade. The American kids went about with ease, their sense of entitlement, their fear of nothing, made us jealous.

Ms. Pac-Man, Space Invaders, and Frogger were beginning to tire us out. We played the same games at the liquor store and laundromat back home. We beat a few gringo kids at Space Invader and enjoyed erasing their initials on the highest score list. "Stupid wetbacks," a blond, blue-eyed lanky kid said walking away. We didn't need to know English to figure out what those two words meant. We called him a "*culero*" (asshole) in return, and kept playing.

Jorge and Pedro went off to play a game of air hockey. They were daring and bold, and not too smart. Lucas and I were the thinkers, reserved. Since I was the most athletic of the pair, I took charge. "I'm going outside for a second," I told Lucas. He was into his game, jostling with the joystick, so he gave me a quick nod. I was hungry. Out on the boardwalk, I saw a crowd gathered around a food court. "Hey Luis!" I turned towards the voice calling my name. A couple of girls from our class, Leticia and Maria, approached me. They started talking about a ride they'd been on, the Giant Dipper. I was jealous.

Leticia explained how to get on the rides: "You need to buy passes at a booth first." She showed me their remaining passes, a proud look on her face. I was cool. "We're just waiting for the lines to go down," I said to them. Lucas came out of the arcade and joined us. "Lucas is scared of the rides," I said to the girls, showing off. Lucas turned beet red with anger. He heard his name, and could tell we were laughing at him. He couldn't do anything. I'd given him plenty of purple and blue marks on his arm at school. Lucas was a regular goof. Plus he didn't speak enough Spanish to make a comeback.

Lucas went off on his own, looking upset. "Lucas, where *ya* going?" I said. I lost him in the food court. The girls left and I was alone. My shirt was moist with sweat from playing video games. *I hope Leti and Maria didn't leave because I smell,* I thought.

I had five, one-dollar bills in my pocket which was all my parents could afford to give me. I noticed a short line at the left of the food lines, and kids standing around with chocolate-covered ice cream cones. I went to buy one, believing it'd be easy. I'd just point at the image of the cone pasted on the side of the cart, give the man my money, and grab my delectable reward.

'What'll *ya* have?' said the gringo man. I pointed. He prepared a vanilla cone. I handed him a dollar, grabbed the cone and turned away. I wanted chocolate, but couldn't complain. I had accomplished something new, a purchase in an American theme park. I felt good about myself, licking the cold vanilla cream, instantly feeling the sugar in my mouth.

Suddenly I heard a call behind me. 'Hey kid,' said the ice cream man, 'you forgot your change.'

I got scared. *Is he talking to me?* I asked myself in Spanish. I turned, wondering if I should flee. 'Kid, where you going?' said the gringo, pointing at some coins in his hand. I stood frozen, his language incomprehensible to me.

'Come get your change!' he said getting visibly frustrated.

'Me, no,' I said, unwilling to complete the broken sentence I had learned, '*Me no es-speak inglish,*' out of fear of sounding alien.

Things got worse. The man saw a security guard pass by his stand. The security guard carried a radio in his hand, wore black khakis, and a grey cotton shirt with the word, SECURITY, in the middle of it. He was a buff black man, thick forearms, with mittens for hands. His swollen biceps stretched out the sleeves of his shirt.

There were two black kids in my class, and the man before me was the fourth I'd ever seen in person. There was a black fourth grade teacher at our Elementary school, Mr. Gibbs. Back in December, on the last lunch recess before Christmas vacation, Mr. Gibbs had put on Michael Jackson at the MTV Video Music Awards. M.J. had unveiled the moonwalk to the world and danced to "Billy Jean." The hype about Michael Jackson's performance had been so widespread. I don't think I would've accompanied my friends to Mr. Gibbs' class otherwise. He'd been called the meanest teacher at the school and I was scared of him.

If it wasn't for Michael Jackson, his charisma and flare, I think I would've peed on myself. Standing there that day, seeing the ice cream man talking to the black security guard, was one of the most unnerving experiences of my life.

'Can you give this change to that kid there?'

'Sure,' the guard said, 'which kid?'

'That one right there,' he said pointing at me.

I shook my head nervously. *No, I didn't try to steal that money from the change jar*, I thought to myself. *Please don't take me.* I'd heard that park Security took you to the police if you did something wrong. The police would whip you, with something called a, "ticket." I imagined getting lashes with this, "ticket." I'd been hit in my open palms with a ruler back in Meoqui, but a whip? *This is serious*, I thought to myself.

Even scarier, I'd also heard of kids getting dropped off at the Immigration Office by the police. I didn't want to get deported.

The black man walked towards me, instantly intimidating me. I was going to drop my cone and make a break for it, but my legs wouldn't budge. It was as if my sandals were stuck to the wooden boards below me. Before he got to me, Lucas reached me from the side.

'Here you go son,' said the security guard holding two quarters in between his index finger and thumb, lowering his tree trunk of an arm towards my caved-in chest. 'You forgot your change.' I didn't want the coins. I assumed he was showing me what I'd tried to steal.

'I'll take it for him mister,' said Lucas. 'Thanks.' *¡No Lucas!* I yelled in my head. *What are you doing?* The man relinquished the quarters.

'Anytime, kid,' he said to Lucas.

The voyage back to the Santa Clara valley was faster going downhill. I flipped from daydream to reflection as we descended the mountain. My classmates were laid out along their seats, sleeping, wasted by the park. Mrs. Garcia turned around to look at us all, always the mother hen, saw me with my eyes still open, and gave me a smile. I returned a less audacious one.

I stared outside the window thinking of Lucas. How he had rescued me from the security guard, the police, and the Immigration. By the time we got back to school, I had decided to never make fun of him again. It was great, being more popular because I was smarter, faster, and stronger. It was entertaining to take advantage of Lucas, speaking in Spanish. Yet he possessed strength none of us (Mexicans) had: The power of English. As I'd learned in Santa Cruz, knowing English is what mattered. Now *I* desired this power, more than anything else.

Aleksandra Djordjevic

Aleksandra Djordjevic is a graduate of Wilkes University, where she obtained her Masters in Creative Writing. She is also a graduate of the University of Scranton, where she obtained her Bachelor's in English. She currently resides in Clarks Summit, Pennsylvania.

Black Agate
By Aleksandra Djordjevic

*L*ily is on the take to cut her hair.

She needs a pair of shears to do it, and she is at the grocery store, looking for some.

She has heard this store in particular has what she needs, and she is so happy when she sees there is one pair left. Evidently, other people in the area have had the same idea as she.

About three weeks ago, Lily went to a salon near her where her stylist was rude and treated her badly. Because of this, Lily feels she wants to take matters into her own hands and try giving herself the cut she wanted to begin with, but didn't get.

Lily goes to the self-check-out and pays for her other items (a comb, a spray bottle, black lipstick, and black eyeliner) and she makes sure she gets her change from the slot down below.

She gets into her car, a '99 Pontiac black Esprit, and blasts a song she has never heard before on the radio.

When she gets home, her mother is baking cookies, a pastime Lily is all too fond of, especially when she feels stressed out and in need of comfort.

"Hi, Mom. Shall I make dinner tonight?" Lily places her plastic Check - 'n-Save bag on the kitchen counter, and sees that all the ingredients for a pizza have been laid out.

"No, honey. I'm just putting the finishing touches on things. You go lie down. I'm sure you must be pretty tired from school."

Contrary to what her mother has just said, Lily is *not* tired. In fact, she thinks now would be the perfect time to get started on her styling.

She goes to her room and takes out everything she bought, then heads to her bathroom where she washes her hair for ten minutes and drapes a towel over her shoulders. She is semi-excited, semi-nervous about how this will all turn out, but Lily knows she has an artist's eye, so she estimates everything will be fine.

By the time she is finished, dinner is almost ready. Her mother is reading in the kitchen and has just pulled out the cookies, where their comfortingly soft fragrance wafts into Lily's room and makes her question whether the black lipstick is too much.

She is all made out now, hair all combed, sprayed through, cut, dried, and styled, and just as she is working up the guts to show her mother, there is a phone call.

"Yes, hello. My name is Irina and I'm calling from *Sudden Queen* magazine. Is Lily there?"

"Yes, she is. Just a moment."

Lily's mother hands her the phone, barely noticing the work she has done.

"Hello?" Lily grins to herself, realizing that she must have done a great job on her hair because if she hadn't, her mother would have instantly said something.

"Hi, Lily. This is Irina and I'm calling from *Sudden Queen*. Your poem, "Battle Cry," completely won us over and I'd like to just read it back over to you so that we can go ahead and publish it in our Fall/Winter issue."

"Yeah, sure. Read away."

"Ok. *Night falls and I wonder where I'm going in the distance of my own orgiastic thoughts. I think of the day and as I look through the window of the breaking-down car I'm driving, I think I see your face among the stars making me want more from my world, my shock wave of a life. If I have lived to understand who I am, then I will have succeeded in my mission. If I have lived my mission, then I will have lived to sing the song of my beauty. Take this, my battle cry, and rest it beside the night where I lie at my grave, curiously hoping for another chance at believing in an unknown star.*"

"Yup. That's it. Seems like there's no mistakes."

"Terrific! Well, keep your eyes peeled for the next issue. I'll be sending one to you soon. And congratulations–you should be feeling proud."

"Thanks. I am."

"Ok then. Good-bye."

"Bye."

Lily puts the phone down and is about to look at herself again in her mirror, when her mother says, "Whoa. Come over here. Did you do something to your hair?"

Embarrassed by how short she's cut it, Lily ventures to look her mother in the eye, but instead takes a pen from the counter and starts to chew it.

"Cut it," she says, definitively.

"Well it looks great. You look like one of your models from *Vogue*–Linda Evangelista in her early years. Am I right?"

"Yes," Lily mumbles, silently smiling to herself.

"And you have just the right amount of make-up on," she says, looking at Lily's lipstick-free mouth. "Wow, I'm proud of you. This has been a great day, don't you think?"

"It has." Lily spits out a piece of plastic in her hand and looks to see when dinner will be ready.

"Just a few more minutes. So what was the poem that got accepted? I heard that Irina say something about one of your poems."

"Battle Cry. I wrote it a few months ago after I broke up with Josh."

"Oh. I see. Well, are you still feeling war-torn or should we cut this pizza now?"

"Let's cut it."

"Ok."

And with that, Lily and her mother sit down to dinner and talk about the classes Lily is taking at her university.

* * *

That evening, Lily decides to draw a self-portrait. She feels she has come to an epiphany about her looks. No longer afraid of them, she feels she has uncovered a beautiful gem stone within herself. She knows that how she looks has an impact on the clothes she picks out, and tonight she has a date...with a guy named Marlowe.

Mysterious and handsome, with green eyes and auburn hair, Marlowe used to be in her Darker Playwrights class, where the students studied, of course, Marlowe. Lily had been quite taken with his ability to charm, the way he moved, and the poems he left on her desk each morning before class. The notes ranged from serious to funny and she couldn't wait to show him her new haircut.

She was meeting him for coffee at a place called Brewed, and she was excited, knowing that he hadn't seen her for close to three months.

She was early when she got there, and she thought she'd read her journal of poems over before he arrived, because there were quite a few she wanted to share with him.

Ten minutes later and Marlowe enters the cafe, wearing dirty black skinny jeans and a black fitted jacket and tee.

Not recognizing Lily, he sits down at a table near the back and orders a café au lait (his favorite) and a raspberry Danish.

"Um, excuse me, is this seat taken?" Lily asked looking at the other tables, then looking at him.

"Oh my God! Lily! How are you? *Man*, you've changed!"

Laughing, he kissed her on the cheek and the two began to catch up on the classes they were taking and the poems they'd written.

At the end of the night, Lily looked at her watch–the café had closed an hour ago, and both had been sitting at a table and chair set outside. They watched the night and its colors weave its spell of enchanting streaks through the clouds, and before the morning came, Lily recognized something in herself. All this time, she had been a poet and it had taken a trip to her local grocery store and a new haircut for her to come to this point. She'd changed, that was for sure, and she knew that she was on the brink of something big: like the night sky, and that her urge to write poetry was her battle cry, and as she parted from Marlowe, she thought she heard a distant sound of singing, like a bard the true Marlowe had once known, and at that moment, Lily began to play chords within herself: I am me and no one else/Beauty lives on the artists' shelf. And with that, she saw him in an alleyway, petting a black cat and saying, "All poetry rests in He/who lives in the Soule's Poetrie." And he disappeared, and she was left to forever wonder whether what she had seen was her imagination or real.

AHMED-HAMID WOODY BAGALA-ALINA

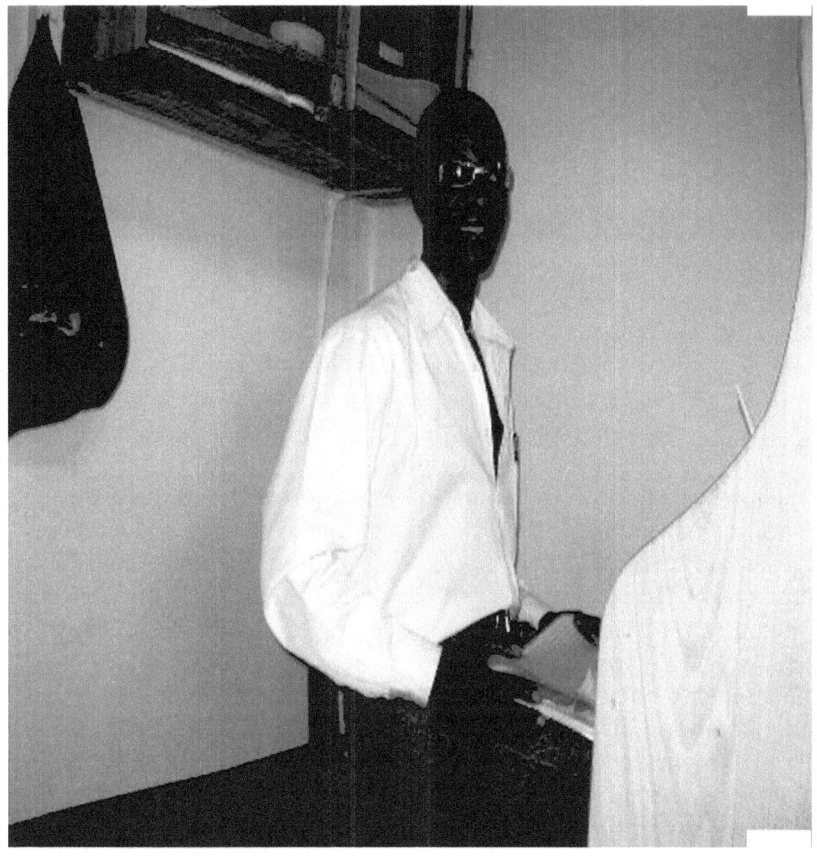

Woody was born in Jinja, a small sleeping town 80kms from the capital. He writes screenplays, short stories, poems and full length fiction/nonfiction books. He lives alone in an apartment fifteen minutes from the Nile and twenty from the Victoria. He sometimes works gigs a doorman, bodyguard/driver, tour guide and has worked as a teacher teaching English to disadvantaged children for eight years; he has also worked in a laundry shop, as a mason, fitness instructor and administrator. One people, One love, One world One God. God is ONE. Creativity is organized random thoughts & aspirations. One people, One love, One world One God. God is ONE. Creativity is or-ganized random thoughts & aspirations.

The Lizard Of Hornland
By Woody Bagala

Once upon a time, long before man made the telephone or discovered electricity, all animals and birds lived together with him. During this period, man did not even have the concept of making his life different from that of his lesser intelligent friends. And if someone where to tell him that in future he would be enemies with almost all the animals, he would have torn the teller to several small pieces and fed him to the nearest carnivore. It would be thousands of years later that he would completely and utterly alienate himself from all but a few of these creatures and he would call it a better life. First he would attempt to kill most of them; either directly or indirectly. Then he would create centres where he could go to watch them at his leisure, denying them their God-given freedom.

A freedom to live wild and free. The stupidest thing about all this would be that man, clever as he thinks of himself, would one day accept that he indeed is one of the most foolish beings on earth. Because in denying wild animals their right to live wild and free, he would slowly kill his own world. The lesser of the wild lived: in seas and oceans, lakes and rivers, streams and ponds, bushes and thickets, forests and jungles, under the ground and in the vast blue sky; the lesser the earth` s ability to sustain him. But as all these things go, by then it will be too late for him to do anything useful about it.

At about this point he would also form various organizations to protect these nearly extinct species of God`s creation from none other than himself. At this point in time, he would lose all his natural enjoyment of paradise on earth, however much he would delude himself and his kin. And he would then always live in fear of the wild and what it contained. He would then start to regret why he did not stick to a simpler diet of animal protein, or completely go vegetarian, instead of experimenting with all kinds of meat. He would also regret, though he would be loathed to confess, his mindless pursuit of wild game in the name of sport and leisure. But then again, this is the whole summary of man` s life story; spoil a good thing the best way he knows how and also mess with scripture: do something he should not then spend a better part of his life regretting and repenting it — all the while doing it over and over again.

It all started with a small not very tasteful fruit and a big perfect garden. Sometimes in April it is very hard to forgive man or look on him sympathetically. Why did Eve not eat a yellow banana? Or a pineapple?

* **

At this time, man had not yet learned to build homes. Well at least not those made from mortar and stone and wood and iron. He used to live down in caves. And up in trees.

And sometimes forests. Or when the weather was good, in open spaces. Under tented skins of past animals with immortal hide and skins, held together by tight strings of dried intestine from drowned hippo. With poles forming the building pillars of his simple land scrappers, the tallest structure of the period was three times taller than man. And he needed the help of giraffes to achieve this. The other animals did not begrudge him his need for privacy and periodical nocturnal isolation. It was a respect thing.

All animals and birds respected other animals and birds, themselves and each other. The animals that were meat for other animals and birds, took it for granted that they had to be eaten. This included animals like goats, sheep, cattle and rabbits. Even the birds did not feel bad about being eaten by other birds or animals; they all knew it was God` s plan and accepted it. Man would always apologise first before hunting down animals or shooting birds or spearing fish. He would always explain that he had to feed his family. Most of the time though, man fed on fruit and vegetables. This fruit obsession would stay with man all his days; and most nights, too.

Eat or be eaten and eat and get eaten were all good. Remember, this was all God` s grand master plan for his creation. This though did not stop this prey to run for their lives whenever their predators appeared. They would make all sorts of noise to try and get spared instead of speared; hoping to die of old age, illness or accidents. And they would run like the wind, if you would take a moment to forget that the wind that is normally in question has no legs to speak of. Or even shut up about, either. Among the most feared animals were man, lion, tiger, puma, buffalo, rhino, leopard, bear. The most feared reptiles were mostly snakes and lizards. Bees and butterflies were among the most gentle of creatures. One devoting time to making the sweetest excrement known to other animals; the other devoting to flying seemingly without effort. And to looking beautiful. In thousands of years to come the butterfly would revert to making hurricanes every now and again out of anger at man` s way of handling animals.

The locusts spent their time eating weed (and not the kind that would e-ventually drive man nuts either) and dying leaves in autumn. But among all these, the most feared was the lizard of Hornland.

Hornland was a place full of trees big and tall and flowers colorful and beautiful. And shallow green rivers teeming with fish that one could catch with a basket and lakes, big blue and deep, full of bigger fish. The trees had very sweet and colourful fruit. The flowers, some with all the colours of the rainbow, were the most lovely in all the lands. The rivers and lakes had the sweetest tasting fish ever with water so green it filled ivy with en-vy and so blue it made the sky shy. The air was so sweet and fresh weaker animals were left swooning from inhaling it. The grass so soft it felt like the fur of a baby polar.

Hornland was a place meant for immortals and those born with a ten-dency and yearning to live long; gods and kings and queens and princes and princesses and gentle non aggressive creatures. Even man did not deserve to live there for he was known for his fits of temper when things did not go in a particular direction for him or when something or someone got in the way of his plans. Perhaps it had been a part of God`s grander plan, not even royals living here. For this was a true paradise. When man got into paradise, he would always get a little wicked, especially if said pa-radise was surrounded with or annexed to bodies of water so beautiful they made one want to cry. And the amount of fruit variety there would add to the complications and temptations anyway.

Hornland was a place that everyone wanted to go; man, his children, animals and birds. It was also the most dangerous place around. Whoever wanted to go there had to first collect a group of friends to escort him or her. The chances of coming back alive were almost always less than half. Man forbade his children from going there under any circumstances. All creation living around here was of the view that Hornland was the original garden. Everything else fit this story except the horned lizards. Normally, when any animal or bird wanted to visit Hornland, they asked for help from the locust family.

The locusts would then go and clear large areas so that if any lizard we-re hiding, it would be easier to see them before tragedy struck. Besides, the locusts and other insects were harder for the lizards to attack, being small-er, able to fly high and all.

The king of Hornland, a horned lizard (obviously) called Big Horn (not very obvious any longer) was the biggest lizard ever to live (no doubt). Big Horn was as big as a hammerhead shark but stronger than six whales wor-king together. Yet big as he was, he was still very fast and agile both in attack and defense. What made the horned lizard very dangerous was that it could climb trees just like other primates; swim faster that a hungry shark and had a poison so strong it made a cobra`s seem like the spittle of a dirty monkey. What made the horned lizard even worse was that it could bite or spit the poison from a distance. It could use its gigantic tail to slice prey into two and worst of all it was very anti-social. It lived in isolation and attacked not only birds and animals and fish and ants and insects but man too. A legend among earlier man had it that thousands of years to come, some men would contract some of the horned lizard traits and would behave in much the same manner.

None of the living creatures believed this. Besides, it was not clear who exactly had foretold this happening. If everyone, and everything, did not fear the validity of this particular legend, they would have tried harder to find out.

It was faster than a cheetah. It could jump from one tree to the next just like a collobus monkey and had a large mouth where a small animal could fit.

It could also use its two sharp pointed horns on the top if its head as very effective impelling weapons. The worst quality about this lizard was that he was willing to use all his power and ability to force other animals and birds and man to fear him and regard him as their king. He and his kind were the hardest animals to kill and they were said to live for a minimum of five hundred years. The crows were their only allies in the quest for lizard supremacy.

Their reproductive ways and cycle was weird; male and female could reproduce but each could only make a baby once every ten years. This though, meant that a pair of horned lizards could make a population of another one hundred in their lifetime. These lizards started reproducing from the age of ten; for that is when they become young adults capable of giving birth. Giving birth to twins or triplets was unheard of among these creatures and maybe that was a good thing for their foes. At this point in time, there were said to be two hundred adult horn lizards and the youngest was one hundred years.

Their king, Big Horn was two hundred fifty years and had twenty five children. The oldest horned lizard was Speed Horn who was five hundred and thirty years old. He was Big Horn`s father and had named his son as king after him. He retired when he ate a python liver that turned out to be infected by four adult cobra poisons which the python had swallowed days earlier. He became blind within days and lost the use of his legs. This had been thirty years ago and everyone, including himself, had expected him to pass on soon after that. Now palace guards taste his cuisine before he had to eat it. This meant that he no longer enjoyed fresh liver but had to eat it three or more days after the guard` s tasting to be fairly sure it was safe to eat. His people feared that in his weakened and wizened state, even the smallest amount of poison would off him so fast he would not have time to say ciao. His medicine lizard, a lizard equivalent of later man`s shaman, even denied him fish bile, a very tasty appetizer for horned lizards. Speed Horn sometimes felt like snapping the fella into six and serving him for brunch.

Though according to lizard custom nothing much would be wrong with this, Speed feared all that poison in Weasle Horn would kill him dead several times over and then do it again; just for tail snaps.

One day, when an elephant accidentally tramped dead a baby lizard, Big Horn had sent two of his most fearsome warriors to Elephant Land and they had killed five hundred and maimed three hundred elephants. Among other causalities were two million grasshoppers, six hundred bees, five million butterflies, one billion ants, two hundred sixty seven rabbits, five dogs, one cat and one child. To be fair to the lizards, evil as they were, most of the dead animals and insects were killed not by design but as a matter of course. Some of these were killed by dead or dying elephants falling. There was no malice aforethought in these actions. When the child fell to his death, he killed five hundred ants, three butterflies and the cat which had actually been his pet.

He had then announced that from then on, if any of the other animals or birds or man hurt a lizard, he would kill a thousand of each species; fish, animals, birds, insects and man. It did not matter whether it was an accident or incident of attack.

By then, man could still talk to animals, birds, insects and fish; and they also could talk to him and each other. Though man was never and never will be the strongest being on earth, he is the most intelligent and if he chooses to make the right choices he can rule over the earth and the heavens. So when he heard Big Horn`s announcement, he called together all the leaders of the different animals, birds, insects and fish for a meeting.

They met at Melting Lake, a beautiful lake that had a shallow pond filled with ice and trees on the shoreline with large overhanging branches. It also had a large strip of land about three hundred meters long and thirty wide that ran from land into it. Melting Lake was an ideal meeting place for everyone and was actually the equivalent of a modern day metropolitan`s City Hall with access ramps for the disabled.

Here, two of a kind from the hawks, eagles, ostriches, falcons, owls, chickens, storks, geese, gulls, penguins and others could perch on tree branches or lounge on the ice or float in the shallow water.

Alongside them were cats, including the big five and the bigger animals. Though a lot of the animals, birds, insects and fish gathered were of high rank, it was only the elephants who were represented by their King and Queen. King Big Tusker and Her Majesty Cherriphant were received with solemn bows and whispered words of condolence. Their entourage had three hundred of the biggest and meanest tusker-carriers ever known. Apparently, they were not taking any chances.

Man made a fervent speech about the lost ones and the threats issued by Big Horn which he went on to explain were not idle threats but words that should be looked at as a promise. He said the only way they could ensure they were at peace and not live in fear would be to attack first. He politely asked the others who were grumbling about the wisdom of this course of action to be patient and calm. He went on:

`` Let me assure you I have reliable information to the effect that there are only one hundred horned lizards alive as of today. On our side, we would have more numbers and better weapons. The horned lizards are very fast but they cannot run or fly for long periods. My friends, those things tire very fast.

We know that their old king is blinded and very sick because he ate a python that had swallowed a few cobras. That means that as along as the cobras are with us we can kill the lizards. ``

`` Are you planning on making pythons swallow cobras then offering them to the lizards? ``, asked Big Brown, the in charge of security in the bunny population.

`` We shall not allow that! ``, hissed Mad Cobra, the handsome diamond back expected to take over the cobra kingdom after his father passed on. A python burped disrespectfully.

At this point there was a very loud and high pitched elephantine trumpet and every one froze. ``

Please allow him to finish and then we can all have our say, `` said Queen Cherriphant.

`` Thank you Queen Cherriphant. As I was saying, we have the numbers so all we need to do is use them right. Though one of my strategies is to use snake poison, it will have left the bodies of the donors. I plan on harvesting this poison and putting it on all kinds of weapons and food favourite to the horned lizard. So everyone here who can give us poison should do so starting now and coming back soon as they have produced more. I shall need the help of porcupines, hedgehogs, cheetahs, kites, hawks and eagles. Everyone is going to have a role to play, some of it very dangerous like the part I want the monkeys to play. ``

How come we always have to do the most dangerous stuff? `` asked Bemba. He was a royal in the monkey population.

`` Because our kind is the real deal, brother, `` thundered Apel a silver back, beating his chest like no one else except his kind could.

For a moment it looked like Growl-Up, one of the bravest lions ever known to live was going to object.

Then Lion-On, his equally fearless mate, put her paw on his tail in what Babbit- a very stubborn rabbit, would later claim was a restraining gesture.

Six months later, man had his army and his weapons. And the horned lizard had not a clue as to what man and his friends were planning. Man, with the help of his friends, had mixed more than thirteen poisons and carefully wrapped them in large leaves. The poison was so potent that when an adult elephant accidentally trampled one leaf, he died moments later. He had not even had to eat the poison!

On the appointed day, like they had earlier agreed, all animals, birds, fish and insects started off at designated areas and headed to Hornland, the monkeys in the lead and the fish staying in the waters.

Whenever necessary, birds given this job would pick up the fish and fly them from one body of water to the next.

Actually as their plans had progressed, everyone had come to appreciate the logic behind using the monkeys as scouts and primary attacking force; they were agile, fearless and quiet when they wanted to be. The idea was that once the monkeys were in position, they would signal the birds who would start flying overhead, distracting the lizards and also dropping poisoned pellets carefully carried in their talons. The fish were to poison the shallows were the lizards drank their water.

Because they set very early in the morning, they found the lizards still asleep, some in trees but most on the ground. The fish that were required to poison the waters around Hornland and their bird helpers that man had dubbed `The force of the air` and that Babbit christened Air force`, had set off even much earlier and by the time the monkeys were set, the water was poisoned. The monkeys, like ordered, ignored the lizards in the trees and started throwing poison pellets that they had carried in large leaves at the lizards on the ground.

As the lizards stirred and started rallying to defend, the birds started throwing their pellets and making a racket of glorious noise. They were swooping and angrily pecking with their beaks, aiming for the eyes as man had suggested. If the enemy is blinded, he cannot fight very well as he would not be sure where exactly you were going to be attacking from.

Because the attack was well co-ordinated and executed by a large force, the lizards were soon in disarray. It seemed everywhere they turned they were being maimed and killed. All the animals were on the attack, even the butterflies flapping their majestic wings frantically and stirring up a lot of wind!

Kristin R. Schulz
Newton, Kansa, United States

Kristin Schulz started writing at the age of 10. She is a sophomore in high school, where she enjoys managing football and boys baketball. Also, she participates in the Writers Anonymous club where she can share her stories and poems with other students who love writing. Outside of school, Kristin enjoys playing the piano or violin; drawing animals and/or scenes from her small town of Newton, Kansas. She also enjoys spending quality time with her family and friends.

Missing Jammy Lynn
By Kristin R. Schulz

*M*onday, January 26th, 1991

Mommy never listens to me. Sometimes I want her to go away. Daddy left today so he could have some quiet time, from mommy. It's because mommy and daddy had a fight and so she got angry and he left. Mommy saw me and started yelling. I tried really hard to tell her why I was downstairs, but she didn't listen to me. Mommy almost hit me. I ran up here and now I want to disappear. But I don't want to leave sissy or brother. But I really want to DISAPPEAR!

Jammy Lynn

Tuesday, January 27th, 1991

"Detective Guy here. What happened?" I reached the old style Victorian home in Massachusetts on that late afternoon. First thing I saw and heard was the owner's wife, crying her heart out. I walked into the parlor and asked again, "What happened here?" And her dark brown eyes slowly moved up and locked on mine.

"My daughter is missing and I think it's all my fault. I..." She started babbling on but it's hard to tell what happened next because as soon as she said "I", screams from outside arose. it took a bit for the wife to register what was going on so the rest of us ran out to see what was happening.

We got out there, and low and behold a huge bear standing in the front lawn. Some of the officers who had come, tried shooting it down with tazer, but they tazed each other instead. It was as if this massive beast had a force field or something that allowed nothing to come through. As soon as the officers were down the bear dropped something on the ground. The woman then walked out of the house, and seeing the bear, fell down in shock. I rolled my eyes. As I turned my head away from her, the bear was gone, like magic. I was only turned away for a split second, and then he was gone.

I walked over and picked up the item that had been left be the bear. It looked like a little girl's wand from a faerie or princess costume. To me it just meant more evidence, but when I turned around to face the mother, at an instance I knew, to her it meant more.

"Can I see that?" She sounded so clueless, but somehow angry at me for even the thought of touching it.

"I'm sorry ma'am, but it's evidence." I felt scared for the second time of my life after that. That face she gave me, so horrible that it reminded me of something. My mother, when I was younger, she used to drink a lot. Whenever she was too drunk, she would come home, see me and give me that same look just before she hit me with the umbrella that my father and given me. I never used one after that.

We stood there for a moment, just staring at one another. Though soon, a bright golden school bus pulled up to the lonely curb. A tall girl, about 15 and a boy, about 9, walked out of the doors and onto the glossy grass. Apparently they thought that I was hurting their mother, for the two ran over and inspected her.

"What did you do!?" The girl yelled. For some reason the girl sounded not angry at me, but her mother. I glanced down at her brother and could tell that he was uneasy about something. I wanted to talk with them but it was getting dark so I retreated to my car and drove off.

Wednesday, January 28th, 1991

"Mom! Where's Jammy? I haven't seen her and I need to give her something." I woke up that day and went to wake Jammy Lynn, but I found her bed not touched. When I went downstairs to ask mom, she was trying to tell Ethan that she was his mother not that other person.

"Hey! Stop that you may have married our dad, but you're not our mother. Ethan, go upstairs."

"Now listen here Elizabeth, I married you father and that does make me your mother."

"You can't understand how wrong you are Debra! Dad married you because he needed someone to look after us. Not try to push out memories of our real mom."

"Look here. A little girl lost in thinking. You wouldn't know a good mother when you saw one!"

"I know you aren't one of those. You're going to die out sometime. Dad will get rid or you before you can do anything else..." I couldn't even finish what I was saying. She could of killed me if I hadn't ran upstairs. But the odd thing was that I ran into Jammy's room. I had even slammed the door shut. When I turned to lay down on the bed I realized where I was. Apparntly Ethan had ran in there too, because he was hiding under the bed. I coaxed him out long enough to calm him down. He sat on the bed but jumped right up again, as if had sat on a tack. I stared at the spot of impact with wonder. There was a small trinket in the shape of a wolf. Ethan tried to touch it, but it just flew across the room. I walked toward where it had landed, and could see that it had a note tied to it. Untying it I could see writing on it. As I read it, Ethan must have gotten worried because he pulled me toward him and had me read it aloud.

Thursday, January 29th, 1991

Elizabeth and Ethan Rosebottom came that day to see me. They looked terrified and lonely. When I asked where their mother was, the girl gave me this look that had a tone, that stated why should I care about her, she doesn't care about us. That look also told a story, a very sad and neglected story.

"I need you to look at this." Her voice sounded so serious and sure. I looked at her and then to the boy. To me he looked as serious as his sister, but I soon learned otherwise.

"Would you just look at it already? Sissy could be hurt and I want to see her!" The first words I ever heard out of that little mouth. So harsh and alarming. Like when a kid tells their parents they want to die.

Afraid someone would come in screaming that I kidnapped the kids, I gently grabbed the item from the girl and held it for the next five minutes.

"You going to do something with it or just sit there staring at it. I mean if you aren't going to help us then we can go elsewhere. Because we NEED to find Jammy, and we'll do that with or without you."

"Now look here. I'm just trying to think of how this came into her possession. You did after all say she never had it before. So why would it be in her room?"

"Does it look like I know? After all I'm just a kid and so is she. Which is why I need to find her. We both need her back home." Before I could reply she whipped her head around and pulled the boy down under the coffee table, and the woman I had talked to earlier appeared in the door way.

"You! First you don't help me and then you take the only kids I have left at home?! You are so in trouble, and I hope you burn in hell! oh, and one more thing, if you don't want to lose everything, then I'd hope you find my daughter." After that she just stomped out of the room. Leaving us with a shocked expression on my face.

"Is Debra gone yet?" Elizabeth faintly asked. When I didn't answer she rushed out of the hiding place and over to my chair. She sat me down, and it felt as if I were in a hospital. It was then that I wondered, why did the girl call her mother by her first name? Elizabeth must have read the question in my expression because she then sat next to me and began telling me the story.

Friday, January 30th, 1991

I had just finished analyzing the wolf figurine when, the telephone rang and surprisingly it was my superior, asking where I'd been.

"Sir", I said. "I'm on a case involving a missing child and I suspicions about the mother. So far the only evidence I have is a few statements, a little girls wand, and a small wolf figurine...No sir...Sir please! Yes, sir; good bye sir." That was the last time I heard from him.

Depressed at the previous conversation I called Elizabeth Rosebottom on her cellular devise. When I told her though, the tone of that voice was just so horrified and sad that I almost walked over to the superior and said, "Hey, I will and can keep searching for that child with or without your consent." I didn't though.

After I hung up, I walked over to my evidence, bagged it and then placed neatly into a locked drawer.

-Eight Years Later-

Monday January 26th, 1999

"Daddy, daddy... What's this?" I couldn't believe what Johnny held gently in his hands. A piece of hair!

Candice had apparently told him to come ask me, and I'm glad she did. The hair in my perspective and guess was from that girl. Man, who was she? Jammy Lynn! That was it, Jammy Lynn. Oh, sorry, where was I...oh yes, so I immediately called off my families vacation.

Tuesday, January 27th, 1999

Detective Guy called me today for the first time in eight years. At first I thought that he called me to say hi, but it wasn't so. He called...to tell me...that he was personally reopening the case of my sister. I asked him if I could call Ethan or Debra. He just sounded outraged. Though, luckily he allowed E-than to know. So once I finished with the detective, I immediately called Ethan and explained everything. Over the phone, I could tell that he was writing everything down. So I instantly told him not to let 'mom' see it or hear him talk about it. After that he said he still has some school work, so I let him go.

Wednesday, January 28th, 1999

Ethan came over today with a bag of cloths and a pillow. He looked so terrified and angry. When I asked him why he was over here, he just went to the guest bedroom and slammed the door. I could of sworn that I had heard him crying.

That evening I got a call from the detective. He sounded really beat up so I invited him and his family over for super. He gratefully accepted. Thirty minutes late he was over with the family and sitting down to eat.

After dinner I pulled Mr. Guy off to the side and asked him, what the matter was. The shrug he gave wasn't enough. I re asked and this time, ma-de him look me in the eye. As he finished answering the clock struck 1 o'clock and they left for their own home. When they left I turned away from the door, and walked over to my room like a zombie.

Ethan tried to comfort me, but it didn't work out so well. He asked what the detective had told me, and again I was unresponsive. I just stayed in my room for the remainder of the evening. Listening to the sounds of the neighbor's dog, Frisky barking at the bush outside of his cage.

Thursday, January 29th, 1999

Mr. Rosebottom appeared at my office today. For the longest time I didn't even think he was alive. I mean, 8 years ago when I was on the case for the first time, he was nowhere to be seen. Now he's suddenly here, in my office! In my field of expertise, that usually spells trouble.

"I'm sorry for the intrusion detective, but I need some answers on a case. Well to get to the point, it's my daughter's case. She has been missing for eight years now. And I know it's been a while, but i need to find her." He sounded so infuriating, how could he do such a thing? Leave for 8 years and then come back and say..."Oh, I need help, my daughter got kidnapped 8 YEARS AGO!" Though the look on his face seemed so frightened. I just had to tell him.

"Sir, I was on that case eight years ago. We hit a dead end then and with only two pieces of evidence, we had to stop. I do have this however from the other day that my son found." Reaching for my pocket, the husband's face went blank. Though when I opened the small parchment to reveal the hair, he went white as if I had shot him.

"Is that... is that what I think it is? My daughter's hair?" He sounded so sure of himself that I nodded my head and smiled. But then he asked to see the others, and the smile faded. i told him that I couldn't do that. That I needed to see ID, and then get back with my superior before I could do that.

After we stood, staring at each other for, oh about 15 minutes, he turned around and stormed out the door. But before he slammed the door, he said that he deserved to know. It was so sudden and full or frustration that I had to do something drastic. Call the police.

Friday, January 30th, 1999

I can't believe this! He has done it again. Detective Guy has astonished me again. He called the cops, on my dad! I mean he did nothing wrong. All he did was ask to see a little evidence. It's not like he was going to murder him if he didn't show him them! True he was angry when he left but so what! That's just, UGH!

For once I actually thought that I was doing the wrong thing by going back to the place where I found the hair. You know to investigate more. Though my son had found it and not me, I had a pretty good idea about where he did. I was just expecting to find a place just how I left it. Not a whole tent, full of circus people.

Though I knew that something was up, I just kept thinking that I need-ed to go and see a show. So I started to walk over to the tent's opening and life the flap. When I did a huge bear stood up and raised a massive paw to knock me down. I turned my face and waited for the pain, but I never felt anything. I turned back around and the bear was down on all fours staring at a girl. She looked about 13 with a tattoo of a paw print on her ankle.

I walked into the tent a few minutes later and over to the girl. She asked me to follow her. I was wary about the request but I followed anyways. She led me to a small sitting area where a wolf put was sitting. She mo-tioned for me to sit, and so I did and she sat across from me next to the pup. When I sat down she started to tell me how she came to this place and what she remembered of her old life. After she was done I knew this was the missing child. She was the one I've been searching for.

When I could finally speak, I jumped up and screamed, "You! You need to come back with me! Your family has been missing you SOOOO mush!" Once I finished screaming, she stood up and said calmly, "Alright. But I'm taking her with me." So she packed up what she had and we left the circus tent without any more fuss.

Once we got back to town I drove over to my office and told her to wait in the study, so I could make a call. She seemed very timid about staying, but reluctantly she stayed put.

I waltzed into the other room and shut the door behind me. Then over to the phone I went. When I dialed the child's sister I suddenly realized my window was broken. Shattered into a thousand pieces, and next to the glass mess was a bloody piece of clothing. It wasn't like a whole shirt of something, but a small ripped section. I knew who it was as soon as I looked into the cabinet that held the other evidence I found.

I rushed out of the room to check on the girl. But as I opened the door, I was approached by a blazing fire. I tried yelling for Jammy but I inhaled too much smoke. Luckily her wolf pup same running over and sort of motioned for me to follow and I did. It led me over to the far corner, near the main door. The girl, um, Jammy was there but unconscious. I knew anymore of this would kill us all so I crawled over to the door and tried to kick it open. First couple of times it didn't work out the way I thought it would. Finally I stopped and heard voices coming up the stairs. I went back in for Jammy and pup. Pulled them our and started to scream to let the men know where we were.

Close to five minutes I waited for them to round the corner. It never happened so I grabbed Jammy and moved toward the stairs. Naturally the wolf followed us and so did the flames. I got to the end of the hall, next to the staircase and whispered to the dog to go get help. It did, thankfully. Once it was out of sight but the fire wasn't, I stood up, scooped Jammy up into my arms and tried to get down the stairs safely and quickly.

When I was near the third floor I could hear footsteps and small barks. I knew then that the pup had truly understood me. As they neared me I started to yell for help so they knew where I was. They came rushing toward me. Fire was already around Jammy and I.

I knew they were there when they appeared in front of me with the dog by their side. I handed them Jammy and they assisted me out of the building and over to a emergency vehicle. And then they rushed us over to the local hospital.

Saturday, January 31st, 1999

I got out of the hospital today. The detective called my family and handed me over. I didn't see my mother there, but it was a huge relief to finally see the rest of them after all those years, and to finally be back in the real world. Don't know why but it is.

Vivian Pang
Westborough MA., United States

I am 11 years old and I love to golf, run, read, and write. My dream is to become a pro golfer on the LPGA tour. I have two brothers who are like monkeys. Soon I am moving to California and I am excited!

Runner's Racetrack
By Vivian Pang

I reviewed in my head all that had happened in the past day. I considered the fact that it was all a crazy dream for the second time. Let me tell you why. First of all, I am sitting in a world above the Earth with an option of being immortal. Lush, green meadows with white flowers are surrounding me.

Well, I am jumping ahead of myself. It all started this morning when I was on the track. My heart was bursting. Like, literally exploding! I was on my fourth mile doing another practice for the ten-mile marathon the next day. I was almost finished with my five miles. I didn't want to use all my energy up for the big day tomorrow.

It was perfectly silent. All I could hear was my own heavy breathing. Then suddenly a giant brown hawk-like creature with puffy feathers and a pointy head came swooping down. Straight at ME! I tried to scream, but I was so shocked no sound came out. The bird creature clasped its giant claws onto my tank-top's straps and lifted me into the air. This time the scream came out without hesitation.

"Help me!" I yelled.

Then what happened next made my jaw drop to the ground. The creature spoke.

"Don't be afraid," he said in a deep, rumbly voice.

I decided to keep silent for now and see what this giant monster wanted. After all, birds don't eat humans. Right?

As you can tell, I'm the kind of person who can believe in supernatural and magical things. I am eleven years old and I still believe in Santa

Claus and the Tooth Fairy even though all my friends tell me it's my parents. So now you can see how I could be so calm with a hawk above my head and me soaring above the clouds.

Suddenly, the puffy bird flew us straight up toward a blinding sun. I couldn't see anything but white light, and before I knew it, I felt like I was a bread crumb being suctioned into a vacuum cleaner. I heard a giant "POP!" and looked around frantically.

Now, this is where reality comes in. Sandy colored paths curve through grassy fields. The sky is a beautiful light blue. I wondered if it was a dream for the third time.

"Where am I?" I whispered timidly.

The bird said in a deep voice, "You are in a world located above Earth called Runner's Racetrack. Only the best of the best runners are summoned to come here. You have one week to decide if you want to stay here and be immortal, but you can never leave or see anyone on Earth ever again.

"Not even my parents?" I gasped.

"No. And you can never change your mind. You will be here for eternity."

The word seemed to echo in my mind. Eternity. I knew it meant forever, but my brain hurt whenever I thought about it.

"Look around," said the puffy bird. "Doesn't everyone here look happy?"

I watched a group of five runners pass by. They did seem content. All of them gave me sympathetic smiles as they remembered their once in a lifetime choice.

"How come everyone here is kids?" I wondered.

"You never age here, and only kids are summoned. We catch them before they become adults. Don't worry, a booklet of information will be sent to your dorm tomorrow morning. Run along now. The path will lead you to your dorm cell."

"Lead?"

"You'll see."

I hesitatingly stood and tentatively stuck my foot onto the sandy colored path. All of a sudden, the randomly curved path led perfectly straight to a white marble mansion. It looked like a castle made for a king and queen. I wondered how big my dorm would be. The mansion seemed about half a mile away. It had a beautiful garden with different flowers of every color in the front lawn. I started jogging where the ruler straight path pointed directly to.

About three minutes later, I stood at the black gate that surrounded my destination. I pushed it open and walked up to the perfectly painted door. I wondered if my family was looking for me. I was homesick. I wanted to ask someone if I could go home before the week was over. My family and friends would be frantic.

A doorman pulled open the front door and said, "Welcome! You must be new here."

"Yes," I replied. "Can I ask you a question?"

"You just did, I might as well answer another one," he smiled. "By the way, my name is JimBob."

I laughed.

"I'm Violet Panley and I was wondering if I can go home before the week is over. My friends and family will be frantic looking for me."

"We'll change what happened yesterday and you'll supposedly be at a camp for seven days."

"Shoot!"

"What?"

"I have a marathon tomorrow!"

"Don't worry, we'll postpone that until next week if you choose to go home. We have lots of marathons here, though. Now, enough questions. A mini book will arrive at your dorm tomorrow. Run along now!"

"Okay. Where's my dorm?"

"Wow, are you a question shooter!" JimBob joked. "Just follow the signs that say "Newbies' Section: This Way" and pick any room. They're all the same."

"Thanks so much!"

I followed the signs up the winding staircase and peeked inside one of the many rooms. I selected a random one and looked around. There were creamy colored walls, a silky violet bed, shiny wooden desks, white lamps, and a very clean bathroom. It looked like a 5-star suite. I was exhausted so I lay my head down on the fluffy pillow. *Just for a moment…* I thought.

Next thing I knew, it was morning. Six days left to make my decision, and I hadn't even thought about it. My heart seemed to stick in my throat. I could stay here, be immortal, and do the thing I loved most every single day in a beautiful world with kind kids and caring creatures. Or I could go ho-me, live a normal life, and be happy with my parents and friends.

I would definitely stay here if it weren't for my parents. I can't even imagine life without them. It seems so selfish to even consider staying here, but if you were in my place, it would be a tough choice too. I'll just wait for the info to arrive. After I look it over, I'll decide. Six days is a long time, I think. Maybe, right?

At around 10:45, after lots of pacing around the room, the booklet finally arrived. I hurried over and snatched it from the ground where someone had just slipped it under the door. It was about fifty pages thick. I sat down at the desk and began to read. It said:

To all runners summoned:

You have exactly one week to decide if you want to stay at Runner's Racetrack or go back to Earth. If you stay here, you will be moved out of the Newbies' Section and into luxurious mansions where you will live with a few friends. Food and drinks will be provided. We have café's, game rooms, movie theaters, and more. The only disadvantage is you can never go back to Earth or see anyone living there ever again. If you decide to go back to Earth, we will respect that choice. Your memory of Runner's Racetrack will be immediately erased. You will never be summoned again, so choose wisely. Keep reading to find out the rules and events here at Runner's Racetrack.

After I finished reading the whole booklet, my head was dizzy with rules and events occurring here. I was unsure than ever what was the best decision. Maybe a walk around in the beautiful weather and fresh air would help.

I slipped on my light green sneakers and descended down the spiral staircase to the tan path outside. I started jogging on the running path. Soon I came across a few runners who looked friendly.

"Are you an undecided?" one of them asked politely.

"Huh?"

"That's what everyone calls a summoned runner who still has the choice to go back to Earth," another one explained.

"Oh. In that case, yes. Any suggestions for me?" I asked.

"I think you should go home," someone said. "By the way, I'm Laurel, this is Lizzie, and that's Linda. We're the Three L's."

"You should definitely go home," Linda advised.

"Go back to Earth. I mean, it's great here and all, but pretty much everyone here regrets their choice and badly wants to see Earthlings again," Lizzie added. "Plus, it's not as great as it sounds being immortal. I would be long gone by now."

"But everyone here is so happy, and life seems so enjoyable and relaxing," I said truthfully. "This is the hardest decision I've ever had to make."

Linda shrugged and said, "It's hard for everyone. But just make sure you choose the right option."

I nodded. "Thanks, guys."

We all continued on our way. It sounded like most people wanted to go home but were stuck here for eternity. That must stink, and I didn't want that happening to me. Plus, I miss my loving parents so badly my heart aches.

My decision is made. I want a normal life with my awesome parents and unique friends. I want to pass away when I'm old. I want to be able to become an adult. I want love more than running. I'm going home.

I give permission to my daughter Vivian Pang to submit her writing into this writing contest.

Raquel Wetzell
Virginia, United States

I was born in Alexandria, VA in 1997 and have lived here most of my life. Now as a freshman in high school, I discovered a love for writing two years ago and now it is a great hobby of mine. Sometime later in life I would like to write a fantasy novel.

Checkmate
By Raquel Wetzell

*T*he court room was silent. The large male judge drabbed in a baggy black cloak stared daggers at the defendant as everyone waited for the ruling.

"The verdict?" asked the judge maliciously. A jury member hurried quickly over to the stand and handed the judge a small folded piece of paper. The judge read it silently with slow precaution and anticipation.

Finally, he read the contents of the paper aloud.

"*Guilty.*"

Aaron's breath caught in her throat. The voices in her head went frantic, screaming, "*Die! Die! You all will die!*" Aaron covered her ears, letting out a bloodcurdling scream.

The judge gave her a strange glance, "Very well then. The defendant is sentenced to life in the Newport State Mental Hospital. The court rests."

*   *   *

Aaron sits in a solid concrete room, staring at the gray cracked walls. There's a single twin sized bed and that's it. No furniture, no window, no toilet. All Aaron can do is sit there and wait for therapy or meal time. That's all the patients ever do in here. Well, the insane ones anyway. On the top floor of Newport State are the mild patients: juveniles who suffer from drug abuse, self-harm or eating disorders.

The metal door swings open and Ms. Ward, Aaron's nurse, has a happy smile plastered on her chubby face, "Come on dear. Time for lunch."

Aaron slips into her straightjacket without complaints. Besides, this time, she's actually hungry. The nurse escorts her to the lunch room in silence.

The lunch room is split into two sections: one side for the minor patients and the other side for the psychos. It's not a big surprise Aaron lands herself with the crazies. Ms. Ward takes off her straightjacket and leads her to the lunch line.

"Have a nice lunch dear,"says the plumpy nurse, locking the metal lunchroom doors behind her.

Great, we're stuck with these people, says one of her voices. Aaron sighs, walking over to an empty table at the far corner of the lunchroom. Miserably, she eats her dry salad.

Someone clears their throat behind her, "Um, you're sitting in my seat."

She turns slightly, looking at a boy her age. He gives her a half smile, brushing away his dark brown hair, "Never mind."

He takes the seat beside her, "New here?"

Aaron nods, losing her appetite. The boy glances at his own meal in disdain, "It's funny how normal patients get the good food and we just get the leftovers."

She crosses her arms, pushing the tray away, "So, what are you in here for?"

Aaron notices the sinister look in the boy's dark eyes, "Schizophrenia. I was five years old when they brought me here. Our dog convinced me to kill my parents. Then he got annoying so I stuffed him in a bag and dumped in the lake behind our yard."

She gives him an uneasy smile, "Wow you make me look like a saint."

The boy chuckles, "Not as bad as it seems, though. I'm Nico, by the way."

Overall, Nico is a pretty good friend to Aaron. He helps her adjust to the crazy life of Newport State Mental Hospital and its patients. Nico lets her know which psychos to stay away from, which doctors to piss off without getting solitary confinement, and the best ways to torment normal patients without getting caught. Little by little, Nico gains Aaron's trust.

They're sitting in the hospital's library looking at an inappropriate story of Ancient Rome. Currently it was open to a picture of a woman who had murdered her dearest friend. Apparently someone had told the woman her husband had been cheating on her.

"Vicious," Nico murmurs. "Killing is one thing but decapitation is an entirely different matter."

Aaron shrugs, "It's still death one way or another. That's how the Romans saw it and that's how the courts here see it."

He shuts the book, placing it back on the shelf, "So… who'd you kill?"

Aaron recoils, giving him a cautious look, "What're you talking about?"

Nico smiles lightly, "Come on Aaron, you got sentenced to life in this dump. That's the same sentence I got and, remember, I murdered two people and a dog."

She sighs, "I— I, well, my friend Katherine came up to me one day. She… she told me to take a walk with her."

Aaron frowns as if trying to recall something from her memory. Nico urges her to continue.

"The voices told me something was wrong. They told me they'd take care of the situation, that all I had to do was turn off my mind and let them take control. I didn't want to listen to them…"

She frowns again, feeling the voices in her head tugging at the dark recesses of her mind. *Continue,* they hiss.

"Katherine told me she was moving to Colorado. I, the voices… we kind of lost it. They told me if I couldn't have her, no one could. The next morning she was dead."

Silence sits between the two patients. Aaron enjoys the silence though. What was Nico supposed to say? Everything's going to be ok? That'd seem fake to her and Nico was the kind of person that told you things straight up. He never tried to hide his feelings.

A small smile spreads across his lips, "Now, you're officially a psychopath."

Later that day Nico and Aaron report to a group session. It's where them and a bunch of other patients sit in a circle and talk about simple things like their lives back home or how they like Newport State.

Ten people are there before them, talking in low hushed voices. Aaron recognizes a few of them from one of Nico's tours around the hospital.

Zoe Williams, a kleptomaniac, greets them along with Riley Bannon, the necrophobic, and Selene Carter, a drug addict. Nico and Aaron take a seat beside them.

The security door opens and in steps Ms. Ward and Dr. Marshall. She's pretty young to be a doctor, Dr. Marshall's 26 to be exact, graduating Harvard with a Ph.D. in psychology. As much as Aaron hates to admit it, Dr. Marshall kind of looks likes her, both sharing the same shade of blonde hair, emerald green eyes and upturned nose. The only difference is Dr. Marshall's a lot tanner than Aaron. But hey, it's not like they'd let her visit the beach or anything.

Dr. Marshall goes around the circle, asking the patients about their feelings. Aaron doesn't pay attention until Nico's name is called.

He glares at her in a defiant manner.

"Now Mr. Di Angelo, how do you feel right now?" she says in a professional voice. Aaron tilts her head in confusion. With the other patients Dr. Marshall spoke in a gentle, motherly voice and now it's all business.

"Mr. Di Angelo feels annoyed," Nico mumbles, matching her tone.

"And what have you annoyed?"

"You," He smirks.

She puts on a tight smile, "And what about me annoys you?"

Nico sits up, still smiling, "Your voice. The soft country accent is constantly ringing in my ears and it's very annoying. Your face, it always has the expectant look on it the same way you'd expect a dog to roll over or fetch a stick. Your attitude, you feel like you can fix anyone and anything but we both know you can't change me."

Tension fills the room as Nico and Dr. Marshall take a few moments to glower at each other. Soon it's all back to normal and Dr. Marshall is smiling once more.

Her gaze focuses on Aaron, "How do you feel right now, Ms. Hale?"

She stiffens at the sound of her last name. Ever since the trial, Aaron's parents made it clear she wasn't their daughter anymore. Just some schizophrenic girl that lived with them for fourteen years before going nuts. Aaron shrugs.

Dr. Marshall grimaces, "Now dear surely you must feel something. By the looks of it you don't enjoy hearing your surname very much. Why don't you tell us about that?"

Aaron sneers, "Why should I? Judging by everyone's faces they much rather be somewhere else right now. Does it make a difference if I share my feelings or not? No one's going to care. I'm stuck in this place for life and no amount of therapy will change that."

Nico gives a large grin as Dr. Marshall scribbles some notes on her clipboard. Dr. Marshall sighs, fixing her glasses, "Very well then. I'll make sure to book you in for a private session later."

After that joke of a therapy session, Nico and Aaron find themselves once again in the library. They scan the shelves looking for another gruesome book. Nico looks at her, "What you said in there was awesome. If I ever said that to her Dr. Marshall would lock me up in solitary confinement for a week."

"Well you weren't exactly a goodie two shoes either."

Nico shrugs, "Dr. Marshall's used to it now. Besides she asked me what I was feeling and I told her but to completely refuse a doctor takes guts. Don't get me wrong, I've done it before but let's just say it wasn't a pleasurable experience."

Aaron leans against one of the gray walls, slumping to the floor, "God I hate this place."

He takes a seat beside her, "I do too but don't worry it's only temporary."

She quirks an eyebrow, "What part of 'sentenced to life in Newport State Mental Hospital' do you not understand?"

"The law," Nico sneers, rolling his eyes. "It doesn't mean we can't escape from the hole someday."

Aaron shakes her head, "You're insane."

"Am I?" he questions. "Trust me Aaron, when you've been in here longer than anyone else all you can think about is leaving this place. One day I will escape, with or without you."

She remains silent.

Nico sighs, "You should start thinking about it. You never know when that opportunity will come."

Aaron spends the new few hours pondering the ideas Nico put in her head. Come lunchtime, she forgets all about it. That's until she meets up with him again.

Nico's constantly glancing behind his shoulder like a Xenophobic as he tells Aaron to hurry up and grab her food. Aaron sits down at their usual table, watching Nico curiously.

"There's a reason why I sit here," he whispers. "For some reason the security cameras can't get a good shot of this corner."

"And you know this how?" she asks suspiciously.

Nico chuckles, "I know people. Anyway, there's something I want to talk about. I couldn't mention it in the library with all the cameras and snitches hiding all over the place."

Aaron crosses her arms, "I'm listening."

"Like I said, I know people. In your room, cell, whatever you wanna call it, there's a stone under your bed. If you can push that out of the way, there's a hole that drops down three feet into an underground tunnel. If you keep going forward it'll eventually lead to the outside."

She narrows her eyes, "Why are you telling me this?"

Nico smiles innocently, "We're friends aren't we? Trust me Aaron, you deserve better than this place."

Aaron looks away, biting her lip. It's a tempting offer yet a dangerous move. What if he's just leading her into a trap?

Aaron quickly dismisses the thought. Nico would never do that.

He looks at her seriously, "I have a therapy session with Dr. Marshall at six. I'm going to do something that'll give you enough time to escape. Are you in?"

She nods abruptly and for the first time the voices in Aaron's head are completely silent.

*　　*　　*

On the security door in Aaron's room it has a digital clock. Currently it reads 5:50. She sits anxiously on her bed, chewing her thumbnail. Sure enough there's a stone under her bed just like Nico said. Aaron wants to lea-ve now but she knows she has to wait. It's only a matter of time.

At exactly 6:01 alarms blare throughout the hospital. Aaron tries to cover her ears but she can hear the speakers turn on, "*Code Red! Escape patient by the name of Nico Di Angelo. He is armed and unstable. The hospital is officially on lockdown for three hours. Patients are to be in their rooms. All doctors and nurses are to be sealed in the cafeteria. Security officials are to secure all exits. No one gets in or out."*

Aaron can't help the fact she's impressed. She crawls under her bed and pushes the stone away from the tunnel's entrance. Hesitantly, Aaron plunges into the darkness waiting below.

*   *   *

"He who is prudent and lies in wait for an enemy who is not, will always be victorious," Nico's father had once said. Even though Nico had killed him with his own two hands, he had never forgotten his father's wise words during their customary games of chess. Nico fondly remembered the way his father always quoted Sun Tzu's legendary book, *The Art of War.*

It was his father's words that spurred Nico to kill Dr. Marshall. It was a rather simple job for him to complete.

He had shown up to his private therapy session three minutes before 6:00. Dr. Marshall had handed him a glass of water along with his regular blue pills knows as Clozapine. It was a rather new medication they had tried testing on Nico rather than his regular antipsychotics.

He pretended to drop his glass, spilling the water on the white tiles. It shattered on impact. Dr. Marshall sighed, making a move to get some paper towels. That's when she made the biggest mistake of her life; she turned her back on him.

It took all but a matter of seconds for Nico to grab a rather large piece of glass and stab it into Dr. Marshall's jugular. He plunged the shard into her neck over and over again, ripping out her trachea. Nico was almost unaware of the blood seeping onto his white hospital clothes.

Nico wasn't fazed by the dark red liquid pooling at his feet or Dr. Marshall's piercing greens eyes that started at him lifelessly. In fact, it brought him a giddy almost high feeling, how easy it was to kill someone he despised.

Nico had left the room after that, smearing his bloody hands on the white prison walls as a warning to them all. No one was safe. The security officials found him soon enough. Nico didn't struggle though, he was satisfied now.

He sat in the solitary confinement room: a 9x5 cell with padded walls, the floor solid concrete. There's a thin mattress reeking of pee and a small shower in the corner of the room. That's pretty much it. Nurses haven't arrived to drug Nico and give him a shower yet, so he's still covered in Dr. Marshall's blood. He rest in a corner with a straightjacket, staring at the wall clock. It's been three hours already.

Nico smiles wickedly, walking over to the shower. His grin widens as he hears a small noise echoing from the small drain. It almost resembles muffled screaming; music to his ears. With hands strapped across his chest, there's not much Nico can do with them. But he doesn't mind. Like he told Aaron before; this isn't the first time he's been in solitary confinement.

Nico kicks off his shoes, sauntering towards the spot he was just sitting at. His foot slides into a small almost unnoticeable slit in the padded wall, waiting until it brushes against a cold metal object. Using his toes, Nico's able to fish the item out of its hole.

It's a screwdriver, aged with rust and dried blood. He's back at the drain, again using his toes to remove the small grate. It comes off with a pop, opening up to a ditch at least a foot in diameter, covered in mold and mildew.

The noises cease, "Why hello Miss Hale."

She steps into the small crack of light, glaring daggers at Nico. Aaron looks far worse than she did a few hours ago. Her blonde hair is matter, cuts and bruises littered across her pale skin. Aaron's lip is bleeding and looks as though her clothes went through a shredder.

"You lied to me," she hisses. "I thought we were friends."

"You're too soft, too trusting," he tells her, "No offense, but you ruin my image."

Aaron's expression is one of pure disbelief, "You're totally insane!"

Nico rolls his eyes, "Well duh! Don't take it too hard though. I really do like you Aaron." For a moment his expression softens at this, "But you confuse me. I don't like being confused."

"So you're going to kill me just because you have feelings for me?"

"Pretty much." He scoffs, "And I'm not going to kill you. Don't get me wrong, I want to give you a quick, painless death but unfortunately my hands are sort of unavailable at the moment. You'll just have to settle for dehydration and starvation."

Her eyes flash a dangerous shade of forest green, "You son of a—" she doesn't get to finish her sentence. Nico slides the grate over the hole once more, leaving Aaron to the rats and dead bodies she failed to notice before. Nico sits back in his corner, tucking away the screwdriver.

It takes a week for Aaron to die. Once again, a satisfying feeling settles in the pit of Nico's stomach.

"Next year ought to be better," he murmurs to himself happily.

The door to his room clicks open and the smile from his face disappears. Nico watches as Mrs. Ward flashes him a disturbing pedophile-like smile.

She's next, a small voice tells him.

Emily Snell
Somerville, OH, United states

Emily Snell was born in Georgia and currently resides near Oxford, Ohio, with her family and dog. She is 13 years old and enjoys reading, writing, mathematics, music, and playing the trumpet. Her favorite book is *The Lord of the Rings*, by J. R. R. Tolkien, followed by *Ivanhoe*, *Les Miserables*, and *The Hunchback of Notre Dame*. She mainly reads fantasy, science fiction, and classic books. She likes to listen to music a lot, and participates in several bands and one choir at her school.

Other activities she is involved in include MathCounts, Power of the Pen, Destination Imagination, and marching band. She enjoys writing poetry and short stories, mostly fantasy. She was lucky enough to have the opportunity to live in the Netherlands for three years and visited thirteen other European countries while living there. Unfortunately, she was young while living there and remembers little about it except for the many different delicious foods.

Ashes to Ashes
By Emily Snell

*G*rief weighed heavy upon the hearts of the soldiers as the dying breathed their last and the living wished for death. Up on the hill that so many of them had given their lives to defend, the exhausted but victorious soldiers wept for all the men who died that day and all the children who would never know their fathers. They knew that in an hour, or a day, or a week, they, too, could be dead, and the knowledge haunted their dreams and troubled their thoughts, deeper and more terrifying than mere dread of the unknown. It loomed over them like some darkling behemoth crawled out of the fiery bowels of the earth, casting its sombre, stygian shadow over their souls, struggling to quench the light of hope that shone forth. Their battle against it would never end. Even when they were old men and this war was ended, they would remember its power and strength. They would never forget the cries of the wounded, the stricken faces of the dead and the dying, the bloodlust of battle. Each had found within himself something primitive and unwholesome, some twisted perversity that hungered for blood and killing. Yet each had also found something pure and heavenly, some righteous force that was unstained by vice. These conflicting emotions raged within each man's soul, each struggling to vanquish the other and reign supreme over his heart. That battle did not end with the war; it continued throughout the long years of each man's life, ceasing only when his eyes closed in eternal sleep. On one side was brutality and mercilessness, the cruel joy of being able to withhold from a fellow man that which he treasured most: the breath and the heartbeat that give him life. On the other was untainted goodness and virtue, the happiness that comes from loving and knowing that you are loved.

They wept, for they were surrounded by anguish and despair and suffering. They wept, for they knew not what would become of them. They wept, for they did not want to kill, but knew that they must. They were not ashamed to let their officers and fellow soldiers see them weep, for they had reached a point where they were not afraid to lay bare their souls to their companions. They shared a bond that could never be broken, a kinship that could only be forged by the flames of war and shared suffer-ing. Their souls were as one soul, their hearts one heart. They would share their darkest secrets without fear of being scorned, tell each other their every dream and hope and wish. Each of them would die for his com-rades. Many of them had.

Among the many bodies, an enemy standard-bearer lay on the rocky ground, the colors of his army still clutched in his hand. A soldier slowly approached the young boy, whose clothes were tattered, and saturated with crimson blood. He knelt beside the boy and gently pulled at the flag, but the boy was not quite dead. He stirred and coughed up blood, staining his uniform further, and struggled feebly to retain the flag. The soldier stopped and gently closed the boy's hands around the pole of the flag, propping him up so that the flag did not touch the ground, which was black with soot and ashes from the fires that had raged relentlessly on the plains. The boy mumbled something, and the other man leaned close to him.

"He makes me to lie down..." The boy coughed again, spraying blood onto the soldier's face. He tried to continue, but could not summon the strength.

"He makes me to lie down in green pastures;
He leads me beside the still waters.
He restores my soul;
He leads me in the paths of righteousness   For His name's sake.
Though I walk through the valley of the shadow of death,
I will fear no evil; For You are with me; Your rod and Your staff, they comfort me," the soldier completed, speaking as tenderly as a mother com-forting her child. He smiled sadly at the dying boy.

The flag-bearer took a deep breath, using the last of his strength to quote a final line from the psalm.

"And... and I... will dwell in the house... of the Lord... forever."

And then he spoke no more, for the light had faded from his eyes. The soldier gazed at him a long time, the pain on the dead boy's face replaced by the peace and serenity of a faithful believer. Suddenly, the boy was more than just a boy. He was every innocent child who deserved so much more than what he received. He was every trusting friend who would forgive each trespass without question. He was every child who desired nothing more than to love and be loved. The soldier gazed at him sadly, mourning the loss of his bright-shining soul. His unseeing eyes were like dark abyss-es, and the soldier was suddenly sure that if he looked into them long enough, he, too, would fall into that infinite void of darkness and lonely souls. He gently closed the boy's eyes for the last time, wiping the blood off of his face and hands with his own uniform. He lovingly eased the flag from the boy's grasp, laying his limp hands across his chest. Another man might have waved the flag triumphantly, but the soldier did not. Instead, he folded it carefully with the terrifying calmness of a man who has seen too many men die who deserved to live. He draped it 'cross the still body of the young boy, then stood quietly and saluted the dead. One by one, the men around him followed his example, and as the sun set on a day of fate and anguish, the soldiers stood and saluted their foes and their allies alike, both dead and living. They stood there silently for a long, long time as they slowly faded into the darkness of the night...

Christian Ramirez
Palm Beach, Florida, United States

Christian Ramirez is a Screenwriter and Aspiring director from Palm Beach, Florida. Just having completed his High School education at Atlantic High School in Delray Beach and entering studies at the collegiate level; at eighteen years old he looks to have a long and enduring career in both the literary and cinematic fields. He is most inspired by writers: George Orwell, Aldous Huxley, Philip K. Dick, and Chuck Palahniuk. And filmmakers: Quentin Tarantino, Terrence Malick, Darren Aronofsky and Christopher Nolan. His favorite novel is 1984.

The Edifice of Complexity
By Christian Ramirez

*W*e all could just stare and watch as life was taken from us. We were the ones chosen to leave our homes, where our ancestors were born, raised, and died. We had to leave Earth that day, and the reason I still don't know, it was supposedly random. I could only wonder what I did to anger God, and to anger fate. I thought of all my sins the night before I left, everything I did wrong, and I pleaded to whatever was listening to me in the seemingly infinite universe, I pleaded for mercy and begged for a second chance. But it was not given. I would wonder everyday what I could've done to cause this, but I would not know, I would never find out the truth.

I had to stay strong for my wife that horrific morning. It helped that I had lost hope, it really did. Watching the sunrise that morning it was as if I saw my own demise. I had heard of what they did to people who resisted, and, let's just say, it really wasn't worth it. I decided it was best to stand in front of the door, waiting peacefully for whoever was coming to take us away. For a wise man once said "The mind is its own place, and in itself, Can make *a Heaven of Hell, a Hell of Heaven.*"

Inevitably, a large vehicle came and drove us for hours, until we reached our assigned spaceship. The spaceship was enormous, about a mile in length. Walking into it we saw that the massive size was only used for one purpose- hypersleep pods, all in uniform order. The only way I could communicate what this massive prison looked like is to say that to see it would instantly destroy all hope you ever had for human life. What was a limited, uniform space, seemed like infinite rows of pods, infinite hell. I could not look back at my wife as I walked us toward our assigned "dormitories" (as they called them). Entering these ominously tight prisons, we all could just stare and watch as life was taken from us.

They told me forty years passed in that wretched sleep. I had a dream in that sleep, a dream that I had felt could change my life, but as I was struggling to get out of that tight space, I exerted all my energy in figuring out how to get out of the things that bound me, and in that determination, I had forgotten what it was I dreamt.

Hearing only cheers and cries of joy throughout the spaceship, I rushed out into the main corridor to see what could be out there to cause such joy among what I thought were fellow prisoners. That's when I saw it. In the moment, I could've sworn that we, humans, had finally completed the tower of Babel, that we had finally built a way to heaven. It was a large beautiful planet, full of life, and anything one could imagine there being in a paradise. They called it- a name that I found most appropriate- EDEN.

In the rush of my emotion, I ran back to find my wife, but for all joy in this world there is equal sadness. I learned this when I found her very ill. The doctors told me she had one week to live. Her last wish was to see as much as she could of this planet as she could, so I took her and together we experienced Eden for one week. And I could say now, that when she could no longer travel, I was not sad, because in that week we had experienced more bliss than I believe anyone had in their entire lives back on earth.

After a week had passed, I took her to our home, so she could await her death in peace. We had learned on our travels that we were not asleep for forty years, but for five hundred years, as this planet was built by men around the star named Tau Ceti, placed in perfect position from that star to provide us with enough light and warmth for life.

As she died, she muttered the following words ""You are free to eat from any tree in the garden; but you must not eat from the tree of the knowledge of good and evil, for when you eat from it you will certainly die."

Her death would bring me many years of solitude in this massive paradise, but I lived every moment in bliss that words cannot describe, UNTIL- I noticed something, something that would show me where I was living.

Walking up to the water one day I realized something as I looked down into the crystal waters, I looked at myself and saw nothing. Could there be something wrong with my vision? I thought so naively. I went to speak to a representative of the ruling official.

Walking into his office, I started noticing the world getting a little dimmer than usually. Was this planet not full of life and light in all ways? A secretary called me in to speak to the representative.

"Why is there no reflection in the water?" I asked politely.

"Is this not a paradise?" He replied.

"How do the laws of nature not apply here? Where am I really?!" I yelled emphatically in my panic.

"Did your wife not tell you? You are free to eat from any tree in the garden-"

A gunshot was the last thing I heard.

I awoke in a bed in a volcanic planet, wretched and plagued with death. I looked in every direction and could only see beds with people asleep lying on them, in what appeared to be peace. We were protected from our surroundings by a glass dome, an incredible magnitude never before witnessed by man. To my surprise, I saw something that made calmed me in my most fearful state- it was my wife, awake, taking care of the dormant population. I called to her, and she came.

"You made it" She said.

"Where am I?" I replied.

"This is where you go when you die. These are the people that died on Eden, and as more people die, we have more people to take care of the sleeping."

I saw her injecting a liquid into someone's bloodstream.

I asked immediately, with fear:

"What is that?"

She laughed.

"It is the only way they can endure. It is Eden."

I ran away to the nearest room I could find. Fear is a diluted version of what I felt at the time, compared to this torturous feeling, I could only wish to had felt something like fear.

I found a wire and I hung myself.

My eyes opened to see myself still standing in front of my door, waiting for the vehicle to arrive to take me and my wife away from earth that morning.

IT IS IMAGINATION THAT IS CRUEL, REALITY BENEVOLENT.

The vehicle arrived in front of my house that morning. Lost in my mind, I walked towards it. Not looking at around me, a soldier walked out and beat me with the butt of his rifle, face planted on the ground, I had only the sight of my wife running away in the distance, and my last thoughts were of how futile her attempts for life were. I saw the neighbors staring through their windows, but- we could all just stare and watch as life was taking from us.

I heard another gunshot, which caused my death.

I awoke again. I looked around at a concrete prison. It had no windows, dim light, one bed, one toilet.

Months passed, and the anger and frustration became unbearable. I went into an animal-like rage, which ended in me flipping over my bed. I walked up to it and saw something strange. I saw a mirror. I saw my reflection. It was on the bottom of my bed. I turned it upwards so I could see myself clearly.

Where was I that I could not escape?

Could death not free me?

My wife?

What did she look like again?

Was that her the entire time?

What was my dream again?

Olteanu Irina
Bucharest, Romania

I began to write since primary school. First, with poems and later with short fairy tales. I graduated the Law School but I discovered that my main quality is the writing. I participated at some international contests for poetry in English but I consider more difficult to write in my native language, Romanian. I like to write any type of story and I feel that this is what I was meant to do. Of course, the writing came after hundreds of books being read. I don't consider myself a journalist or a column writer. But just a writer.

My name is Teddy
By Olteanu Irina

—*T*eddy! Teddy Wilson! Come here boy when I call you. Fanny calls out loud her son but he keeps riding his two wheeled scooter like nothing could ever bother him. She calls her son with his last name almost every day. There are a lot of Teddys in the park and Fanny feels some kind of strange need to distinguish him from the others.

- Sophie, come here baby! Fanny emboldened her one and a half year to take some steps towards. Sophie is more obedient than Teddy so she goes to her mother. She already knows how to walk; now she wants to run.

Teddy and Sophie are both blond blue-eyed. Fanny's husband, Bill is responsible, because she's brown eyed, brown hair type of person. She's in the mid 30's but the way she dresses and talks make you think she is at least 10 years older. Together with her husband managed to lease an a-partment in a new residential area for the kids. It's outside the city, the air is much cleaner and the buildings are new and better built.

-Hi, Fanny! Hi, Teddy! It's Mary, Matt's grandmother. She also lives in the neighborhood, but in a duplex with her son, daughter in law and of course, her nephew.

Matt is a good kid. He never pushes or talks in a bad way. He listens to his mother and grandmother and he's Teddy's best friend.

-Teddy!

-Matt! They are both really happy to see each other although the last time they met was just yesterday. They both go to kindergarten. Teddy to a public one and Matt to a private one. Matt seems to have learned more than Teddy, but maybe because he's a few months older.

-Matt, will you come to my birthday? Teddy hopes for a positive answer.

-Yes, of course, if my mom lets me, answers Matt prudently. His grandma was looking to him with "the look", so he knows he must be careful with what he says.

Mary doesn't like Fanny, nor Bill very much. They were both born at the country but moved to the city. Mary was also born at the country, but at least doesn't look or think anymore like she used to. She had changed, in her opinion, in a good way.

-Fanny, guess what? We have a new neighbor. I heard they bought the condo with 70 000. It's half the price you paid, isn't it.

Fanny wants to answer but she doesn't. She knows she already told Mary how she bought her house, which, in fact, isn't hers, until she will pay the rest of the lease. Now Fanny is in child care leave, but her company is in bankruptcy. Bill is working without legal papers and the only help she gets is from her mother. She left to Italy after she divorced Fanny's father and she sends her daughter once in a while money.

- You know what Mary? I don't even care about the condo. I think every day about how to get rid of it. She is so bitter because if she waits maybe one year more, the economic crisis wouldn't have put her in the situation to hate her home. Because she really does now.

- But how could you do this? I can't imagine you can find anyone to take over your lease. It's too expensive.

Mary is now mean indeed but Fanny doesn't notice.

-Maybe I can talk to the owner of the building or to the bank or with the bank to reevaluate our contract. This bank loan really kills us.

Fanny is usually really open and sincere to everyone. But Mary is still mean.

-But you will lose a lot of money…

Fanny knows. She paid three years already, she sold her car and she still fights everyday for the last cent.

-I know. I guess we will search for a rent condo. At least we won't pay so much. And she ofteaza.

-Teddy, come here to drink some water, it's too hot.

It's already noon and she has to cook the launch.

-Ok, kids, say bye. Sophie waves her hand and Teddy says bye to Matt.

They all go to the supermarket. Fanny is so tired and Teddy runs around making him much harder to watch. But Fanny is already used to him.

-Teddy is still a boy. Teddy ignores her like always. He knows she has to watch Sophie so he can do whatever he wants. Now he's playing with some toys he spotted on a shelf.

Fanny grabs a frosted chicken and tries to get out quickly from the shop. It's already late and she has to cook some chicken soup for dinner. They all go home and Fanny puts Sophie asleep. Now she can concentrate on her soup. But Teddy, as usual, doesn't want to go to bed. So he plays for a while but:

-Mom, I'm getting bored. I want to play with something else.

-But I bought you yesterday the car. Fanny tries to keep him still.

-Mom, I want to go outside. I saw some kids from the block in the park.

They can see from their window aside from the park, so Fanny tries to be reasonable.

-OK, you can go out and I and Sophie will come in half an hour. She hopes she can carry on with her soup in time. And it's not like it's the first time he goes outside alone. He's almost five and he knows really well the neighborhood.

-Thanks, mom. Bye, mom.

Teddy leaves the house really happy with his scooter. Fanny watches him for a couple of minutes and she goes back to her routine. Almost an hour had passed since Teddy left outside. Fanny had finished her soup and Sophie is awake so they go outside with the stroller.

They cross the street and Mary is in the park.

-Hey, Mary! Had you seen Teddy?

-No, I arrived just 10 minutes ago.

-Teddy! Where are you? I don't have time for your games. But Teddy doesn't answer this time.

Keagan Campbell
Ontario, Canada

My name is Keagan Campbell and I'm a 24 year old writer from Brampton, Ontario. I'm currently studying at York University as an English major with a minor in creative writing. Though I'm usually inspired by events in my every day life, I more enjoy writing fiction and poetry more than anything else. My hyperactive imagination has always helped me in doing so and I hope to be able to entertain and inspire others with inventive and original stories the way I was inspired as a child. There is no greater joy for me than knowing someone enjoys my work.

Slip of the tongue
By Keagan Campbell

*W*illiam stood surrounded by a jungle of unfamiliar . Hangers of pinks, purples, whites, blacks and reds were all around him as far as the eye could see. Intimidating designs, complicated size numbers and mysterious styles adorned with clips, ribbons and latches for purposes that he couldn't understand had surrounded him. Glossy eyed, he scanned over the lace, sheer, and other fabric garments that sought to swallow him whole with sheer numbers. La Sen-za was his own personal hell. While William contemplated the horror of it all, Carla returned from the dressing room behind him.

"The black one fits, but the blue one is a little small. Sucks. I really like the blue one."Carla's head swivelled back and forth almost mecha-nically between the two bras in her hand

"Oh my god, I hate bra shopping so much!" William said, his eyes wide and shiny, drowning in tears of despair. "It's the single most frustrating thing in the entire universe."

"Oh come on! It's not just bras, there's other stuff here too. Is it really that bad?"

"It's torture. Its red-hot pokers slowly jabbing my eyes while I scream for mercy. It's-"

"Alright, alright. Jeeze!" Carla put the blue one back in the bin and continued perusing the various styles that remained. "I don't get it. What's so bad about this? You get to pick out sexy stuff for me to wear for you later." Carla leaned in towards William and slipped her arms a-round his waist in a playfully seductive manner. William's face remained unchanged.

"You, more than anyone, should understand how great a hindrance I think clothing is in general. All those clips and straps are just another thing that gets in the way when I'm trying to -"

"Will!" Carla nudged William with her shoulder. "We're in public, keep it clean". Carla leaned on William resting her head on his back and gazed at a nearby frozen yogurt stand while contemplating the male psyche. "Well then if that isn't at least entertaining, what about the scenery?

There's plenty of eye candy around too isn't there?" William immediately dropped his head and looked directly at the ground.

"Shit!"

"Whoa! What happened?" Carla snapped her arms out at the ready, waiting for action.

"Now I can't look anywhere! Yah, there might be girls he-re...which...uh...I don't admit to there being any pretty ones...or any...at all. But if I look at 'em, I know you're going to get jealous eventually. God only knows what might happen then!"

"What? I'd be totally fine with it!" William turned towards Carla with a look of disbelief on his face.

"Last time you caught me looking at a girl, you bottled it up for three months until you pushed me while we were walking to the movie theatre one weekend 'cause I joked about wanting to stare at Natalie Portman all day. It was icy. I nearly cracked my skull open. How do you not remember this?" William's bewildered tone brushed the moss off Carla's memory.

"Oooohhhh yyyaaahhh! I remember that now. Shoot, my bad." They both stood there in silence as if to acknowledge the stalemate. "Well I still need some bras. I really thought this would be more fun."

"It would be fun if store policies didn't take away the only good part! I'm not allowed to be in the change room with you to watch!"

"I thought you didn't care about looking at me in lingerie?" Carla jokingly taunted William for his hypocrisy while poking at him randomly in her usual antagonistic manner. William recognised the hole in his logic and began backpedalling.

"Well, er, sometimes I guess it's kind of hot. Either way there is that wonderful point when you're changing and you've taken off one thing, but haven't quite gotten to trying on the next thing..." Carla laughed and slapped William on the arm.

"Shut up!" Carla picked out a blue bra much like the one she had to put back and checked the size before putting it back in the bin. "This should be more fun but it sucks! Who puts this much thought into an excursion to a lingerie store?" William turned back around to poke through some bins behind him while he answered.

"Why the hell wouldn't I? No matter where I am I have to take your feelings into consideration. That's what you do for people you love, right? And I'm considerate, so this is hell for me! Hell I tell you!" William turned back around to meet Carla's locked gaze– stunned and motionless. "What? What's the matter?"

"Oh my god. You love me?" William stopped and reviewed his words in his mind and realised what had just happened. A look of fear washed over his face.

"Oh. Crap. Crappy shit. Um, well I kind of. Fuck, it really wasn't supposed to come out like this."

Carla, not listening to a word he said, threw herself at William and hugged him as he remained in the throes of panic. "I love you too!"

"Listen, um, I know what that sounded like but..." William searched his mind fervently for the best words to convey his confused state to Carla without hurting her. With her arms still wrapped around him, Carla pulled back to look William in the face. Her calm joy was now masked by doubt and confusion.

"You don't love me?"

"Well ya, but no. I mean, I do but...Ugh! It's so hard! I don't understand it at all. I just, I care about you so much that its confusing and I'm not sure what to call it, if anything yet." William put his hands in his pockets and looked towards the ground. "I'm sorry. This is awkward." William attempted to turn and leave but was met with the resistance of Carla's arms still wrapped around his waist.

"Hey, it's okay you know."

"No, it's not. Now you said it. I can't say it. I have to say it!"

"You don't have to say anything. Look at me." William looked up at Carla's face, her light brown bangs dusted across her soft empathetic expression. "Can you imagine a future where I'm not with you?" William locked in on her brown eyes. They often brought him comfort in uncertain moments, but today they were unable to fulfill their usual duties. The ease of Carla's response left doubts hanging like Christmas tree ornaments in William's mind. He wasn't sure how serious Carla really was, if she was at all. Love was not a word William took lightly, and now he was less sure Carla felt the same. William couldn't help but think that Carla was underestimating the word that he had foolishly let escape the confines of his mouth. Perhaps, he was afraid that despite his firm stance on the subject, he had underestimated it as well. William could feel the pressure welling up in the pit of his stomach as the milliseconds crept by, giving way to nausea. William swallowed hard to fight his reaction to the tension to no avail. He felt the weight of the answer on his tongue as it spilled out.

"You know I can't. I don't even want to try."

"And what's your favourite part of any day?"

"Now you're just fishing for compliments." Carla smiled at William's re-mark as he brushed some of her hair off her face. She leaned forward and kissed him softly.

"Then you don't have to say anything. I can wait." William sighed in relief.

"That's a load off my shoulders."

"But I am coming back to it eventually."

"Aaaannnddd the load's back on. Can we at least not do this in La Senza next time? People are staring at us." William and Carla both looked around the store to see the patron's eyes averting from stolen glances. The light whispers of conversation seemed to swim around them through the air a-mong the mall sounds of music and footsteps of passing people. William was still uneasy but for now he could only hope that when they did revisit the conversation, all those doubts would be packed up and put away for good. William could tell Carla was unease by the stares surrounding them, attempting to penetrate their privacy. Carla quickly agreed.

"Deal."

"God, I hate bra shopping. It's nothing but trouble."

Miranda Leites

Lehigh Acres, Florida, United States

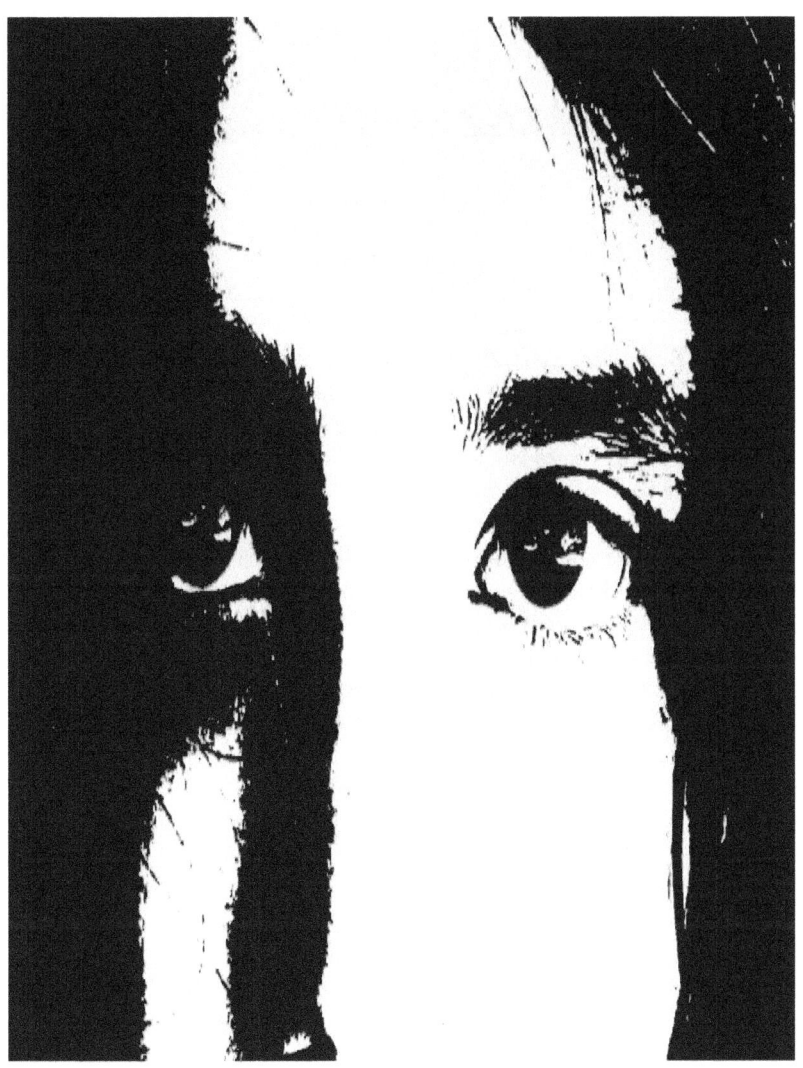

The Dream Organization
By Miranda Leites

*W*here am I?" asked Saia, not being able to see anything in the pitch black abyss. "You are here," said a soothing voice.

"I don't understand," said Saia. "The time shall come when you *do* understand, but now is not the time," said the voice, fading. "No, don't go. Please..." Saia started feeling drowsy.

When she opened her eyes, she was in a lab. People were experimenting on her. But they were all looking at a screen that led back to some wires connected to her forehead.

The screen they were looking at suddenly started beeping and they quickly turned to face her. When she saw that one of them had a needle in his hands, she tried desperately to fight back. She managed to kick a few of the doctors, including the one with the needle, but the others quickly held her back. She kicked them hard in the faces and they fell back, unconscious. One pressed an emergency button and an alarm started to ring.

Saia desperately tried to find a way out, when she spotted the door she ran as fast as she could to it. She ran into a long, white hallway with clear glass walls to be able to see into the small rooms on either side. Inside the rooms were more "doctors" watching screens with people lying on surgical cots.

Suddenly, she saw operatives dressed in all black outfits and taser guns charging at her from both sides of the hallway. Just as they were about to reach her, it seemed like time stopped and the light of the room faded into pure darkness. "Now is the time," said the voice. "How did you stop them?" asked Saia.

"I simply interrupted time."

"How?"

"Now is not the time to explain that. I have something else I wish to inform you of."

"And that is?"

"These people, no, these *monsters* are harming people across the globe."

"What are they doing to us?"

"They are taking away your imagination. And think, without the ability to imagine, to create, how are people going to think for themselves? They won't, and that is exactly what they plan on doing."

"What do you mean? What will they make us do?"

"They will make you believe false things. They are planning to start a war with the rest of the world by making you believe that the other countries are evil. Many people's imaginations have been taken away already, but I myself am in no condition of fighting back. So you shall do that for me."

"Alright, so what do I have to do to stop them?" said Saia, still not quite understanding.

"You must kill the leader of the Dream Organization."

"Dream Organization?"

"That is what they call themselves, because they can only do it while you are dreaming, otherwise it would be too obvious."

"So where is the leader then?"

"He should be in the northern most room of the building, his office."

"But when you unfreeze time, I'll be trapped by these operatives."

"That is the only time I can help you. I will trap them in time and then you must run, understood?"

"Yes."

The darkness in the room disappeared and when Saia looked behind her, she saw all the operatives frozen, but not in ice, more like as if they holding a pose still.

Like she was instructed, she ran to the north. Everywhere, she saw operatives, doctors, and everyone else frozen in time. That is, until she reached a door labeled "Head of Organization" on it. On the end table beside the door there suddenly appeared a knife. She forced herself to pick it up, and walk in the room.

There stood a young man dressed in a suit. He had a very kind looking face, and Saia suddenly feel her grip on the knife loosen. "Why are you doing this?" asked Saia. The young man thought for a minute. "That's classified," he said, he looked to be about twenty five years old. Saia walked up to him and held the knife to his stomach. "Really? Would you really be able to do that to me?" asked the young man.

Saia felt a hard shove and suddenly opened her eyes to see that she was back in her apartment, unharmed. She sighed in relief. *That was only a dream,* she thought, *a silly, silly dream.* Suddenly, she heard her bedroom window break open, in spewing at least twenty operatives. "You've seen too much," said one of the operatives, jabbing a knife into her heart.

You have failed me, Saia.

Eduardo Cerviño
Phoenix, AZ, United States

Born in Havana, Eduardo Cerviño has resided in the US since 1968. He has worked as an architectural designer, and traveled both for work and pleasure throughout the US, Canada, Latin America, and Europe. He has written and published numerous short stories, as well as two novels, titled HARRY'S FURY and IN MY OTHER BODY. Two additional novels will be completed in 2011. He writes under the pen name E.C. Brierfield, and lives in Arizona with his wife and collaborator Lesley Sudders, author of THE BRODICK FOLLIES.

About his writing style, Eduardo says: I'm in the business of death, mutilations, ghosting, blood, and putrefaction. That's what I'm all about. Living dangerously and fast. Imagining what goes on inside my neighbors' houses, what terrible things they dream about doing unto others but do not have the guts. I offer them the opportunity to roam through the darkest corners of their minds. If you want sweet escapism, don't read my stuff. If you are planning to kill someone and get away with it, I'm your kind of author.

The Companion

By Eduardo A. Cerviño

*A*SINGLE CAN LIGHT hung from the ceiling, out of reach. Its narrow beam projected a shiny spot on the concrete floor in front of my feet, and barely illuminated the base of the three barren walls I could see. Behind me was the door. Shadows loomed above it all. The lack of windows confused my circadian clock and I lost track of time.

A green nylon rope held my feet to the legs of a metal chair. The same rope snaked in circles around my legs, waist, and upper arms, and tied my swollen hands behind my back.

Pulsating pain crept upwards from my beaten soles. An acrid smell permeated the sweltering air. My only comfort was the cold concrete in contact with my bare feet.

In the zone where light and shadow kept a synergetic relationship, a somber soldier sat on the floor in the lotus position. He wore no boots and his feet showed at each side of his knees When my captors were out of the room, we talked softly. Occasionally, I found the strength to lift my head from my chest just enough to see him. His hands, resting on his knees over the camo-pants, were clean and white, with long fingers.

"Can you tell them what they want to know? It would help your situation, don't you think?" he asked.

"I don't have the information they want."

"I'm sorry to hear that. Those two guys are determined to make you confess, although I think they would be disappointed if you told them anything and they had to stop." "Would they stop if I lied to them?"

"Maybe for a while, until they find out, and then . . . well, you know. Tell them something and see, but remember that what they do to you feeds the darkness in their souls."

"Can you dry the sweat on my forehead? It's rolling into my eyes...

please." A fly buzzed around my head, landing at the corner of my eye.

"Sorry, I can't. It's not permitted. I'm not here to make you comfortable. I'm here as an observer, to keep you company."

The soldiers returned. When the room was briefly flooded with outside light, the pesky fly hurried away, to be replaced by talons of fear tearing at my entrails.

"Hellooo," said one of them.

A piece of a rubber hose appeared at the corner of my eye. It came from behind with great velocity and wrapped around my shoulder, molding itself to the contours of my flesh with morbid exactitude.

My scream lacked conviction.

I waited for the next blow. It didn't come. "I'm thirsty," I croaked, not expecting water.

"Tell me the names of the guys working with you, and I will give you water, a big glass of ice water," his throaty voice said, inches from my left ear.

My right ear had been ringing persistently; it didn't bother me anymore. He filled a glass, letting me hear the ice cubes tumble from the plastic jug. After noisily drinking, he tossed the rest on the floor; the ice cubes shattered where I could see them.

"I told you. I don't know what you are asking of me."

The soldier pulled the hose from my body; it slithered away out of sight like a harmless garden snake. This time I knew it would return with the force of devilish satisfaction. It didn't take long for my vision to be fulfilled.

Lacking surprise and saturated with pain as I was, the malevolent act did not elicit a guttural expression and I remained silent. The light spot on the floor seemed to contract, while my mind mercifully closed down.

I awoke when a bucket of water wadded my hair and washed away the sweat over my eyes, neck, and shoulders. It made my skin slippery and the rope gave a little, making the tiny needles of nylon prickle the wounds in my pectorals. With the tip of my tongue, I collected the moisture from my lips.

As a third man entered the room, daylight outlined on the floor the distorted angles of the door at my back. The temperature differential drew fresh air inside the space; it had a salty tang.

I felt gratitude for the gift the nearby sea had sent my way.

As he closed the door, the bright rectangle on the floor diminished until the last sliver of light died. In that fleeting moment, while my eyes adapted to the near-darkness, I caught another glimpse of the soldier seated on the ground. The guards remained oblivious to him.

I thought his presence was an added psychological attempt to mess with my mind—a way to encourage me to hope that help could come from this mild-mannered person, so that I would confide in him whatever they thought I knew.

A microburst of air outside the door shuffled the huge leaves of the palm trees by the building. I imagined these majestic palms gently swaying in the wind. The rustling sound tricked my mind and I felt the breeze's cooling effect roll over me.

THE WIRE CAGE cell where I was held was exposed to the celestial dome. This was the third time the soldiers had taken me from it and brought me to this room. As before, we had followed the winding road at the edge of the palms, to the building with trimmed hedges and manicured lawn. From the instant the two bulky officers, neat in their freshly pressed military uniforms, showed up at my gate, the etheric realm connecting me to them told me about the bestial instincts they intended to unleash upon my body once again.

The viciousness and duration of this session exceeded the previous ones.

"Save yourself some trouble, and talk to us," said the new man in the room. Before I could protest my innocence, he held the back of my head and with his free hand covered my nose and mouth with a wet rag.

"Don't be an idiot. We have others who said you knew of the plot, so we will be here until you change your mind."

This third man's face loomed over mine. His long hair fell forward. His clenched, tobacco-stained teeth showed under a graying mustache. Suffocation filled my senses with panic.

My heart thumped wildly; however, the asphyxia was having a sedative effect and from a full gallop my heart began to change into slow-motion.

He asked the same question as the other men had done before, but did not let go of my head or the rag. I rocked my head from side to side. My eyes bulged, my resolve weakened, and I contemplated implicating others in the plot they kept talking about, whether true or not.

I imagined other men taking my place. As quickly, an inner voice spoke to me. Why hurt others? Let go; it is your time, not theirs.

My heart was now misfiring. The movement of my head was not an indication of my refusal to talk, but a desire to shake away the rag and breathe.

When he let me go, my lungs were on fire and I gasped for air. The ropes around my chest were too tight for my lungs to be able to exercise their full bellowing action. The gulps of whistling air were insufficient.

A knock on the door halted their handiwork.

"You all come out for a minute," said someone standing outside the door they had opened. "We have new orders."

They left the room, but the door did not fully close after them.

A thin ray of daylight on the floor ended where my companion sat. It bisected his body from head to crossed legs. His bald skull was shiny, his eyes had a calming luminosity; there may have been a faint smile on his lips.

I heard the voices outside; one sounded authoritarian, the others compliant. "Are you sure about that, sir?"

"Yes. We have to stop. It was a mistake and those are the orders. Are you questioning me?"

"No, I'm not..." "No, I'm not what?" "No, I'm not. Sir!"

"Do as you are told, then." "Yes, sir."

I heard the steps of a man walking away, but did not understand what the other three were arguing about outside the door. Surprisingly, I had lost interest in my surroundings and only the gaze of the man on the floor was of any significance to me.

His large green eyes were full of compassion. One tear rolled from his right eye, while a second nestled on his eyelashes. His mouth opened a little; the smile included his eyes and cheeks. A tender puff from his mouth bridged the distance separating us. I opened my lips; I knew he wanted me to. The streaming breath entered my lungs with the refreshing sensation of the morning dew, and yet the pain I was feeling in my arms and chest told me that my heart was tired of the abuse it had sustained.

What was that, he said? I thought. Oh yes, "Forgive them, Father, for—" The rest of the phrase came to mind, "for they know not what they do."

My heart thumped once more, and went silent. It didn't matter to me as long as the eyes of the stranger kept crying for me. He rose and glided over the floor toward me with the ease of a cloud in the sky, and extended his hand to me, inviting me to stand up. Mine were tied so I did not attempt to take his.

His smile grew into a soft, amused grin. "Do you prefer to stay in the chair?" I shook my head–I was free of the rope. I accepted his help and stood.

The door swung open and the soldiers came inside, stopping behind the chair. This was the place from where they had dispensed their cruelty with malign complacency—making menacing comments, cocking their pistols, or, more to their liking, flogging me.

I felt refreshed and free, and enjoyed the soldiers' expressions of concern when they saw my lifeless body. One touched my neck, checking my pulse.

"Damn, look what you did," he said, pointing at the moustachioed soldier.

"We did as we were ordered."

"Yes, it was our job. But we were supposed to keep him alive. Look what you have done."

"The commander will understand. I got carried away. He will stand by us. Surely it has happened before."

The engine of a plane flying low over the building screamed and faded in the distance. The two soldiers looked back at the open door and saw, framed by it, the silhouette of the craft, gaining attitude over the Caribbean Sea.

"Was that the commander's plane?" asked the third man, looking up at the ceiling where the can light swayed.

"Yes, he flew in this morning to review this guy's files." "I'm sure he will be back; we'll talk with him then." "Are you sure about that?"

"About what?"

"That he will return to the base; he is not stationed here."

"Do you know where he is stationed? Do you know his name?" "He never said, and I never asked. Damn."

There was no answer, only concerned glances at one another. They turned their eyes toward the door; the plane was a dot on the horizon. Close to the shore, a pod of dolphins romped on the waves.

"I really didn't know what you wanted from me," I said to them one last time.

My companion touched my arm; the wide open door beckoned us. He eased his way through the soldiers. I glanced one more time at my corpse in the chair.

"Excuse me." I mumbled, and followed him outside, no more concerned than two fellows leaving the neighborhood bar.

A fast-developing monsoon rain pelted the tin roof of the isolated barracks. Steam hugged the ground that the noontime sun had been baking minutes ago. Beads of water rested on the giant leaves of the banana trees; there, they fattened up, then rolled, fell, and pooled on the ground below. A hummingbird darted across our path on its way to collect nectar from a wild orchid; steady in the air, his wings beat the rain into a delicate spray.

"I can't feel the raindrops," I said to my companion.

"Of course not; what do you expect? Wait until your next incarnation."

THE END

Dante Long
Lansdowne, Pa, United States

My name is Dante Long I am a 2011 Penn Wood HS graduate. I was born on January 12th, 1992. I enjoy writing and drawing as my hobbies. I am of Cuban ancestry. I was inspired by the writer Jorge Borges and his writing.

The Battle for Relevance
By Dante Long

*T*oday I get my mail sent by my school informing students of the 2010-2011 school year. For one reason only I was excited –I was going to be a senior. I promised myself I was going to join an after school activity for a change and to have the best year possible. I didn't want just a good year academically, but socially as well. I even figured I join an after school activity, I didn't have a job or plans after school really anyway, so I figured why not. Since school starts on Tuesday, the 6th of September, I planned to return to my normal 11:30 sleeping routine-better than 3 am like last year I thought. Normally around the start of school I hype myself into believing I'll be super organized, my book bag, papers and locker…It's just those things never happen.

A black collared shirt and blue jeans were what I decided on wearing the first day. As I grabbed my jeans, my phone vibrated on my dresser. I got a text message "So was sup when ya go back to school," the message read. I replied sarcastically by saying "In an hour, wearing no UNI-FORMS," I said.

I figured she'd be mad at that one, her school Lamberton required uniform, and at least Penn Wood High had no uniforms. That put my school ahead of hers on the cool scale that we made up. "You got home room 109," my sister asked. Yeah, "so I guess you do to," I said. Since we're related so that was no surprise to us. Melissa is more sarcastic than Vee is so I just assume she's joking with everything.

I pull out my X-box and grab a game to play…"crap," I said. My X-box was defective so I wasn't playing anything. Instead, I walked around Lansdowne with Melissa and Ray-our mutual friend. I met Ray In July, and he was cool company. As we were walking, Melissa made fun of the weird sty-le of clothing people chose to wear. I thought most of the attires were funny, but Ray did most of the laughing. 5 minutes later I decided to go home and iron my clothes for the start of a year I would make mine. When 9 o' clock hit I turned to Wrestling, I'm a big fan and the main event was a table match. As weird as it sounds, I kept thinking about school.

The last thing I did before the night was over was text Taylor. Taylor was a graduate of Penn Wood, and very pretty with green eyes. She was actually one of my first female friends I had who acted like a female. I was interested in her; just I wouldn't allow myself to tell her. After things fell through with this other girl in the summer, I subconsciously stayed in the background. Before that, girls only talked to me through Facebook sometimes. This year I was looking to change my luck with females. So after I sorted my clothes I went to bed.

When birds chirp, that's 6 0'clock to me. The sun light seeped through my blinds, so I got up. Without my normal drowsiness I got up quick. I got dressed, brushed my teeth and started to wash my face. Since as long as I could remember, I developed a skin condition. At first I thought it was some form of Acne, but I was told by my doctor it had characteristics from it and some infection underneath my skin. For that reason, I cheated myself out of many things, I was kind of shy already, and this irritating condition did help anything, just cost me extra money I didn't have .To some people I deserve this punishment, because the classic "He don't wash his face." Theory creeps in. After I finish washing my face with an aggressive cleanser, I ate breakfast and left out to school.

As I walk down Price Street in Lansdowne, I see other students walking to school. While I see the change in others in just 3 months-I remained the same. Same height, same weight…everything. My school had the most unique setup of a student body. We had the real smart kids; average smart kids-just lazy, students who live alternative life styles and students trying to be tough when it doesn't call for it. I really didn't know where I fit in, but I knew I had to be my own person. As l walked in the school and go to 109, my homeroom, I hear a voice. "You, boy" said Dave. Dave was a friend of mine and we had similarity in personality, difference was he was all out hilarious. I looked at him and said "hey, what classes do you have?" Dave asked. "A lot of electives; I got statistics, psychology and English too, my only cool ones," I said. I look and ask him the same question. "A whack current issues class and electives like you," said Dave.

After talking we went to our homerooms. 20 minutes later we went to first period. First period was Economics class, and it was ok. About 4 hours passed then it was time for 5th period lunch. I had 5th period lunch last year and didn't know anybody. I remember I had a crush on this one girl who sat in the front of the cafeteria. I never had the courage to talk to her…the feeling sucked, trust me. This time around 5th period lunch was different, I knew mostly everyone and had Dave and Yushi, my friend at my table. Yushi stood out from traditional style. He was his own person and didn't care who liked it. 2 hour later, school ended. It was a good day I was just exhausted.

After a good first day, I went home and was welcomed by my mother, Tina. "How was school today?" said Mom. I told her it was busy and that I couldn't complain. My grandfather Russell hugged me when he saw me and asked if I joined my school's art group, NAHS. "I didn't check it out today, I'll see about it tomorrow," I said. He looked at me and patted me on the back, got his jacket and went to the store down the street. My grandfather looked tired when he left; I just figured that because he worked long hours. Later on, I sat on the couch and reminisced on the day and told myself I would join NAHS, the National Art Honor Society. I don't know, but sometimes I like to be in groups of less people. Since I had this annoying skin condition, that wasn't attractive, I didn't feel like people stared at. An hour later my grandfather finally came home and I asked if he was o.k. I knew something was up, he was a military guy at heart, I should have known he'd be too modest to admit anything.

Mid-September, I finally was a member of NAHS. I've been to three meetings and saw some familiar faces; along with some new faces too. By being at the group's third meeting, I already improved my record, last year I only attended one meeting. Then after that I dropped out because I wasn't sure I had the commitment the group required. However, this year was different, I 'm staying put in. I got on my computer and started searching for colleges that had health study courses that I wanted to major in. I can't lie it was tough, I wasn't actually where I wanted to be. I mean my class rank and G.P.A weren't where they could or should have been. So because of that fact, I can admit I hardly applied to schools. I knew what I wanted-just not how to get there.

After school Wednesday, around 3 o'clock, I get a call from my mom. She says it's about my grandfather, and that they were at the Veterans hospital downtown. She told me to just be at the house and that they would be home shortly. I was nervous and upset "I knew something was wrong," I said out loud. When I got home I sat around concern so I started my work for psychology...my favorite class. Most of the people in there were cool and active, despite being an early class. The teacher was cool too. The class to me felt like a recycled version of my history class last year. It basically had the same classmates.

It was about 11:00 pm when my sister and my mom returned. "Hi, they said he needed a blood transfusion," said my mom. "I wondered what caused him to need that," I said. My mom looked at me and said "we asked the same thing." Melissa said she wasn't going to school the next day, honestly I couldn't blame her. I said goodnight to them and went to sleep.

Over a month had passed since my grandfather had been home, my mind really didn't process it. He hasn't been in the house since September

15th. Now October 15th after a long day at school and hospital, I crashed on the couch- I was that tired. When I woke up I saw Melissa standing over me with money. "Ezar and Ezra gave this to us when he heard about what happened to granddad." I was overwhelmed with gratitude. Ezar and Ezra were twins and real good friends and master video game players. I really appreciated what they did, they really didn't have to-but that's how they were.

It seemed like no time has passed in school. Whatever problem I had, goals and aspirations before the year, I knew one me thing...they suddenly gotten tougher. I thought to myself there was no way I was able to join NAHS.I was great at drawing, just not a painter really. I entered the art room on Friday and only 6 people knew who I was, I wasn't really a standout guy at the time, but I wasn't going to leave the group.

On Halloween night, my sister, mom and I met my uncle, grand mom and aunt at the hospital. I remember my grandfather wanting to speak to me by myself. We talked about everything, like school, the family, and the media. I never mentioned his illness. I missed him around the house. I remember my mom told me he had cancer when they found out. Everyone was up-set. My grandfather told me he loved me and that he was proud of me. I took his words and stored them in me forever. I told him I loved him and that I was still going to college to be a doctor. I wished I was a doctor then to help him, but I wasn't. I hugged him, but not too long, because he was hooked up to the equipment .Later on I got dropped off to my friend Greg's Halloween party. All my friends were there. "Dante," I heard some-one say. I looked up and saw it was my friend Miriam. I said hey back to her. "What are you dressed as?" I asked her. She told me she was a reality TV star. We both laughed and all went in the Living room to see what was on TV. On the TV everyone saw a commercial about a state essay contest sponsored by PWA. The commercial promised $15,000 dollars for first place, plus a scholarship in journalism. After that everybody was excited. One person at the party googled the full details for the essay competition. The details stated the contest was exclusive to high school students in Pennsylvania. The essay had to be a minimum of 6,000 words, doubled space and due December 1st.The essay asked students one question. That question read "How would you preserver during tough times and why is college important?"

On Monday that was the talk of Penn Wood. I talked about entering it at lunch and Dave and Yushi thought I was joking about entering. Yushi told me it was 6000 words like I should have been intimidated about enter-ing. I looked at him and said "why not? Some has to try." I picked up a registration slip after lunch and signed it, and then I was officially in. I checked the sign-up form and only 50 students entered. I saw about 13 names of really good writers, and one guy even was the son of a teacher. I didn't care, I liked competition. In late November, things started to change for me in the right direction. NAHS started to include me in more activities and allowed me to draw their logo for their t-shirt. I actually felt like I had a place with the group for a change. I can tell they saw how hard I was working. My friend Cliff and I stayed after school working on paintings and projects for NAHS.I got my progress report and my grades did a complete 360, my hard work in class was paying off too. It was still going to take more to get into college, but I was ready to continue my hard work.

The one thing I thought about and needed was competition, and the mo-ney and notoriety that came with winning it. Slowly but surely I started to shed my skin. The more I talked about my issues and how I'm working on them, the more respect I got. With my life turning around, I finally felt important again. I know it sounds weird, but it's the truth. With a few hours until the essay start, I was gathering my thoughts, thinking how I would say I dealt with everything.

For the essay contest, all students had to go to their respective schools and write the essay there in person. The contest would only offer 3 hours to write it. The winner s, 1st and 2nd would be announced early January, via e-mail. For the last two weeks my arms were sore from writing, but I was obsessed with wining.

Going up to my school the day of the contest was nerve wrecking, like the SATS. Most students talked about the contest and had their pick in mind. When I got there I grabbed a computer and got down to business. After the second hour, everyone was tired, but they were still writing. By 12 am everyone was finished and essays were collected. I left Penn Wood High and went home feeling, feeling-complete.

When I got home I told myself even if I didn't win at least I entered. Looking back now, I had changed .I mean I couldn't change my skin condition. My life was one thing I could change. If I learned anything, it's that change is very possible if you have the necessary tools.

On January 2nd I stepped outside to check the mail. When I sorted through, I saw my results. When I opened it said "congratulations Dante Mason, from Penn Wood High School, you have won second place in our PWA essay contest." I rejoiced and felt that all my work was worth the effort. I was so excited I forgot the scholarship that comes with it. I achieved my mission to change the mediocre person I was. The next day my friend from art Samantha congratulated me, along with my other friends. I decided to put the winnings to my college fund and spend 2 grand on a celebration of my struggle throughout senior my year. Before I did that I took a trip to my grandfather's grave and placed my certificate on his grave and I then walked away with more confidence for the future ahead.

Monique' Y, DuRant

Buffalo, New York, United States

My name is Monique' Y. DuRant and I reside in Buffalo, NY. I have worked for the Adult Education Division here for over sixteen years. I have been writing stories and poems since the age of thirteen. My preference is young adult and children's fiction. I have completed two works thus far. I go to some of the local elementary schools and read my stories to the children, and they love them. I write a weekly column for a local newspaper. Currently, I am a full-time college student on the Dean's List. My goal is to finish a series of children's based on my main character, Porgy Lloyd. I absolutely enjoy writing and plan on doing so much more. Next year I will be fifty years old so I think now is a good time to start looking into publication.

Have No Fear
By Monique' Y. DuRant

Chapter One

While walking home from school Aapri seemed to be deep in thought, paying no attention to the ground underneath her feet. In front of many of her schoolmates she suddenly had a chance meeting with the curb. Outbursts of laughter surroundded her. If anyone really had the power to disappear Aapri wished it were she. The other kids gathered around her, and their laughs kept her glued to the ground. They chided, teased, goaded and made her feel the way they always did. The way a microorganism must feel, very small. Separating herself from the ground seemed to take an eternity. The chants became more audible. "Did you have a nice trip?" an unknown voice sang out. There was another out-burst of laughter. Aapri wiped herself off and tried to ignore all of the laughing. She thought to herself this is just another thing they will have to tease me about. She continued her walk with her head down paying close attention to the mocking pavement.

As she walked into her home she was greeted by her mother and father, Nicole and Kenneth. They asked her how her day had been. Aapri shrugged her shoulders while saying "it was okay". They could feel a sense of defeat surrounding their daughter. Nicole wanted to cheer her daughter up so she went out to the store to buy some of Aapri's favorite comic books. After arriving back home Nicole called her daughter downstairs to the living room. "Honey, look what I picked up for you. I have three of your favorites" mom said. Aapri instantly perked up and started smiling. She was so happy to get the new comics. Her favorite ones were the gruesome, horror comics. These particular ones looked to be very enjoyable.

Have No Fear

She felt very comfortable snuggling under the throw on the bed as she proceeded to read the first comic book. It was great! It had her looking around the room every time she heard the slightest noise. One of the characters in the book had his eyeball ripped out. Once the book was finished she arrived at her favorite part – the back few pages of the book. There is a lot of advertising on these pages and there are certain items you can order. As she glanced through these items her eyes came across something of interest. For $3.95 you could actually order your own "boogeyman", it was a straw-filled doll. There was something about the eyes on this doll. It seemed like they came out of the page right into her room. She ran to her jewelry box to see how much money she had in her secret compartment. Finding more than enough money to purchase the boogeyman she prepared her envelope. Sleep was upon her now so she lay down with a great feeling of calm and comfort. In the morning she would give her mother the money and ask her to write a check and mail off her order.

Chapter Two

Everyday for a week Aapri would run home paying attention to every step she took and ask loudly, "Did it come yet"? Her mother gave the same response everyday, "No, I will let you know as soon as it comes". Aapri could not understand why it was taking so long. She decided she would just be patient and it would be there soon. There has to be a certain amount of days for the order to even reach them, she thought.

Have No Fear

Things were still not going that great at school. There was a group of kids who continually harassed her. It seemed as if they knew she had no brothers and sisters to protect her. They ridiculed her clothes and even talked about the ponytail in her hair. It was the same group of kids who laughed at her when she fell. She tried to avoid them as much as she could.

In the classroom she would sit in the front of the room so the teacher would be able to see any taunting. This did not always work; they usually found a way to bother her from behind. It was usually to pull her ponytail or put signs on her back. She always hoped that one day they would just leave her alone or just disappear. Especially during recess when the same kids pushed her back and forth under the radar of the watchful teachers

The only things she liked about school was being in the library and talking to the school counselor. Ms. Vickers would help to build Aapri's esteem. Aaprihad two good friends in school their names were Samy and Shalah. Sammy was quite small so everyone called him little Sammy. Shalah was well liked by all of the students and Aapri was glad to have her as a friend. Shalah would stand up for her if she happened to be around when the children were picking on her. They would instantly stop bothering Aapri because they had respect for Shalah.

While walking home together Aapri told Shalah about the doll she had ordered. Shalah expressed her fear regarding horror books and spooky things. She told her how she often had nightmares about the end of the world. Dreams of fire throwing clouds and water covering the entire earth were very common visitors.

Have No Fear

While reading a book if things started getting scary she would instantly stop. If a new scary movie came out she never wanted to see it. They had a lot of things in common and liking scary stuff definitely was not one of them.

Chapter Three

It was Saturday night and Nicole took her daughter to the show to see the newest horror movie. It seemed like Nicole screamed every few seconds while Aapri just laughed. This stuff was not scary to her it was actually very funny. It was funny because she knew these things could never really happen in real life. That is why she enjoyed such gruesome things because none of it could ever be real. Or so she thought!

On Sunday Kenneth asked Aapri if she wanted to go skating. After thinking about it she told him she did not want to go. She knew some of her classmates always went to the rink on Sunday and she did not want to run into any of them. He decided to ask her if everything was going okay for her. Of course, she told him that everything was fine. Kenneth decided to let it go for now he would wait until she was ready to talk to him. "Okay, well if you are ever having a problem just know that you can come and talk to me about anything" he said.

Monday morning Shalah was at Aapri's doorstep to pick her up bright and early. The school day was long and seemed like it would never be over. In between classes, Aapri ran into Mrs. Vickers. She wanted to know how Aapri's day was going and how her weekend was. "I guess everything is all right, I did go to the movies this weekend", she said dully.

Have No Fear

Mrs. Vickers let her know that her door was always open if she was having any issues. She watched Mrs. Vickers walk off and decided she was very glad she was here.

Today there was a new transfer student in school her name was Daisy. At first glance she seemed very shy and withdrawn. From the sound of her slight voice you could tell she was scared to speak out loud in a group. It was barely audible when she said her name to the class. The regular bullies lit into her immediately. They chanted "Daisy, Daisy sure looks crazy". Aapri talked to her and even sat next to her. Daisy thanked her for being so nice. Together they helped each other make it through the day, each feeling glad they had met.

One thing they had in common was that Daisy also liked scary stories and movies. Aapri was very happy to have a new friend who had the same interests as she did. Everyone else was so squeamish.

Chapter Four

Aapri walked alone Monday after school. She quietly bypassed her tormentors and made her way towards home. When she arrived at a major intersection she noticed an elderly woman using a walker. As she looked down the street she noticed a large eighteen-wheel truck sort of speeding out of control. She moved to the middle of the street after seeing the elderly woman start walking in the street with her walker. Looking up the street Aapri could see the truck still careening towards the woman. The woman never looked up and never saw the truck.

Have No Fear

Aapri raced to the other side and pulled the woman out of the way just in time. The truck smashed into the woman's walker and on the side of the truck you could see the words B.G.M. Distributions. Whoever was driving the truck slowed up just long enough to look at Aapri with big, dark eyes and say "Don't worry Aapri I am on the way. I will see you soon." There was something very familiar about those eyes, she had seen them before. She wondered how this person could possibly know her name.

This was probably the first time Aapri ever felt any type of real fear. What just happened seemed very surreal. Did her imagination finally get the better of her? She turned around to make sure the elderly woman was o-kay. Low and behold there was no one there. What happened to the woman she was just there seconds earlier? There is no way she could have just disappeared, unless it never really happened. Aapri walked the rest of the way home in shock and disbelief. Did it happen or not? She decided she could not tell her parents about this incident, for fear that they may think she was crazy.

As she walked in the house she pulled herself together so that no one would know anything was wrong with her. Nicole saw her daughter and asked her how was school. Holding it all together Aapri just shrugged her shoulders as if to say okay. Her mother noticed that she did not ask if her doll had come in the mail but she made no mention of it.

After doing her homework and chores Aapri went upstairs and called to chitchat with Shalah.

Have No Fear

As soon as the conversation started Shalah could tell her friend was not her usual self. She tried to get Aapri to open up and tell her what was going on. But she would simply say over and over that she was just fine. Soon as Aapri hung up the phone she picked it right back up and called Daisy. She told Daisy she thought she was reading too much horror, and that she was going to stop for a little while. Daisy was curious about what it was that sca-red her friend like that. After asking several times what happened she never did get a straight answer. The last call she made that evening was to little Sammy. He mostly talked about football and how he was going to play in the NFL one day. She always kidded him and told him he should play baseball and be a shortstop.

Chapter Five

Sleep took a long time coming that evening. Aapri tossed and turned for quite some time. Finally, she could feel herself starting to drift off. It felt as if she were lying on slow moving water similar to a waterbed. As she slept she felt her body being lifted up off of the bed and carried downstairs through the dining room. The front door opened up as she floated quickly out of the house. She realized that a gigantic hand was carrying her, and she was lying in the palm. At this point she started screaming for her parents, her screams went unheard. The hand carried her up the street and she pa-ssed several of her neighbors. She hollered for them to help and to call her parents or the police. They looked directly at her but it was as if they could not see her. A neighbor's dog barked at her uncontrollably, it was as if he could actually see the big hand carrying her.

Have No Fear

The hand kept going as if it had a specific mission to carry out. She no-ticed there was what looked like a red rubber band on one of the fingers of the hand. It went through Sidney Park and carried her closer and closer to the Gibson Falls. She heard the sound of the rushing water getting closer and closer. She heard herself screaming louder and louder. Why couldn't anyone hear her or stop this? Suddenly, she felt water splashing in her face as the hand held her at the top of the falls. It was then that she stopped thin-king it was a dream. At this point she started screaming at the very top of her lungs. She hollered "Oh! My God! This is not a dream. This is really happening, somebody please save me". The hand pointed downward as she plummeted hundreds of feet into the mighty waters.

The next felt sensation was Kenneth picking his daughter up from the floor as well as the spilled pitcher of water from the nightstand. Between the water and the sweat she was absolutely soaked. Her father explained to her that she had a terrible nightmare but that she would be okay. She told her father all about the dream and asked if he would stay with her for a little bit longer, he agreed to. They sat and talked about things that were going on in school with her. She told him about her tormenters, Mrs. Vickers, Shalah, little Sammy, and Daisy. Kenneth explained to her that he would contact the school to deal with the bullies. He also expressed his happiness that she had friends that she got along well with. Aapri kissed her dad goodnight, changed her pajamas and climbed back into the bed. As she lay down she felt something strange under her pillow. She lifted the pillow up and started crying because she realized it was a very large red rubber band.

Have No Fear

Chapter Six

Aapri was up all night after discovering the rubber band. "This cannot be from the finger of that gigantic hand" she thought aloud. But what other explanation can there be. Has she been dreaming or was there something dark and disturbed going on in her life? She was red from pinching herself to make sure she was not dreaming. It was now time to get ready for school. Aapri dressed very slowly unsure of what the day was going to bring.

Shalah met her at the front porch at 7:30 a.m. They walked along quietly as they passed all the usual markers. As they arrived in their homeroom they could instantly tell something was wrong. There was loud chatter going on everywhere. Sammy and Daisy walked over to them and asked had they heard what happened. At that moment Mrs. Vickers entered the classroom. She asked the children to quietly sit down. Mrs. Vickers let the class know that it was true that four of their classmates had been missing since yesterday. When they disappeared they were not together, they were each in different parts of town. No one had any ideas or explanations for what had happened to them.

As Aapri looked around she felt this horribly eerie feeling. She noticed that the only students missing were the four classroom bullies. These were the students who filled her life with misery everyday. Those were the four students Mrs. Vickers was speaking of. Mrs. Vickers let the children know if a-ny of them were having any problems dealing with the disappearance they could come to her. Aapri was hot on her trail as she left the room.

Have No Fear

Aapri asked Mrs. Vickers if the police knew anything. She told her they really had no leads but, there were some peculiar similarities in the cases. "Similarities like what" Aapri questioned. "Well, it seems like the last places they were seen each had a red large rubber type thing just laying where they stood. The police have no idea what this symbolizes. They hope that it is not the work of a serial killer. It is all a little overwhelming", Mrs. Vickers stated.

Once back in the classroom Aapri caught back up with her three friends. She told them everything that had happened to her in the last few days, even about the red rubber band. She told them everything that Mrs. Vickers had told her. The only reason she shared everything with them is because she cared for them deeply and she felt they would not judge her. They all told her she was imagining everything and it was caused by her abnormal interest in scary things. She pretended to agree but she knew this would happen if she tried to share her experiences with anyone. The rest of the day slowed to a crawl. As soon as the bell rang she was the first one out of her seat.

Chapter Seven

The next day at school Aapri knew something was wrong as soon as she entered the building. There were policeman everywhere she looked as well as reporters. She wondered what it could be now. The hallway seemed to stretch longer and longer as she walked to her homeroom. Upon arriving at the doorway to the class she could hear the cries coming from the room. It seemed like there were only a couple of students in the room today.

Have No Fear

Aapri heard someone say the name Shalah. She moved closer to hear what they were saying in regards to Shalah. As she walked towards the students talking she overheard the name Sammy. It was then that it donned on her that Sammy, Shalah and Daisy were not in attendance. At that point the substitute school counselor came into the classroom. That feeling of imp-ending doom hit Aapri like a ton of bricks. The counselor told the students and the teacher that there had been many disappearances the preceding evening. She confirmed that Aapri's three best friends were among those missing persons as well as Mrs. Vickers. This seemed to affect Aapri very personally. She wondered why something would happen to all of her best friends. Also, why had something happened to the people that harassed her?

When she arrived home her parents were so grateful and happy to see her. They told her that they heard of all the disappearances. She was assured by her parents that they would not let her go to school alone, or come home alone. They promised not to let anything happen to her. It was at this point that she told them everything that had happened to her from the very first incident. She wondered at what point in her life did everything she had come to know change. It seems like it was after she ordered the boogeyman doll. Her parents told her that everything was probably just a bad nightmare from too much scary fiction in her life.

Chapter Eight

Sleep came very slowly for Aapri that evening. She tossed and turned for several hours. When she finally fell asleep the gigantic hand appeared again. The hand picked her up by the collar and carried her out of the house.

Have No Fear
There was no sense in screaming because she knew no one would hear

her to wake her up out of this dream. She looked sadly at all of the neighbor's houses as she drifted past. There was no fight left inside of her. This hand seemed to know exactly where it was taking her. Aapri had no idea where she would end up this time. She just prayed that when it was all over she would be back in the safety of her bedroom.

The hand carted her to a dark and desolate area of the town that Aapri had never been in. Nearing the end of a road she could see there was something very large and dark up ahead. As her eyes started adjusting to the starry skies she noticed there was a figure in front of her, and it was well over eight foot tall. She let out an audible cry as she realized it was an exact replica of the doll she had ordered. The doll leaned over and said with a grimace "I'm here". This doll was definitely not made of straw.

The doll explained to her that he was behind all of the disappearances. Aapri mustered up the courage to ask the gargantuan doll why he did this. "I am the boogeyman you have always searched for. I have always searched for you also. I took away those bullies because I did not want anyone to hurt you. Your friends were taken away because I did not want to share you with anyone. From here to eternity you are mine alone. And, just in case you are still unsure – this is not a dream. Aapri screamed a bone-chilling scream and was never to be seen again.

Have No Fear

Chapter Nine

About a year after the disappearance of their daughter Nicole and Kenneth decided to go into her room to box some of her items up. It was a tedious task because they just could not let go of the hope that she was still alive. They boxed up clothes they knew she would not be able to fit anymore. The hardest part of the job was when Nicole had to box up the comic books.

As she thumbed through the magazines she wondered why her daughter always had such an interest in these gruesome articles. One magazine that she had never seen happened to catch her eye. She was immediately drawn to the back few pages of the book. There were so many different items that you could order. She thought about the doll her daughter had ordered and wondered why it never came.

On the last page Nicole noticed a peculiar looking doll. She looked closely and realized the dolls eyes looked very familiar. They were eyes she had seen many times before. They were eyes that had come from her. Kenneth came running as he heard Nicole hit the floor while screeching "Oh! No it's Aapri."

Aireen Grace Andal
San Jose del Monte City, Bulacan

Aireen Grace Andal is a graduate student of Demography at the University of the Philippines. She graduated from college with a bachelor's degree in sociology last May, 2010. She is currently working as a technical writer and research assistant. She reads books on social sciences and humanities. Her favorite authors are Plato, Michel Foucault, John Braithwaite, Slavoj Žižek, Fyodor Dostoevsky and Leo Tolstoy. The Holy Bible (King James Version) is her favorite book. Her fields of interest are sociology of deviance, world politics, mortality, migration, child studies and comparative literature. She also engages herself in painting and reading manga series.

1978-1993
By Aireen Grace Andal

1978-1993. This is all about her.

I find her to be fair. She's beyond anyone could imagine. Perfect. She is Isabel.

I first saw her at the university. 1978, she's at her first year of studying comparative literature. I was then at my third year as a student of political science. Her hair is brown, long and wavy. Her eyes, black. Her smile, tempting. Her presence owns my attention. I met many girls but when I remember her, I forget about them.

I am Rolando, but they call me Rolly. I never told anyone about her. My mother frequently set me up on a date with her friends' daughters. She believes that if I marry a girl from a family we know, our relationship will be stronger than otherwise. But I already had my Isabel.

1979. I met Luisa when I was graduating from my bachelor's degree. She is a fine lady. She paints. I saw her paintings and they were good. She is at her best in portraits. I saw beautiful young ladies painted. Fair and sweet they seem. But never shall they be the most lovable compared to my Isabel, in her second year then, whose face is like the sun that brightens up the day. Her dimpled smile pacifies a troubled heart. Any dress suits her. That is why when she joined the university theatre group, she appeared like the star of the night in every production. I am a fan. If I am a painter, I would fill my room with portraits of her. I made it cum laude with Isabel as my inspiration.

1982. I met Sandra at law school. She was my classmate. She's smart. I am stunned sometimes by her timid looks whenever she's asking me about a certain law or provision. At times, she scares me with what she knows. At times, she intimidates me by her high scores in exams. Indeed, law school was one, if not the worst hell-on-earth I ever experienced. But these were nothing compared with the day when I saw Isabel, graduating with a degree in Comparative Literature, crying when her father died. My heart was shattered. I was like a worm crawling upon the ground. I felt so void. I was crashed. I felt broken. The pain was more than the hurt I felt at my first failed examination at law school. I never wanted to see Isabel crying again.

1984. I met Ria in my first job as a legal officer at a local government unit. She's the resident psychologist. She's good at people. She can make them talk about their past, their highest hopes and wildest dreams. But she can't move my thoughts. The only person who can direct my thoughts is Isabel, who was then a high school literature teacher at a public school in our home town. Only Isabel occupied my mind. Only Isabel can make me laugh, cry and shout. Only her.

1987. I met Margarita when I lost my first case. She's a pianist at a bar near the office. I was drunk. I told her my disappointments about myself. I thought I was great. She offered to play a mild piano piece so that my heart will feel ease. I listened to her music. It was soothing to the ears. I was like floating and it lightens my burden. But Margarita is no better than my Isabel who was then awarded as the best teacher by the town head for her compassionate teaching. Her smile and laughter fill my ears like music and drives all my sorrows away. Only Isabel can make my heart sing. Isabel puts melody each day I see her.

1990. I met Maria when I got accepted as a lawyer in a well-known bank in the country. I really aimed for this job. I became very proud of myself. This is one of the happiest moments in my life. This means career. Maria is the human resource manager. She congratulated me and told me that she's impressed by my job experiences in the government so she opted to cast her vote for me during the final deliberation. I did not know what to feel. I think I owe her the joy I had that time. But what she did for me was nothing compared to the bliss brought to me by Isabel, who just got engaged with someone. Isabel never failed to make my heart jump and shout for joy. It was like no other else. But she's not mine.

1993. I met Ana, my nurse, when I learned I had Alzheimer's disease. I was shocked. I am just in my early thirties. Those were my saddest days. But Ana gave me the care anyone would wish to have. She knows how to take good care of the sick. She will be a good wife. My family also offered care for me. They bring me food. They bathe me. They showed a lot of care. But never can all these be compared with Isabel, who is now married and about to give birth to her first child. Isabel's presence drives away my sickness. She makes me well. She is my medicine.

The doctor said that my memory will soon fail me. I will forget people important to me — my family, friends, workmates, former classmates; I will forget everything about my job; I will forget my properties; I will forget about those girls I met in my life.

But I am certain that the last I would forget is my dearest one. I met many girls in my life but she's different.

1993. This short life I lived was filled with her memories as I watched her at school, at town when I arrive, at different gatherings.

1990. My love for her is as a seed that grows bigger each day. But she's going to give birth... not my child.

1987. She filled my life. But she's engaged and counting days before marriage.

1984. She's the most beautiful teacher in town. I am a bachelor. But we never talked. I dreamt of holding and kissing her. But we never held hands. We never kissed.

1982. When I saw her cry, I wanted to comfort her. But I never touched her. I never felt the warmth of her face.

1979. She's my favorite actress. I wanted to be his knight. But she never felt my love. She never felt my hands.

1978. I met her. I saw her smile. But Isabel never knew me. I never went near her. Never.

I wanted to promise myself never to forget her. But I don't think that time would allow me to do so.

Yet in all these, I never regretted a single instance that I loved her. Yes, the best I can do is to watch her; to observe her graceful smile; to stare at her sweet face; to remember her in my remaining days. I have had many wonderful times. But none of these is comparable with the times I had from 1978 to 1993.

About a hundred boys
By Aireen Grace Andal

" While we try to teach our children all about life, our children teach us what life is all about. "

A. *Schwindt*

*I*was 19, turning 20 when I conducted my undergraduate thesis inside a youth detention. And for about three months, I met about a hundred boys.

It was a whole new world. They live inside a detention home for children in conflict with the law. Some commit murder, some theft; some got into robbery, some inflicted physical injury; some raped girls, some took drugs; and some possess deadly weapons. They are minors when they assumed the roles of children in conflict with the law. I cannot tell their names but I can tell their stories... who they are... what they have...

They were all wearing white. I started to meet them one by one as I get to interview them for my study about their attitude toward the Philippine criminal justice. But as I decide to take a break, I was able to know them mo-re. As I look upon their eyes, I felt this issue running inside me. I was frightened by their acts. But I was also tapped by their ingenuousness. There seems to be a strange invisible wall that they climbed to be in conflict with the law at young ages.

But as I get to know them, I forgot that they once crossed forbidden lines.

They were ordinary boys as one could imagine. Some are friendly, others are snob. They love basketball. Some play the guitar. Some sing. Some play chess. Some are talkative, some are silent. They have favorite television shows, they have movie idols. Some share favorite foods, some share the sa-me favorite cartoons. Most of these boys stopped going to school; some worked — legal or illegal, some stayed home and became idle. They talk a-bout their families, school and crushes. Some have families; some have none; some are adopted; some are abandoned. Some wanted to have a mother because they have none. Some wanted to have a father because they have none. Some wanted to have families because they have none.

They taught me.

They are brothers. They depend on each other. They love each other. They share stories of anguish and fear as well as of faith, hope and love. They show patience, they show gratitude. Of course these boys fight. During fights, they give cold shoulders to each other. But it doesn't last until the sun goes down; sometimes for minutes, sometimes for hours but never a day. They said that girls fight longer than boys. They forgive. I admire them. I realized that I was blameworthy of easily finding faults. These boys reminded me of being human.

They understand. They have different religions but they respect each other. One can pray without being teased. They show no prejudice, no discrimination. They show acceptance. They embrace diversity. They welcome differences, they show who they are. They treated me as an older sister. Even if I am very different, they never left me out of place. I pay them gratitude for they reminded me not to judge easily as I tend to be narrow-minded about beliefs other than mine.

They picture. Growing up experiencing grief-stricken poverty, some of these boys still dream. Some dreams are high, some are low. To be lawyers, doctors, teachers and priests; to drive a *jeepney* or a bus, to sell food and to put up their own store. Some just wanted to be happy, to be at peace. However, some do not hope a lot, but they showed contentment of what they have. These boys imagine. I esteem them. I became more appreciative of what I have, and I think I can have. These boys tapped my back.

They are men. I saw the responsibility of a parent, as some were already husbands and fathers. Though never officially married, they address their girls as wives. They love their sons and daughters. They see their wives as princesses. They want them to have the best education possible, but they grip on the uncertainty of this chance. I salute these boys.

They are creative. They speak of words I do not understand; it seems that those must be broken into codes, a thing I cannot do so they taught me some of those words I never knew. I felt like a foreigner in a place I am not familiar. They seem to be citizens from another world I never heard of. They also communicate through sign languages I fail to recognize so they taught me some. Two thumbs up! They showed inventiveness.

They are about a hundred boys. They live on and created a world so different from mine. They are boys. They hate being laughing stocks, they are sometimes ill-tempered; they eat a lot. They cuddle each other's hair, they shake each other's hands, they laugh as if there's no tomorrow, they frown as if they're going to hell. They went here and there, they had this and that, they met him and her.

Upon learning these, I felt immature. I felt ill-educated. I felt I was a stranger in a world so small. As I immerse inside the detention, I learned a lot from them. In their homes, some were treated not as children, some were neglected, some were despised. This is something I will not learn outside the detention for I was never been beaten hard, I was never made hungry, I was never been punched. I never received harsh words; my hands were never tied. They opened an avenue for me to comprehend life a little bit more.

I have no idea how they will go through life.

But, even for a moment, they showed me how naïve I am. Sometimes, I envy these boys. It seems that what they know about the world is richer than mine. Sometimes I wonder if they are boys or men. But upon remembering them, I can recognize the "boy" inside them. After my thesis, some of them were released, some stayed. I might not meet them anymore. But I will never forget them and they are about a hundred boys.

Paola Luz R. Tolentino
Manila, Philippines

I'm Paola Luz R. Tolentino. I live in Philippines. I would like to present my entry entitled "The Poor Boy" it is categorized as Fiction.

The Poor Boy
By Paola Luz R. Tolentino

I'm going to tell you a story that I've heard somewhere...
There once a poor boy who said to himself that he is the most miserable and unfortunate human in the world. He also reprimands God because of his situation.

One day, the poor boy is very hungry, but he has no money to buy food, that's why, he decided to climb the tree to get a fruit. Unfortunately, the tree doesn't have fruit. Because the poor boy was very hungry, he picks the fresh leaves of the tree and he eats those leaves.

While he's eating the fresh leaves, he notices a poor child eating also leaves under the tree where he is. But compare to him, the poor child under the tree is eating dried leaves. He looks closely to that poor child eating dried leaves.

Suddenly, he felt ashamed to himself,

Because the poor child under the tree eating dried leaves is disabled. He has no legs, which can be useful to climb the tree and pick fresh leaves to eat.

That moment, the poor boy realized that he is not the most miserable and unfortunate human in the world. He said to himself that he received special things than others.

This short story always reminds me that we are blessed in many things and many ways. The problem is... we remember this blessing once we've seen a person much more miserable than us.

God can work many miracles, for us to realize that we have everything, all we need to do is to pray and say "thank you" to Him and believe in his holiness and will and we can easily understand this beautiful life. A part of a song says about how we should live our lives...So we just hold on fast and acknowledge the past, as lessons exquisitely crafted, painstakingly drafted to curve us an instrument that play the music of life...". We should live our lives with happiness and contentment, because it will help in a small way to free us from burdens of this sinful world.

Christina Marie Sloss
Houston, TX., United States

THE SEARCH FOR MEANING

A Manifestation of the SUN

The Dream
By Christina Marie Sloss

*U*nder a new moon, lounging with the infinite expansiveness of the stars; Petunia sat in the middle of a road, on a cheap lawn chair...on a rich lava rock surrounded by the largest ocean on Earth. Consumed by a meditative trance, she connected to the universal source through the use of her breath. Staring up at the sky from a cheap and rusty folding chair she watched clear and hazy thoughts flitter across her mind like the passing clouds speeding above on the Interatmosphere Cloud highway I-55, without giving any of the thoughts even a moment's consideration. Eventually the clouds above her cleared the sky completely revealing a figure eight crafted of stars plastered across the sky (probably blown in on air currents from Japan). The stars formed an Ouroboros, the primordial unity, representing that which has been and always will be, speaking on behalf of life, death, and rebirth. The Ouroboros, a symbol that appears in many cultures and disciplines throughout history, is also depicted as a snake devouring its own tail, and the stars morphed into scales poising on the ceiling of the Earth, looming just long enough for a crowd of Japanese tourists to gather into a mob of flashing light pollution bright enough to permanently blind an infant.

"awwwwwwwwwwwwwwwww...
uuuuuuuuuuuuuuuooooooooooooooooooooooooooooo".

Clickclickclikckclickclickclickclickclickclickclickclickclickclickclickc
lickclick.

The starry snake seemed to contain all the known and unknown diamond studded stars and galaxies of the universe within its circular boundary. In the sky, choking on its rattles, the neon serpent god was an infinity symbol in the night sky lingering boldly in the darkness, a hicky on the roof of the world engraved by a serpent's tongue. Petunia gapped at the grotesque projection of mental dream static artwork displayed before her. She just sat there and waited for something to happen that would explain this unidentified insight (if any) that was manifesting. Where was this miscellaneous insight trying to lead her? North or South? Desert or tundra? Africa or the Patagonia? Yerba Mate or Earl Greyer? She was waiting on a path.

An empty clay vessel with voluptuous curves bursting waterfalls of potential energy, Petunia studied the dream emblem contemplating its relevance to her life, when the sun suddenly rose up in the midst of the night chasing the snaky, slinky Ouroboros out of view, the way it chases hookers off of Sunset Boulevard. The sun raced to climax at the apex of the twelve o'clock throne in the sky, before cannon balling down to Earth. Destination = lava rock in the middle of the ocean. The sun was actually dropping out of the sky from 93 million miles away.

The out of sync behavior of the sun confused the mighty sea, causing the tide to rise and carry in swells and tsunamis that seemed to sprout from the ocean's depths. Petunia abandoned her lawn chair in the street, sacrificing it to the god of the sun. Taking off at a sprint, she led a herd of blank dream faces away from the coast towards a shack at the navel of the island. A primitive bungalow centered in the jungle….a Jungalow in the path of the falling sun.

The Sun is the boss of astrology, it's the creative life force; it's the ego, the source of expression. Petunia's first instinct was to fear the charging of the sun. She wasn't exactly sure why she was running from the sun (A four and a half billion year old burning Hydrogen mass of fire reaching ten million degrees in its core), but it seemed to be a chase. The feline of the sky chasing a flower through the jungle.

Darting artfully thru the brush, Petunia leaped and danced through the trees a natural matriarch. Leading the race from the dive bombing fireball so integral to this universe.

Led by a familiar, quirky dream state enlightenment (found to exist only during the subterranean of the night) Petunia led lost souls to safety. As the herd entered the Jungalow, Petunia exited immediately through the back door onto the rear porch. She threw on a rain poncho (with undoubting faith that it would preserve her delicate skin from exposure to the unrelentless scorching of ultra-violate light).

Unexpectedly a light pierced Petunia's peripheral vision drawing her attention to a mysterious stranger on the porch… come to think of it, he wasn't strange at all…enigmatically tranquil certainly, unfathomably peace-ful…maybe… but definitely incredibly harmonic. The dreamy details were hazed over by a golden aura radiating from an angelic physique. His eyes lusty brown eyes had deep and shadowy craters of wisdom that beheld her lavishly beneath the hood of his rain poncho. The sun came down, loitering just feet above the two souls on the porch. With their heads bowed down to the ground in reverence, the sun danced and twirled above, showering sparks in all directions declaring them leader's in a movement of peace. It must have been opening night for the big Broadway in the sky, the sun with the opening act performing a knighting ceremony from an ancient mythology. Maybe something important had just occurred… maybe not (the New York Time's critics will determine that in tomorrow's issue), but for now, one thing was for sure; life for Petunia was beginning to bud...

Dream Symbols

The moment Petunia regained waking consciousness, it was 3 a.m. and she was mumbling "don't fear the sun" to herself over and over. She sprung up in bed and searched around blindly locating a scroll in the dark. A double sided aqua blue embroidered notebook that folded out into a ten foot span of blank white pages across her bed. Petunia reconstructed the dream images across a fresh white page, translating the dream into English as best she could. She was trying to hold onto the memory of it all. This wasn't just any dream; it was one of those dreams that add warmth, color and inspiration to your memories leaving you with a great story forever changing you in some way. The dream left Petunia with a residual halo of idling cosmic energy that followed her into the kitchen, where she found her Aunt busily banging around, moving about like a mad woman searching for an imaginary ticking in the cabinets. Petunia and Aunt Mili were flying off to Spain in the morning.

"I had a bizarre dream just a few moments ago" Petunia interrupted thickly as she began to prepare a sleep concoction of Chamomile, and Lavender tea. Petunia's voice was sweet and had the viscosity of molasses. Words rolled and dripped off her lips, sometimes attracting stray honey bees (which sometimes freaked people out). Petunia tried out her finest attempt at sharing the events of the past hour of sleep from her now epic dream. When Petunia had finished she noticed a change in texture... or was it luster? Her Aunt Mili's eyes, had glazed over, and become glassy, almost spiritual looking if you will. Mili had traded the 3 A.M. I'm leaving the country tomorrow morning, mad woman approach for something different, something Petunia couldn't quite read yet.

"Have you heard the story of Fatima?" Mili spat, barely able to contain herself

"No" Petunia confirmed.

Fatima it happens is a small sacred city in Portugal. It is said that on October 13, 1917 a miracle was performed in Fatima. One town witnessed a miracle from the sun. Three children in Fatima were receiving messages from God via apparitions from the Virgin Mary and they claimed that this miracle was a message from Mary to motivate people to pray for peace in order to prevent a terrible world war.

O Seculo, Portugal's most highly regarded publication at the time released an article by columnist Avelino de Almeida reporting "Before the astonished eyes of the crowd, whose aspect was biblical as they stood bareheaded, eagerly searching the sky, the sun trembled, made sudden incredible movements outside all cosmic laws - the sun 'danced' according to the typical expression of the people."

A writer for the Ordem, Dr. Domingos Pinto Coelho, an eye specialist wrote "The sun, at one moment surrounded with scarlet flame, at another aureoled in yellow and deep purple, seemed to be in an exceeding fast and whirling movement, at times appearing to be loosened from the sky and to be approaching the earth, strongly radiating heat"

In O Dia, the Lisbon daily, the special reporter on October 13 commented "...the silver sun, enveloped in the same gauzy grey light, was seen to whirl and turn in the circle of broken clouds...The light turned a beautiful blue, as if it had come through the stained-glass windows of a cathedral, and spread itself over the people who knelt with outstretched hands...people wept and prayed with uncovered heads, in the presence of a miracle they had awaited. The seconds seemed like hours, so vivid were they."

Pouring herself a cup of bubbling sleeping potion, Petunia dwelled on the sun's mystical cameo from her dream and the sun's seemingly perpetual message of peace to the world. Sipping tea and listening to a chorus of Koki frog lullabies, Petunia replayed the dream over in her head, focusing on all the details that were filling her with wonder. Mid-sip Mili interrupted the loud silence, "You know Petunia, we are going to be in Fatima in five days." Petunia's jaw dropped wide open and silent shock dripped from her gapping mouth into her mug. In a few hours they were leaving for Spain, but Petunia had not been aware of Mili's pre-meditated escapade over to Fatima, Portugal. Paralyzed, Petunia tried to picture what Fatima was like, a place that she had never seen or heard of (so you can image the bizarre images that must have been running through her head, of what this holy city might look like...well... maybe not for Petunia did have a rather obscurely wild and highly active imagination as you might well have noticed by now). For the remaining wee hours of the morning the two women sat chatting under the darkness of the new moon, enchanted by life's seeming coincidences and sipping tea until dawn.

Maroula Blades
Berlin, Germany

Maroula Blades is an Afro-British poet/writer living in Berlin. Ver-brecher Verlag, TAZ and Cornelsen Verlag have published her stories in Germany. She has received awards for poetry. Poems have been published in Germany and abroad. Her Poetry/Music Programme has already been presented on several stages in Berlin: the Planetarium am Insulaner, IFA, Der Haus der Kulturen der Welt and Volksbühne to name but a few. Maroula has read at the Black History Month Festival 2010 in Berlin and at the Berlin Poetry Festival 2010.

The World In An Eye
By Maroula Blades

*D*aniel walks the muddy tracks to school from his kaki waterproof home to the caravan where the orphans learn to read, write and draw camouflaged Leopard 1 tanks and M16 rifles; the same colour as the mud.

"Have you found me a mummy or pappy yet?" He asks his teacher.

"Sorry Daniel, this time is not your time. The Roland's want a girl, look Sharon is crying because she must leave Issy behind, her two-year old sister."

Issy's body is balled in a cupboard under the sink; she's sucking her thumb as if it were a whole world of sugar.

Not too far in the distance a motor changes several gears. The cream Volvo is stuck in the mud. The mud is splashing its metal carcass, just like the barrage of bullets Daniel had heard, cracking the air, and splitting his mother's brow. He watched her falling from the tips of her toes to the soft ground where the mud kissed his shoes. Slowly the mud dried and cracked like a beauty pack from the Dead Sea.

"Go along Daniel," his mother whispered. "I'm just going to rest here for a while."

A tear caressed the side of her cheek as she expelled a puff of breath, which lived longer than she did. Higher and higher the little curl of steam rose and then disappeared out of reach on the road where angels tread. It was the first and last time that Daniel appreciated the mud, the way it held his mother moulding to her form like an orthopedic bed, letting her sleep in cushioned comfort. He hoped for an eon.

'Medecins sans Frontiers' (Doctors without frontiers) nursed the bullet scratch on his left eye and wrapped his mother like half a pound of Edam in a dreary, old oilskin sheet.

Daniel doesn't remember exactly when he became an orphan or how old he is. The numbness set in when his twin brother Tommy died. Tommy took with him the sun, the tears, and the fear that used to strangle them both as they hid in old cupboards in derelict houses. They hoped the sound of the chewing woodworm would not give them away, but Daniel thought they did because a grenade fell and blew open Tommy's cupboard like the japing jaws of hell. Daniel could not identify his brother. Blood, wood, and cement were everywhere. There was not even a bucket of sticky mud to preserve his brother's face. At that point Daniel's hate for the mud set in.

Daniel hates the caravan, the wheels that are sunk down as if to the earth's crust, never once turning, the musty odour of patience sitting within the children's clothes, and the toilet that makes the mud even muddier. In single file children with old eyes walk silently through the door and spring into the muddy world where the sky splinters and cracks, leaking driving rain. They say good-bye to Sharon with sullen drenched faces. Sharon strokes her sister's soggy hair; a kiss would hurt too much. 'America', she thinks as she climbs into the tainted Volvo without looking back, 'the land of milk and honey.'

Daniel looks around the camp between curtains of rain, where orphans had morbidly painted on every tent except the lazaret. The paintings depict skeleton armies advancing without mercy, stomping over the sun, trees and over bodies. Only four colours are used in the pictures, red, white, grey, and black. Each victim's initials boldly capitalized in red. Wild jaw snatching animals seize and eat flesh; they pounce in frenzy through the darkness. The pictures are bizarre and sinister, leaving the viewer numb and plaintive. Tanks, the form of crocodiles, deplete woods with metallic revolving feet. The Leopard I tanks burn and change the face of the land to muddy swamps. Only the fortunate are able to escape to concrete valleys in faraway lands and Sharon is one of them.

There's no mud except in the graphite clouds passing above Sharon's window frame. They remind her of the tents, tanks, drawings of school friends, and the sister she left behind crawling in the uncertain light.

© Maroula Blades

Jayaprakash Raghavan Pillai
Kerala, S-India

Three books of the Author have been published by "Publish America." Many Articles and Poems have been published in the web sites. His writings reflect the experiences that he had while he was an Expatriate Teacher in foreign countries like Ethiopia, Africa, and Maldives.

He is a Post Graduate in English Literature. He had his secondary education in Kuala Lumpur, Malaysia.

The Young Princess
By Jayaprakash Raghavan Pillai

Chapter 1. The Plane Crash.

*I*t was her first flight in a plane. That too, in a Droner type large domestic aircraft owned by an Industrialist in Delhi, her father's friend. He believed it was the largest that could be used for long trips across the ocean for hours at end. Now Parvathi, only ten years of age; had often wondered how it would be to fly like a bird, see the land from higher up and wonder at the marvels of nature, the landscape, sea, hills and mountains as tiny dots far down below; a bird's view indeed. She always needed freedom and that was denied to her. Her Parents felt that as a Princess she was not entitled to mix with others of her own age. Her father had provided everything she wanted but she just did not want to be kept within the precincts of her Palace. She wanted to see the world and she had pleaded and pestered her father to give in to her wish. She had told her father, the Maharaja of Travancore that she wanted to see the world as a bird; to see from up above the clouds and look down below at the sights of the valley and view the beauty of nature as a bird would see it on flight. Finally the Maharaja after much persuasion had agreed and he engaged the services of his most trusted pilot Jehangir to take her to Europe.

"Jehangir," the Maharaja had said, "You are like a brother to me and my family. I trust you will take care of my daughter as you are the only one in the plane besides her in the twelve- seated Droner aircraft. Jehangir simply smiled and said, "Your Highness, Trust me".

As the aircraft was airborne, Parvathi felt that she was lifted higher up by an unseen power. She felt enthralled and looked down below from the aircraft. She gasped in astonishment at the sights of the buildings, land; palm trees that appeared as tiny as the plane started its ascent higher up. She marveled at the sights far down below.

"My goodness!" She exclaimed, what a beauty from here. I really feel as if I'm an eagle majestically soaring the skies for a pleasure. I always wanted freedom this way.

"What a life a superman enjoys!" exclaimed Parvathi to Jehangir, the pilot seated beside her in the cockpit. They were the only ones in the aircraft.

"True! But he is only an imaginary character," Jehangir explained.

"What! She retorted, "You mean he is not real!"

"Don't you know that?" Jehangir said.

"Know! Really thought he was real. I mean as real as any of us," she replied.

"Really!! What a wonderful thing it would be if he were real!" he remarked.

"I have heard those ladies at the court talk highly of him. The talk of Superman is gossiped around the palace and I have always wanted to meet him," she said.

"You will meet him soon enough," he jokingly said, "He always seems to appear at the nick of the moment to save people in danger."

"What do you mean? She asked alarmingly.

"No! No! Young Princess, It was only a joke."

No sooner he had said it than they saw a huge bird with large ugly talons heading straight in front of the plane, rather like a nose-dive at their small aircraft. The pilot tried to swerve the plane out of its path but failed in the attempt. A sudden jolt and a violent shake as the plane lost its balance. Jehangir immediately steadied the aircraft.

Parvathi, terrified jumped up from her seat, yelling "What went wrong? She asked, "Is the bird hit?"

Jehangir could not reply to her entreaties straight away as he was preoccupied with the thought that something dreadful had occurred. The plane had hit the large bird that flapped its wings in agony, getting entangled in the front moving propellers. The sharp blades moving at supersonic speed had entangled the remains of the huge bird's carcass in its propellers. The gravity of the situation was realized and at the rapid approach of an impending doom, Jehangir started perspiring. Drops of sweat rolled down from his cheeks. The propeller would stop at any moment and the aircraft would zoom down to its destruction. Parvathi, although too young grasped the truth when Jehangir did not reply and so she prayed, "Oh Lord, save me, I don't want to die now."

'Sweet Krishna! ," she cried imploringly, "I want to live. Oh! I wish my hero Superman was here to save me! I wish to God he was real."

Jehangir, on hearing her wailing felt helpless but he was aware that nothing could be done. So he acted immediately and tied a parachute strip round Parvathi clipping it firmly in place. "Dear Parvathi, just do as I say," Jehangir said.

"Jump out of this plane now. But don't forget to press the button on the strip so that it would loosen the chute as you jump," he said

"What about you? "Parvathi asked anxiously.

"Don't worry," Jehangir said, "I will make it."

Parvathi tried to attempt the jump-out but she felt nervous and giddy as she looked down.

"I can't do it," she implored.

"Do it now," Jehangir shouted at her and guided her to make the jump.

Try as she would, she could not bring herself to make it. So Jehangir ma-de her get ready for the jump. Next moment before Parvathi realized what had happened; she was plummeting down into space. Jehangir had pushed her out after pressing the button attached in the chute. All of a sudden, Parvathi felt the whole world around her spinning and reeling. She lost consciousness and did not know what had transpired during the fall.

Chapter 2. Shocked Beyond Belief.

A leopard eyeing the object hanging from up the tree smelled raw meat within its grasp that was sufficient enough to satisfy the rising hunger within its belly. After circling round the tree, the leopard waited for a movement from the object of its prey hanging from the branch. When Parvathi regained consciousness, she was thunderstruck to see herself hanging high up in a tree for the parachute had landed there and got firmly stuck up there. She started struggling uneasily. She could not surmise where she was. A sudden growling sound from below and she felt a shiver run down her spine as she saw the leopard eyeing her with interest. The leopard was all set to scramble upwards and pounce on her. Parvathi, horrified, closed her eyes, waiting for the ultimate end, as everything would be over in a minute.

Sounds of loud shouting and shrieks caused her to open her eyes to see a strange sight down below. The leopard had been speared by wild savage men who wore loin cloth that covered the body below the waist. They were jumping, shrieking after the slaying of the leopard. They were completely very dark in complexion and wore beads of strange ornaments. Parvathi did not know what to make out of it. Why had the Lord Krishna saved her? Was it to escape the frying pan into the fire?

No, it could not be that. No sooner was she immersed in thoughts than two of the savages scrambled up the tree and loosened the chute. She found herself landing on a strong carpet mat laid on the ground to check her fall. She got up unsteadily and stood up facing them.

What a surprise she had; for all these wild men prostrated themselves before her kneeling down. Parvathi was perplexed. What could they have imagined? The truth was stranger than fiction. She had been mistaken for their Goddess that had dropped from the heavens. They made signs to her to follow. She did not know where she was at the moment nor did she care. She was definite about something... She was in a deep forest from where es-cape was impossible... She was at the mercy of these savage people who hardly looked human. They were scantily dressed other than a piece of leopard skin to cover a part of their body. They were fierce and looked frightful. But nothing else could be done. She followed and in this overgrowth foliage of trees, tall bushes, walking was extremely difficult and Parvathi was carried by the men in a primitive model stretcher. Parvathi felt terrified and panicky as she could not imagine how she could last amongst them. After hours of trekking through the forests, they entered a hilly mountainous region. Finally after half an hour, they entered their village where mud houses with thatch roofs were seen in all directions. Women and children, half naked, gathered curiously to find out the catch their warrior men were bringing in. The children were shouting in a language that was clearly unintelligible to Parvathi. The women looked on but kept in the background till the men whispered something in their ears.

What an astonishment for Parvathi as all the women knelt down before her as if to greet the Goddess that they had known would descend down on them one day. This was the great day they believed. The men and women were hard at work making a royal chair made from branches and covered it with soft leaves of trees and plants to make it cozy and comfortable. When the chair was accomplished, the women knelt before Parvathi and uttering strange hysterical sounds made Parvathi to sit on the chair. A make-belief head-dress of leaves and flowers was put on her head.

Then slowly the women and men started their dance around her in a hysterical wild manner that Parvathi merely ten years of age felt to tremble and shiver owing to fright. But she knew that these natives meant no harm. From the mannerism of these dark-skinned natives, Parvathi had a feeling that she was in the darkest part of Africa. She could scarcely imagine the fate of her pilot. Is he alive? What would her parents be thinking about her at this moment? How long would these natives treat her this way? She realized her desperate situation for she was cut off completely from the world she knew. She was lost. She could not understand the language and making her understood amongst them was something that she could never succeed.

The news of her disappearance might now have been flashed all over the globe and searches may still be going on. But she had landed in a queer place and neither could she find out anything about her location nor was there any way she could communicate with them. Parvathi felt they were jabbering like monkeys and chimpanzees she had seen once in the zoo.

More distressing was the fact that the news of her disappearance and the searches made for her; could not be traced to her as there were no means of communication available in this dark hideous place. The more she thought about it, the more desperate she became when she realized her condition.

Neither did they want to know anything from her for they believed that she had brought them luck. Fruits and other eatables were placed before her but she did not take it up in their presence. Thinking their Goddess was not pleased, they brought all the fruits they could gather and placed them at her disposal. Parvathi could not resist the temptation to eat as she was almost starved. She started picking one by one, tasting them and had her appetite satisfied by eating the tasty ones. The natives were excited when they saw their Goddess eating. They danced round in jubilation.

To the natives, Parvathi seemed as a beautiful Goddess. They admired her fair complexion, so fair a creature they had never seen before. Compared with their dark bodies, they knew that her soft delicate and lovely body could only belong to a Goddess. She had appeared to them as a Goddess to bring good luck on them all. Parvathi did not feel uneasy as she was used to being admired even in her country.

Whenever she chanced to go out with her parents, they was escorted by policemen who were everywhere on guard. A gathering of an immense crowd of ordinary people always gathered to see her and her family. The queenly treatment was not something new to her.

But here in the deep forest the people are living a life more or less like the wild animals. Parvathi was a little embarrassed to find the importance these savages were showering upon her. What would have been the state if they realized that she was after all a human being like them?

Chapter 3. Marthanda orders the search for his daughter.

Parvathi belonged to a royal family. Her father, Marthanda Varma was the Maharaja of Travancore and her mother, Gowri was the Mysore Maharaja's daughter. By birth, Parvathi was a Princess in her own right of Travancore, the land of Gods. .

The Maharaja was a tall handsome man in his mid-forties. He was pacing up and down endlessly unable to control his emotions. He had given her all the comforts available in the Palace. He never failed to give in to her wishes. Foreign Teachers were invited to stay as guests to teach his daughter. They taught all subjects and she was brought up to be more cosmopolitan in her outlook and behaviour. Now he felt that he should not have permitted her to travel alone. With the death of the pilot reported from the site of the plane crash and no news about his daughter's body, he was led to believe the impossible.

"Marthanda!" his wife Gowri burst out. She seemed to be also a middle aged woman, fair and extremely attractive in appearance.

"Any news received about of our daughter Parvathi."

"Not yet, my men are scouring the length and breadth of the globe. No news other than the crash. They have relayed photos of the remains of the aircraft that crashed and Jehangir's body in it," he said.

"Then what could have happened to our daughter?" she asked.

"I don't know? We will know soon. My men are everywhere."

"Oh! My daughter! Where are you?" She cried out.

"Stop it! Try to control yourself. We may know everything soon," he said.

"She is the Princess and the country needs her as she is the rightful heir to the throne of Travancore and she is our only daughter," Gowri pointed out.

"Please stop it! Don't make me mad. I hope she is safe," said Marthanda.

"Maharaja!" his valet entered and said, "Two men are in to see you, and may I allow them to come in".

"All right, send them to the rest house."

As Marthanda walked into the rest house, the two men got up to greet him.

"Your Highness! We are honoured to be able to do some service for you, Sir." One of them said.

"Are you both C.B.I. detectives?" Albert asked.

"Right, Sir", they said.

Both were extremely tall and well-built and both seemed to be men who looked capable of dealing with emergencies.

The elderly man was called Ashok and the other slightly younger called Selvon.

"I hope you know why you were called," said Marthanda giving Ashok a file. "All the details of the plane crash and my daughter's photo are in the fi-le. She is still alive, I believe since her body has not been found. Find her and you will be rewarded."

"Sir, we will try our best and we are starting immediately to site of the crash" Selvon replied.

They left Marthanda for a trip to Kenya in Africa where the aircraft had crash- landed and exploded. Traces of the pilot's body were in the wrecks of the plane but no traces of Parvathi's remains.

Both the detectives had felt that they should start at the site of the crash.

They had been puzzled to hear that the body of the Princess was not traced at the site where the plane had crashed. No clear evidence was there to deduce that the princess had perished in the air crash. Had the Princess jumped off the plane while on flight? If that had happened, was she alive and where was she?

They had to find out. They send Radio messages everywhere to all parts within the vicinity of Kenya.

After days of combing over the place, nothing fruitful was gained from their laborious search.

Chapter 4. Among the savages.

The day was drawing to an end. Still there was no possibility of a way out. Parvathi felt that she would rather die than continue here any longer.

The village of these native settlers was situated on a hilly terrain. The landscape of forests and mountains were visible from where she stood, gazing down at the sights far off.

The landscape was so beautiful, the rivers far down below looked as if snakes were crawling and the sun's rays reflected on them sparkled like eels swishing through a watery surface.

As it was dusk, the sun's golden rays made the bits of clouds scattered about to glow like golden red, yellow and orange bringing out the magnif-icence of the sky as though heaven was preparing to welcome the closing of the day for darkness.

As darkness enveloped the place and no lights were there, the primi-tiveness of the village terrified Parvathi, who accustomed to the most luxu-rious ways of life, found that this place was really a hell-hole for her. A most frightful nightmare that she hoped she would wake up from it all.

But it was true and she could hardly bring herself to stay alone in a mud thatched house given to her. The house had all the facilities the sav-ages provided for comfort befitting their queen. But Parvathi abhorred it as the flooring was mud with no air passage. Doors and windows were too small and securely fastened to keep away wild animals.

In the hut all alone, it was pitch black. Nothing could be seen and Par-vathi groped her way in the darkness. She made sure that the doors were fastened.

No sound emanated from the surrounding places and all was quiet. The quietness and absence of sounds frightened her and she lay awake thinking of her home. What could her parents be thinking? Maybe they might be thin-king that she was not alive.

A sudden hysterical cry heard of wild animals prowling near to her hut aroused a fear in her. The laughing cries of hyenas were audible as though the creatures were circling her hut. She felt trembling all over as she knew that hyenas, the most dreaded carnivores were outside. Any moment those creatures might try to enter inside. She waited, not uttering a sound. Were her protectors, the natives not aware of the danger she was facing.

A scratching sound convinced her that the creatures were trying to force their way inside. She thought of screaming but thought it better to remain quiet.

After some time, the scratching sounds were not heard and she slept soundly from the fright and exhaustion of a tense-filled day.

When she woke up, the rays of the sun had penetrated her hut to reveal that the inside of her hut had been rearranged with fruits and other eata-bles placed on the floor.

Three native women greeted her as she got up from the bed. A pot of water was brought for her to wash her face.

Parvathi wanted to drink coffee but how was it possible in this impene-trable forest. But she was mistaken as the native women understood that she wanted a drink.

The women brought a jar and some cups and started grinding coffee nuts into powder on a narrow pot. Then they boiled it and they served the steaming coffee in a cup to Susan.

Parvathi was surprised as she drank it. It tasted real coffee and sweet. But what did they use for sugar? She was really surprised even though no traces of milk were added to the coffee.

Parvathi then felt an urgent need; the need to excrete. But to uncivilized women, how can she make them understand?

She just walked out and just rushed to the forest area among the euca-lyptus trees. Three women had followed but kept a distance. There she excreted and felt a sense of relief. She really wanted to wash her under-garments as they were the only ones she had and she had to use it till she got another. These barbaric women wore nothing except skins of the wild animals their men had killed. They had looked on admiring the beauty of the white skin-ned complexion of their Goddess. They knew that none other than a Goddess could have such a glamorous beauty.

Chapter 5. Strangers hold her for Ransom

As Parvathi was eating some fruits, a distant rumbling sound was heard. Gradually the noise was somewhat deafening as the sound of a jeep traversing the jungle path. Parvathi could hardly make out whether she was dreaming.

But there the jeep was and three men, brownish in colour, stout and immense in size. Their eyes gleamed in expectation of seeking some object that they had come for. Pistols in hand, they advanced forward from the jeep parked nearby. The black warriors taken up by surprise picked up their spears.

Parvathi could hardly believe what she saw. These three men were civilized and may understand her.

She heard shots and as she ran outside, the three men had shot down three black warriors dead. The savage natives were really shocked as they heard deafening sounds followed by a flash from the hands of these strangers. Before they started firing further, Susan approached them. On seeing her, they stopped firing and gazed at her in stupefaction. They had read all about her disappearance. So this was the real Princess of Travancore, they thought. Parvathi was not aware of their real intentions. These men on learning about her knew where she could be traced and they had reached before anyone else.

Parvathi asked anxiously, "I hope you know Travancore. I am lost and need help."

One of the strangers said, "We know about you and have come to take you home."

Susan on hearing this said, "do you know my father?'

"Sure," he said, "He only called to search for you. We are Africans from Kenya."

"Where am I really," asked Susan.

"You are in a hell-hole, a part of Africa in Kenya where no civilized people are known to settle except savages of the jungle."

"How did you know I may be found here?" She asked.

"We have combed the entire country where your plane crashed but could not trace you".

"My plane crashed!! Is the pilot safe? She asked anxiously.

"No," I am afraid his remains were found in the crash site."

Parvathi almost burst into tears but stopped exposing her emotion in front of these men and native tribes.

"Come on," he called Parvathi. "Get into the jeep before these savages regain their senses.

Parvathi lost no opportunity in walking quietly to the jeep as the natives curiously looked on. Before they could react, the strangers got into the jeep beside Parvathi and rushed the jeep out into the jungle road speeding fast.

The savage tribes, on seeing their goddess being taken by these strangers gathered their spears and started pursuing the jeep. But the strangers were able to outrace the jeep away from the village. Soon the pursuing savages were seen as tiny dots as the jeep rushed at terrific speed out into the jungle clearing.

For some time no one spoke. Then the leader of the strangers introduced himself as Sasi to Parvathi.

"I am Sasi and both of my partners, Vaidhyan and Gurudev are here to help me."

"Nice to meet you all," Parvathi said, "Could You call my Dad now".

"No, no, not now, later," said Sasi.

They had passed the forest area and traveled along a tarred road. On both sides of the road, teff, the main food grain was seen in plenty. The beautiful yellow golden colour flashing in the sunlight promised adequate supply of the food grains all over the country.

Around noon they stopped at an inn by the roadside. Parvathi was asked to accompany them. Food was ordered and Susan ate ravishingly as she tasted real food. Extra food packets were bought for the onward journey.

.

As they continued the journey, the men were extremely quiet and Parvathi might have dozed off, for when she awoke, the jeep was speeding through the jungle again. All around, thick forest spread out darkening the place. The sun in its glorious red spherical shape was descending down the horizon and streaks of dazzling colours were flashing in the clouds scattered here and there. The shrinking rays of the setting sun had brightened the sky to reveal the magnificence of the glory that may be Heaven.

The men were deeply engaged in conversation unmindful of her listening to it.

"Why don't we call him now and let him know we have her.......?" Suggested Sikes, "Let us demand a ransom of fifty million pounds," said Gu-rudev, "He would give any amount to get back his lost daughter."

Parvathi was shocked. So these were evil-minded scoundrels. She wanted to strike back at them by a volley of words but thought better against it. She was then phlegmatic for a moment but then shouted at them, "You would never get away. I heard all what you said," she said,

Chapter 6. Holed up in a dark cave.

"You can't put me inside a hole like that," she said, trying to resist them as they tried to make her enter a large cave on a hill by the side of the road.

The men forcibly pulled her into the cavern and warned her, "We could kill you if we don't get what we want," said Sasi

Saying so, he pulled her into the cavern and pushed her that she fell sprawled out on the dirty muddy floor. Drops of large bones, presumably the remains of animals were seen lying scattered. Evidently these foolish men were drunk or they would have seen through it.

In the darkness the three men were planning a scheme to get the ransom. They had threatened that Parvathi would be killed. Parvathi helplessly crawled to a corner aware that some impending doom was near at hand. A disgusting stench that was unbearable to Parvathi's nostrils almost caused the tendency to vomit. While she was ruminating over the sad happenings of the past few days, she doubted whether she would be back home safe.

A deep roaring sound repeatedly made by wild animals was faintly heard at the entrance. Absence of light made the whole place pitch black. Darkness prevented seeing beforehand what was entering in it.

The men were drunk but sensing something was amiss drew the pistols. A roar that froze the blood shattered the silence of the night followed by a rush of feet as three heavy objects landed on top of the men. Shots were fired blindly and the loud yelling and cries of the helpless men pierced through the stillness in the night as they were torn asunder by sharp jaws of a lion and two other lioness. The men were killed instantly. Almost immediately the ferocious carnivores dragged the bodies and started feasting.

Parvathi left in a corner fainted utterly oblivious of what followed.

She was unconscious for many hours. When she awoke, it was day and the lions were gone leaving bones and pieces of flesh they had left over. Tho-se were the remains of the men. Of that she was sure. She shuddered to think of it and left the cave silently fearful of the approach of the lions at any moment.

The lions might have sniffed at her, and the lions generally do not attack or kill those that are unmoving or seemingly dead. Providence has a hand, Parvathi believed and how long can she escape the dangers that she may be liable to face again.

Chapter 7. Contact with the Outside World.

The jeep was parked outside and it has not been mauled or disturbed in any way. Parvathi opened the door and got inside and locked herself inside. Now she felt safe and if at all the lions return, it would be only at night. She shuddered to think about what had happened.

She had to escape but how was she to do it. She had often seen and heard her father using the phone attached to his car. Taking the phone that looked strange to her, she started the engine first and switched on the phone.

A voice was heard, "Hello!

Susan got excited on hearing a reply. "Hello! Please help me! I need help fast!"

"Please give your location" he asked.

"I don't know. I believe that I am deep in the jungle. Call the police fast!"

'Ok, Hold on! Police will take up your call."

Parvathi was excited. She waited for a long time. Then she heard a voice on the phone, "Hello! Hello! Police Inspector is on the line."

Parvathi replied crying out, "Hello! I am lost in the deep jungle. I can't tell where I am. Find me fast or Lions may kill me."

"Hold on the phone! We will trace the location and come fast."

Parvathi suffering from anxiety and having had nothing to satisfy her hunger for the last two days was in frenzy that she day-dreamed a load of rich food spread out before her. She felt thirsty for a drink. Her throat was dry and she felt like she was travelling in a desert with hardly any water anywhere to quench her thirst. She was like a damsel in distress and as in the fairy tales; she wished a Prince would come to rescue her. She dreamt of the dancehall she had performed often at home. But all these were wayward dreams now.

Dusk was fast approaching and glimpses of the lovely sun's golden rays spreading over the cirrus clouds brought out the beauty of nature one could marvel at.

Any moment, it will be pitch black as darkness sets in. The lions would return and no hope of a rescue was in sight.

The distant roars of a male lion and lioness made her panic-stricken. She started to quaver in her seat but then a rumbling sound was heard from the sky of thunder as if it was going to rain.

But then the sound was not intermittent but continuously sounding lou-der. She noticed a small speck in the distant sky. As it approached, it became larger and a gigantic helicopter propelled above the jeep. Parvathi, overexcited at the sight, jumped out of the jeep, hailed the copter by shout-ing and waving at it.

She was overjoyed to see it descending down near to her. As she turned to look behind, a pride of lions that had gathered, took to their heels as the tremendous noise of the revolving copter frightened them to flee a mighty monster that was seen coming down at them.

Tom and Henry stepped out of the Copter with an Inspector of Police and two other men armed with rifles ready to fire in an eventuality. Tom greeted Susan by embracing her and said, "Don't worry, you are safe now. We are here to take you home".

The Princess turned back and saw in the distance the lions watching and waiting. She was escorted to the copter and within seconds the propelling huge blades started revolving in a strong momentum and amidst a rushing of strong wind that rushed around the place, the helicopter rose to the sky like a giant bird taking the Princess to Nairobi, a town in Kenya.

Chapter 8.   Happy reunion with her Parents.

When she got out of the domestic plane that was her father's, her Dad and Mom were there to welcome their daughter who had been thought dead. Important politicians, members of her family from the palace thronged the airport to see their Princess. A large crowd gathered there to see her. All cheered as the Princess embraced her parents who were overjoyed to see their only daughter return. Gowri was weeping with joy at the excitement of seeing her daughter alive. She could hardly believe it when her husband had told her that Parvathi would arrive at the airport soon. Together they had rushed to the airport in their own limousine driven by one of their chauffeurs.

Cristina Frincu
Bucharest, Romania

My name is Cristina Frincu, I eat, drink, sleep, work and live in Bucharest, Romania.

I am a passionate reader and a clumsy writer, but it makes me happy to write short stories. Some things to read, to make one laugh, smirk, or frown and then eat fries and drink a beer.

I am sending this story of Nymphadora and Anhedonius just to stop the voice in my head that says I am not taking chances and I always wait for something to happen.

Nymphadora and Anhedonius
By Cristina Frincu

ymphadora looked at me and said she knew the most ridiculous love story ever. It was about her and her boyfriend, Anhedonius.

We went for a drink in the old town when she offered to help me with some article I had to write for a ladies magazine.

Nymphadora is young and willing, but Anhedonius is just young. Actually, he always assures her of his love but he wouldn't touch her sexually under no circumstances. I wonder if the subject isn't too private, but she assures me that her only care is to make her look desirable in the article, as she knows she is.

"As long as you don't write about a flaccid Nymphadora, with unshaved legs and no sex-appeal, then I have no problem sharing this. After all, it's like my boyfriend, who used to eat with much pleasure my beef stew, now refuses without explanations to even grab a bite."

She looks amused while talking about Anhedonius. He thrashes at her when she's naked, calls her a nympho and refuses to pronounce the word 'sex'. He purses his lips and shakes his head, as if that's the forbidden word in his eerie world. He sucks the 'erotic' from any sensual manifestation, like a casual massage, and leaves a plain kneading.

"Two minutes of squeezing and almost painful kicking, if only I had some motor oil and three plugs, the massage he gave me would have been the perfect car overhauling."

Still, what's the deal with Anhedonius? Nymphadora laughs saying something about a government experiment gone wrong. He won't tell her and unfortunately she forgot how to read minds, that's if she ever knew that. The beginning was exactly the opposite. They lived in a sexual exuberance and it was great, until two years ago when the apocalypse came and erased from his mind all the lust. No prophet could have seen that havoc coming. On top of all, the words that he could have used for blending an explanation were buried in the world of no space and no time, guarded by seven basilisks that were sworn to kill the humankind if anyone tried to discover the answer.

Nymphadora likes her beer and she seems on fire after a while. She takes a funny face and announces that she's going to impersonate Anhedonius in one of his abnormal behaviors.

"Honestly, Anhedonius, you're impossible. Why do I have to be fully clothed whenever I'm near you? "

"Why wouldn't you?"

"Don't you dare start again throwing back my own questions! Do you think I'm hideous? Am I a monster?"

"No, you're not."

"I know I'm not a monster, you idiot! But do you see me as a monster? And if not, then what the hell is wrong with you?"

"What would be wrong with me?"

She mutters angrily for herself something about tennis, but I don't see any connection. Released from the usual sexual thoughts, Nymphadora's mind expanded and grew many unusual connections between childhood memories and present frustrations.

"When I was twelve I had to take tennis lessons, but beside one compliment about my calves from the instructor I wasn't even able to gain the right to play at the wall. I had as a partner a wire wall. It was pretty large but all my balls got on the other side where it was a cemetery. And here I am now, not a kid anymore but a grown woman, throwing questions at a wire boy that doesn't want to play with me. Is it my fault? Maybe my interrogative inflexion is ambiguous and Anhedonius simply doesn't hear a question, maybe that's the reason he won't answer me. Or I'm not the kind of girl that can handle the truth and my dear Anhedonius tries to protect me.

She throws the cigarette with a grimace, it's not menthol light. I let her go get a pack of those green cigarettes that taste like chewing gum. Nympha-dora promises me tasty details for the next hour, so I order another round of beers. I like the way she handles this problem, but I can tell it has been an ordeal for this girl and she's just using an umbrella in a cloudy day.

The theory says that sex is not vital, it may create life but it doesn't sustain life. Sex depends on weather, month of the year, geographic area, society, education, career or even what we ate at dinner. Nymphadora is not in any death threat. She can invest all the energy usually wasted in sexual intercourse into more meaningful activities, a better job, a thinner figure. It may be for her best.

But the umbrella sometimes breaks and Nymphadora finds herself in the same cloudy, almost rainy day, definitely a grey day.

"Still, this is a thing I want to do and I can't. I'm a healthy woman and I like to eat, drink, dream, love, have sex and laugh. I sleep in his arms every night and he says he loves me. But he just won't make love to me. Maybe if I hired a gunman

to threat him... And here I am, feeling pity for not having sex while the whales are dying. This is wrong, maybe I am a bad person.

I tried to keep a diary of reasons for not happening. It. Not today, I haven't take a shower...not today, it's Wednesday...not today, there's a good movie on TV...not today, I have to meet with the guys...not today, just not today. He is funny sometimes, when he covers my eyes if there's a hot scene on TV. Kind of like my grandmother.

Yes, the equipment is functioning. It's very responsive. But he yells at me if I touch it.

I used to scream too, but from the opposite reason. I gave up screaming about it because my neighbors began to frown at me. And obviously screaming while my forehead vein is pumping doesn't help his libido. But I tried, I thought he'll be scared enough. "

Nymphadora rests now. Even I got tired of not happening, and I can't help her with anything but listen. Maybe they should try a therapist.

"Maybe?"

She bursts in the fullest laughter ever.

"He would better crawl on the ground instead of going to a therapist. I understand it wasn't easy for him to lose his mother at a young age, but I don't find the right words to explain I am not his mother. And he can fuck me.

I like to cover myself in bed sheets and imagine I'm in the arms of a superior being for whom the sexual drive is merely a DNA impulse for assuring its future existence. We may procreate valuable memes, instead of conventional genes. The future may be us and here I am, grumbling about my petty wish for mating.

It's all right. I can live like this. Technically, it's not affecting me."

She almost finished all her cigarettes, the third beer, and the story. She'll be drinking a large coffee soon so she can think of something else and forget about all these. She should be happy with what she has, tenderness, affection, somebody to change the light bulbs. Anhedonius is always with her, she doesn't even think he knows the concept of a mistress.

"But I would prefer he had a mistress. Honestly, I don't feel any better knowing he's faithful. This thought warms me up just like the faithfulness of my lamp."

Chinwe Morah
Baltimore MD, United States

Chinwe I. Morah (b. June 22 1990) was born in Benin City, Nigeria to Igbo parents, as the second of three children. She has spent the last nine years in Baltimore, Maryland. She graduated Summa Cum Laude from Morgan State University, and is currently in her second year pursuing a Master's degree in English at Morgan State. She enjoys spending time with her family, reading sleeping, and attempting to understand Modern British Literature. She currently works as a research assistant at Morgan State University and as a secretary for her sister's book keeping company. This is her first work of fiction.

Monday Morning, or How I Realized that I was Just One More Unimportant Cog in the Mechanics that is the Universe.

By Melody Danvers

Associated Press
May 11. 2235

*T*he following is a copy of a letter saved from the basement of the old Library of Congress, after it flooded on December 23*rd*, 2219 during the rainstorm that devastated the eastern United States. The letter has been reconstructed by several historians, and is printed here in its entirety.

To whoever may have fished this out of the Chesapeake Bay:

I have always believed that I am special, and everyone and everything in my life has merely confirmed it. My parents have told me all my life that they believe that I and my siblings were created by God for a special purpose. My teachers, from elementary through college, have commented on my quick mind, my brilliance, my capacity for understanding difficult readings, my modesty, and my maturity, which was apparently beyond my years. Even the high school bullies merely shored up my belief in my uniqueness by saying that they targeted me because I was different, and my mother confirmed this by pointing out that they were probably jealous of my good grades, and the admiration and respect I earned from students and teachers alike. So is it any wonder that I have always been certain that I would be spectacular in life?

I never believed in dreaming small dreams. No, small dreams were for losers and the mediocre members of society. For me, nothing but the biggest dream would do. I dreamt that I would be an actress and would win an Oscar and an Emmy for my performance, preferably before the age of 17; the fact that I cannot act did not stop me. I dreamt of winning a Tony and a Grammy, and my tone deafness and inability to sing in any pleasing fashion never deterred me. I wished to graduate from high school by the age of fifteen, and go to whichever university pleaded the most, because I firmly believed that by the time I graduated from the 12th grade, Oxford, CALbridge, Harvard, Yale, and Tokyo University, would be beating a path to my door, and begging me to grace their CALpus with my presence. Suffice it to say, that I am not intelligent enough for that. When I finally tuned into the fact that my skills laid in literature, then I knew without a shadow of doubt, that before I turned 21, I would have won a Nobel Prize as well as a Pulitzer, for my contributions to literature. Unfortunately, creative writing makes my stomach ache, and purple prose riddled with clichés is the only thing that comes out on the page. I never dreamt of wealth, instead I wanted to be recognized for the great achievements I was sure I would perform, which I knew would make the world a better place. I suppose high school should have been the end of my overly grandiose dreams, but the truth is, it only reinforced them.

I only applied to college because I knew it was what my parents and teachers expected. Truly, all I wanted to do after high school was go into a library and read through all the romance novels there. But I did as expected, took my SATs, got a really high score, applied to two good colleges which were fairly close to my parents' home, and within three weeks I received notices from both colleges that I was accepted, and that I was to be given a full academic scholarship, as well as room and board, and some money to cover textbooks. I assumed this was the normal course of things for most people, so when I heard tales from fellow students about rejection letters, and loans, I was confused. Finally, my English teacher asked me whether I had received acceptance letters, and then explained to me that it was unusual to receive a scholarship without even applying for it. This erased any doubt about my future greatness, after all, had two universities not acknowledged their belief in how wonderful I was? So I left for college, a few months after I turned 17 to pursue a degree in chemistry, certain that I would blow everyone else out of the water with my brilliant mind, and they would have no choice but to declare me the greatest student ever seen.

Let me assure you that college was nothing like I believed it would be. Oh, I did more than fairly well in my classes but the debilitating problem which I had suffered from, since the eighth grade only worsened in the new environment. Allow me to backtrack. From the way I write about myself, you might assume that I am brave and feisty with many friends, just like the traditional fictional heroine. Let me dissuade you from any such notion. Before the eighth grade, I went to a juniorate convent which also acted as a boarding school in my home country, and I had a best friend, other friends and acquaintances, rivals, favorite teachers, and even people with whom I pulled pranks, and planned ways to escape from our dreary school days. When I started the eighth grade, I was in a new country with people whose American accent was virtually undecipherable to me. My middle school was a private one, and my classmates had known each other for years. They were not unkind, but I felt excluded, and I reacted by acting as if I did not want to attend their parties, spend time at the mall together, share lunches, or talk about what was on TV last night. I buried myself in any fiction book I could lay my hands on, and before I knew it, middle school was over and I did not know the names of my classmates. The exact same thing happened again when I high school came around, because I attended a public high school and a lot of the students knew each other from middle school. I comforted myself with the certainty of the greatness to come, and also, it helped that I firmly believed that I was apart because I was just that much brilliant, and I intimidated others. Come College and I realized I had virtually no people skills. I could not stand in front of a class to speak, I could not work in a team with others, and joining organizations, even those I was genuinely interested in, and which were interested in having me, felt absolutely alien to me, so I never joined anything. It took me a while to figure out that I was afraid of people, but I dealt with it by living in my books, and in my imagination. All to the further deterioration of any social skills lurking in me.

My stint as a chemistry major was brief, and I quickly changed majors, and found a fairly comfortable niche in the English department. There, my imagination simply bloomed as it was wont to. My written work was more than adequate, and as usual, social interaction stumped me. I had one or two people I could talk to, but in retrospect, I feel that any acquaintance I made was accidental, and was probably pity on their part. I hid myself in my imagination, and refused to come out of my self-induced isolation, which really had changed from a choice to be alone, to the only way I could survive around people I didn't know. As my third and final year CALe around, I realized that I was terrified of graduating, because graduation meant having to talk to employers. You see, at this point I had never had a job, my bank account only had birthday money from my parents, I did not drive a car, I lived at home, had never been out on a date, and the only people I spoke to with some frequency, were my parents and my older sister. I did not know what to do with a degree in English, but eventually the idea CALe to me that I would be able to teach high school with a Master's degree, or even college with a doctorate. This idea did not erase all my overly grandiose dreams, but the idea of graduate school did not just make good sense to me, but it left me excited, and eager to learn more. As I made plans for graduate school, I recalled how horrible going to new places was for me. So I applied to only one graduate school: the English graduate program at the college I went attended, though I really wanted to go to a university out of state. My plan was that maybe between the age of

20 and 22, something would happen and would get over my chronic shyness, and would be able to function with other people. I was of course accepted, and offered a research assistant position, which CALe with pay (technically my first job) and a tuition award. I was alone but excitedly nervous, and that was enough for me. With this in mind, a month and a half before I turned 20, I graduated from with my B.A. in English Literature. I graduated, summa cum laude, as expected of me, though the 4.0 GPA I wanted did not come (science to this day makes me weak about the knees).

Before I go on about graduate school, let me say that for all my talk of being alone, I had my family. My younger brother and I were best friends before he continued the family tradition of going to boarding schools, and my sister took over the position of best friend. My father loves me, and really would give me everything I needed, and was always willing to give advice though I rarely took advantage of this. My mother! What can I say to describe someone whose sole wish for me was that I simply be the best at whatever I wanted to do? She believes to this day that I am absolutely talented, and have a great imagination and great energy which I don't unitize to its full extent. I disagree, because what she calls talent and energy, I call a tendency to become overly excited, and to live in my head instead of the real world. Nonetheless, she has always been there for me. Everyone in my family supported my decision to get my Master's degree, though a few surreptitious comments were made about the usefulness of a degree in English. Both my parents and sister chauffeured me to and from my classes, and made comments about how happy they were to see me excited about what others would call terribly tiresome treatises on literary criticism. I enjoyed the challenges presented by my classes, and I did get better at interacting with others. The very small class sizes, 3-5 students, gave me no way to fade into the woodwork. I got better slowly, but surely. I abandoned dreams of recognition for my contribution to music, the stage, and even that Pulitzer. Now, I just wanted to know every bit of Modern British literary trivia available, but was not willing to do the work necessary. I know, I'm lazy. This was just about a month ago. In fact, as of last week, I was certain that once I finished relaxing and shaking off the requisite tiredness of my first and fairly productive year of grad school, I would spend the rest of the summer delving into the mystery of Romanticism, as well as finally finishing the several books I have on cognitive theory. So, the question on your mind is, how did I come to realize that I was without a doubt unimportant in the running of the universe? Well, it began this morning.

I woke up at 5:00 AM, got dressed and was ready to go on my 3.5 mile early morning walk. Ten minutes into my walk, I saw the corpse of a red breasted robin lying on the roadside, and two minutes later, I had an epiphany and it felt as if my world moved. I knew without any shadow of doubt that I was unimportant. For the first time since I heard the phrase, "nature red in tooth and claw," I felt as if I understood its meaning. I was just one more person in the universe, and I had not been ordained by any higher power, with whatever it was that made some people pioneers, and made other followers. Even if it was about hard work and not special dust from the heavens, then I did not even have that. I was lazy, arrogant, narcissistic, and could best be described as one more spare part that is always left over when assembling IKEA furniture. If I got struck by lightning, the world would not end. It wouldn't even have the decency to change from its usual pattern. For thirty more minutes I contemplated my life, and realized that I was not that special. I do not like rock music, pop music, or Ferrero Rocher chocolates; but I like country music and Cadbury dairy milk chocolates. I like fantasy books, I love space operas, I want to learn how to dance and I love Korean dramas, but I hate horror movies, and cannot stand reality TV. There are many things I like and even more I dislike, but no one asked my opinion before they started doing anything. My 21st birthday is in a week and a half, but I do not drive, I do not drink, I have never been to Vegas, and I have no friends. I am just a piece of lint on a white blouse. No one notices me, and my presence does not affect whether the blouse is worn or not. This was eye opening and terribly depressing. My great dreams felt like chaff in the wind, and my smaller dreams felt like wisps of clouds. For one moment, I considered crying, but why should I waste a tear on an uncaring universe? So, I kept on walking and walking, and eventually I CALe home, and moved on with my life.

When you find this letter sealed in a bottle in the Bay, do not for a moment think that because it is terribly depressing, that it must be a suicide no-te. On the contrary, it is a surrender flag, which I am waving to the universe. I submit to its will, and will act out my part in it. I will live day in and day out, safe in the knowledge that I am unimportant, and will forever understand that I do not matter. I will graduate with my Master's degree, and maybe a doctorate. I will probably get married, and have children. And one day in the future, when my child, grandchild, or maybe niece or nephew co-mes to me with their big dreams and hopes, I will smile and be supportive. But when their backs are turned, I will give a wry and bitter smile to the universe, because I know and understand that we are all unimportant cogs in the universe, and life will continue no matter which dreams do not come true. You are probably thinking to yourself, do not give up. You are just twenty one. Most people achieve their life dreams after the age of twenty. You have at least eighty years to change the world: that is a lifetime. I don't deny this. Maybe I will achieve something. Maybe at the moment I am just hysterical, and merely work up on the wrong side of the bed this morning. Maybe. Probably. Does it matter? All I know is that I feel horrible, and I want to tell someone.

Resignedly Yours,

CAL

Afterward

This letter was found among other letters in the basement of the Library of Congress, along with other letters from important heads of state in from the early 21st century. Historians have argued about who CAL was since the unearthing of this letter in 2219. There are three groups of historians with three different opinions on the identity of CAL. One group believes that she was Corianne Analise Linterson, the woman who reinvented transportation in 2076 with her invention of the individual flying saucer, though they offer no convincing explanation of how her letter came to be in the Library of Congress. Another group believes CAL to be a pseudonym of the first president of the Americas, Sandraline Meercamp – Cumberbach, who first wrote one of the most memorable and most profitable fantasy series, the Degeric Revolutions, in 2098 using the pseudonym Celine A. Loontwill. This might explain why this letter was in the Library of Congress. The most convincing theory is that espoused by historians including Ferdinand Rodriguez, the historian who unearthed the document. He believes that CAL was his great grandmother, Caligula A. Xing, who worked in the Library of Congress, and whose maiden name forms the initials CAL. She was a housewife, but is most famous as the oldest person to be sentenced to death, when she was convicted seventeen counts of first degree murder at the age of 103 in the year 2107 for setting her nursing home on fire, because as she claimed in her confession, she "did not like the shade of pink on one of the flowers on the curtain."

Regardless of the identity of the author, this letter is an important part of history because it shows the apathy and madness that permeated the youth of the 21st century. If this letter is dated to the first quarter of the 21st century, then its author was one of that generation who dropped seven atomic bombs in the space of three months, and fought three world wars. The scars left by that generation endure even today in the mid-23rd century, in the form of mutations, and even the current war can be traced back to disputes begun by that generation of people. To allow our children today to be brought up in the same way that CAL was ensures that the mistakes of the 21st century will be repeated again and again. This is why I advocate that the current isolationist education system needs to be revamped once more, and a return to community based schools, where children are taught social skills, and interaction with each other becomes a vital part of education. To allow our children to feel unimportant and un-wanted results in a disconnection from the world, and will only hasten our destruction.

This report was contributed by Melody Danvers, best known for winning a Pulitzer for her news reports in the 8th World War. This report was filed from her hideout.

Nehemiah K.H. Wong
ShenZhen, China.

Nehemiah grew up in the region called South-East Asia. So that, at an early age, he had absorbed a multiculturalism which is richly diverse.

English wasn't his mother tongue, but it was the official medium of his education. He was a passionate young reader; but when it came to writing, he struggled with an art demanding perfection.

Though baffled he never stopped relating to English as an integral part of his life. He first started his professional career as a young writer, scribbling for a men's magazine.

Later on he studied theology which exposed him to many important branches of human knowledge, including: archeology, semantics, linguistics, philosophy, psychology and rhetoric.

He then stepped into his second career choice, caring for communities in the region. But more recently, having reached a chronological milestone, he has again an urge to write creatively.

He's now musing on the charming discovery, how life can come one full circle without intending. That no matter, how far one has advanced on the timeline; one can't fully escape from the pull of his or her roots.

Nehemiah is happily married and is an Australian citizen, residing in a suburb of Melbourne. Presently, he is working overseas in China, with his devoted wife and companion, Grace.

MONGKUT

THE STORY OF A SIAMESE FIGHTER FISH
By Nehemiah K. H. Wong

CHAPTER 1

INTRODUCTION

*C*rown jewels may begin their history as lowly extractions, but e-ventually they would end, brilliantly, on a royal head. Mongkut's story is that kind of story.

Legend has it that his story started in ancient Siam, after the greatest Khmer civilization of all, located at Angkor Wat had collapsed. Its behemoth city great network of cities, a wonder of the ancient world, was swallowed stone slab after stone slab, by jungles, vines, and creepers pos-sessed as if by the ravenous spirit, of a gargantuan python.

MONGKUT'S BIRTH

Mongkut's history began when Mongkut's mother strayed into his fa-ther's territory. He then immediately initiated courtship as the waiting had been too long this time. The mating dance, was a masterful display of col-orful flowing fin-fabrics, tossed here and there (rather like some charming dances of an oriental court), and a hypnotic glance now and then given in the direction of the drab female (as most females of this species are).

Mongkut's mother, a plain albino, with a milky white body, had the merest suggestion of red and Mongkut's father a bi-colored male, sporting the most beautiful iridescent blue and red, with radiating fin patterns.

With just a few darting strokes, Mongkut's father succeeded in arousing her. She signaled her interest by a twisting swim. The nuptial embrace, initi-ated by the male, consisted of a press or wrap around the female. After en-circling the female's body with his own, a mutual limbo results for several seconds, and permit fertilization of the squeezed eggs with milt.

This dramatic "love-play" stops only when her swollen abdomen be-comes flattened. During suspension, the male normally emerges first. Re-suscitated by the sight of sinking eggs, he dives, scooping them into his mouth. Several do-zen are squirted each time. The nuptial rigor ends only after hours of sapping work. In giving life, guess, not all is pleasure.

Then Mongkut's mother had to leave. That's fundamental. The female never remains. Her presence would only provoke male ire. "No point risk-ing injury or death," she reckoned. This rather heartless male behavior post union is basically protective. So she didn't mind. Giving a last back-ward glance at her lover, a very handsome male, she swam away, never to look u-pon her family again. And she resumed her solitary, nomadic, ex-istence.

NURSERY DAYS

After each press, Mongkut's father had the eggs regurgitated, inserting, them into a life-giving bubble-raft. For gills to fully form, the eggs had to be chambered here for two days. Any premature disconnection with this nursery meant certain death. Gulping air deeply, Mongkut's father, kept feeding an unending stream of viscous sticky bubbles, to maintain the raft. What a meticulous and proud father he was.

In his egg-sac, Mongkut's eyes, just two little black dots, blinked. He twitched so slightly. You could see his little heart palpitating. That's all he could do in such a confined space.

One time, a dugout paddled by, ripping a segment of the nest. Mongkut with others were dragged haplessly down. The breakaway wasn't noticed initially. When his father did, quick as a charging eel, and several pinpointed digs, downward and forward later, he retrieved the embryos. Legend would have been poorer indeed, if Mongkut had died here.

On the third critical day the fries burst free from their sacs. And the glories of our world welcomed them warmly. They often huddled together, sticking densely just below the viscose waterline, like a forest of pins, absorbing oxygen.

About then, Mongkut's father had a sickening feeling. He kept picking up fries and spitting them back into the raft. But they kept wriggling and wiggling and falling back into the water.

A sense of futility signaled the end of his paternal role. Time for leaving had come. Should he stay he could turn cannibalistic. Mongkut's father didn't want that. And that was the last, he saw of his father.

Their home environment, with humic acid at an ideal level, was a boon to Mongkut and his siblings. Leached from decaying leaves, peat mosses and rotting vegetation, it assisted in the prime growth of the fries. The rich minerals, helped their bodies and organs reach optimum growth. They couldn't have asked for more. Small crustaceans, water fleas, daphnia, bugs, and micro-organisms of all kinds thrived in that equatorial soup. A kind of rare tubifex (small clustering worms) happened even, to live there. These worms gave them low oxygen capability.

This anaerobic ability proved decisive throughout their lives — as when locked in a mortal combat called the "Kiss of Death." When this happened, both fighters would have inter-locked, mouth to mouth, tightly shut. Tugging at each other in a see-saw battle, they swim horizontally, lying on their side, in the direction of the stronger fish. Till one surrenders. Then, unlocking snaps into place. Strength, endurance, lung power and even courage of each combatant were tested by this rigor.

But sometimes, a victor wouldn't unlock. And the drowning, resulting, is a pity, of course. Normal protocol, between fellow species, mostly prevents things going that far. Ichthyologists cannot say for sure whether this is an e-rror of hormonal overdrive or otherwise.

CHILDHOOD GAMES

The siblings lived close by at first, hiding among the thick weeds and kelps growing in the stream; and coming out only to spar in mock battles. But these bouts quickly become earnest, especially when their colors emerge.

From these innocent games, they learnt a lot about maneuvering, and ho-ne their physique and skills to perfection. Skills, upon which, their lives depended on. And from dull fishes, not dissimilar from anchovies, their fu-ture colorations emerge, becoming more and more radiant, culminating as adult fixtures.

In adulthood, they impress you as one of the most strikingly beautiful fi-shes in the world. The possible whole colors and mixtures of colors and pa-tterns are almost impossible to catalogue: green, purple, white, black, steel blue, turquoise, yellow, apricot, chocolate, orange, lavender, red, roy-al blue, pastel and even opaque. And this list doesn't even begin to include the myriads of mixed colors and patterns.

Most of Mongkut's male siblings inherited their father's color schemes in varying degrees. Branching colors, of differing hues and shades, also asserted themselves. His female siblings aped their mother. Except for Mongkut, who had a pearly white body and ruddy fins.

GENETICS AND DESTINY

Albinos are genetically disadvantaged for combats. They bruise too eas-ily and the bruises show too eagerly. Injuries become lock-on targets for futu-re attacks.

Like a cut eye or a swollen cheek, on a human boxer, would. Siamese fighter fishes would attack such injuries purely on the working of instincts.

Many an albino had lost fight and life, or became crippled because of this. Hence, the albino's rarity as a top echelon fighter. Body wounds fester easily: and death can come from any of the many water-borne diseases.

But one thing augured well for our protagonist. His eyes weren't red albino eyes. Such eyes are weak: sensitive to light and lacks sharpness dur-ing fights. With poor eyesight, victory becomes problematic. Nature had in fact, favored Mongkut with a wider angle of vision than most. Better positioned, his eyes gave him greater forward and hind vision.

Frequently, just having peripheral vision, was all Mongkut required, to step out of the way, or to be ahead. This gave him distinct advantages in tar-geting, hitting and evasion. Many of his opponents were simply quite unnerved, really, at his speed and accuracy and frequency in hitting or evading. They hadn't experienced anything at this level before or thought it possible. This created early frustrations which later become fear in the hearts of even the stoutest fighters.

But a more insurmountable handicap seems to be Mongkut's size. He, unfortunately, inherited his mother's physical dimensions. This means, Mongkut was noticeably smaller than other males of his species. So the blows he absorbs would hurt him harder than others. Conversely, his hits were less damaging. Surely, top rankings would be beyond his grasp. But in a world of reversals and contradictions, strengths can be weaknesses, and weaknesses strengths.

Nature had, in compensation, given Mongkut greater speed for the loss of size. And certainly greater courage. The thicker girths of his opponents meant that their movements and reactions were more ponderous. And before their blows arrived, Mongkut easily got out of harm's way. (A comparison from the human realm would be the victory of the English navy over the Spanish Armada under Sir Francis Drake.

The Spanish galleons were superior and more formidable in every way, but unfortunately, also clumsier and tardier and were out-maneuvered by the smaller but faster English ships). The bigger males were indeed slower in circling and cornering, when trying to chew on their opponent's gills. Mongkut could always out-turn them, and hit before they got to him.

DANGERS AT HOME

In their home-stream lurk dangers posed by different predatory species. These remorseless hunters, so much larger, could make easy meals of them at any time: Barramundi, Mekong catfish, Siamese carp, Featherback, Snakehead, and others. Mongkut learned stealth skills, enabling him to be concealed. Survival tactics became critical components of his personal strategies. He developed calmness, patience, and alertness: qualities absolutely handy in the future.

Many of his species, his siblings included, died prematurely, precisely because of failures in these departments. Death, being undoubtedly, the har-shest teacher of all, with no repeat lessons from his textbook. Avoidance, not confrontation, is therefore a first principle of self-defense. And this isn't a coward's creed, as Mongkut grasped the early truth that, discretion is the better part of valor.

LESSONS FROM SIBLINGS

When Mongkut watched his siblings spar, his understanding of combat grew. He extracted, distilled, and formulated many ground-breaking techniques for fighting. The habit of observation became one of the earliest keys on his personal journey to superlative excellence. It has been said that, "Curiosity is the playground of geniuses". By watching, he understood the principle of winning a fight without fighting; to win sometimes by psychological means, sometimes by superior techniques, and sometimes by stratagems, is the very art of warfare.

The first technique which he developed, giving him supremacy and recognition, is the "Water-thrashing Technique." It's the tech-nique of creating water turbulence, thus fooling your adversary, about your size and power, and scaring him into ending the duel quickly. Another cutting-edge technique, never seen used, is the "Abdominal-attack Technique." Instead of swimming parallel to his challenger, as others would, to engage in a fight, Mongkut would dip, swimming lower at the level of his opponent's abdominal line instead. His mouth harassing the opponent's unprotected under-belly constantly. This not only frustrated the opponent (who could hardly see and target him) but also unnerve him.

Another useful technique is the "Zigzagging Technique", which prevents the enemy from getting close and attacking: for by darting left and right continuously(at each turn to the right or left, depending on where your adversary is) it keeps the enemy at bay, yet you're speeding away from his territorial markers, forcing him to turn back.

A technique which took longer to master was the "Tail-flip Tecni-que," which uses the opponent's body, as a fulcrum to launch a sneak reverse a-ttack, with added force. Transferring an enemy's force or energy against himself, is a master-level expertise in self-defense. A "judo-ka" for example could execute this move with a snap. Not the least, were the "Clamping Techniques." Most fighter fishes would punch or peck at the gill-flaps. Mongkut developed the techniques of grabbing and hanging on them (or other vital parts), causing terror to his opponents. The stranglehold interferes with the opposition's breathing process, causing the fish to pass out ultimately.

CULTIVATING A SPIRIT OF EXCELLENCE

How did Mongkut develop this spirit of excellence? A spirit manifestly seen on winners, and champions. In truth, while others were dozing in indolence (and they love doing that), Mongkut would redeem the time, spending bitter days on ends, developing and streamlining fighting techniques secretly. "In dark keeping will one shines," as the saying goes. Often he could see visions, and could turn them round and round inside his head, to explore possibilities. In perceiving novel moves, he was patient, persistent and disciplined, trying this or that. And they don't always work out. But he never gave–up, and never sought to display his skills openly. Ultimately, both skills fused together; the conscious ones and the instinctive ones becoming seamless as one.

LEAVING HOME

The day came when Mongkut felt that he should seek a safer place under the sun. On a day while the sky was still a pale wash, Mongkut departed forever from his beloved birthplace. The decision wrenched at his heart. But he knew he was growing. Maturing. Life had to move on for growing to continue. He knew, only by exposing himself to new things and new tests, could he then reach his fullest potential.

Mongkut thought it best to hug the embankments and follow the currents. Doing this he ran into many solitary males, bigger and more matured than him. And each, more dazzling than the other. Only his stealth skills helped him from dueling with them and to observe their ways. This way, he built an impressive archive about the males of his species.

He discovered fishes that fought frontally, others by stealth, others still which favored strength. And some that applied cunning. He saw tacticians, and strategists, and also speed magicians; even political fighters that forged brief alliances. And amusingly, those that fought willy-nilly. But there were a handful that was so outstanding; they could improvise their strikes on the spot, tailoring moves in tandem with the style of their opponents. In the last category, he recognized the best fighters of his species: whose styles of fighting were so fluid, that they had the softness of water to shape themselves to win fights. Mongkut felt a strong affinity with this last group.

Mongkut also gathered critical knowledge of when and how to inflict lethal or crippling blows; and when to inflict less critical ones. He learned the principle of proportionate force. To use force only proportional to the aggre-ssion or danger. And not to hurt more than necessary.

THE OVERCOMER

In his journey, Mongkut encountered dangerous currents that could have drowned him. Sometimes, the nights were black as coal and the air cold as ice when he surfaced for air. Sometimes, there weren't anything to eat. Days passed before he had any nourishment. Mongkut faced deprivations and terror alone, but he neither gave up, nor did he indulge in moods of self-pity and blame.

He somehow knew, such emotions didn't help him in the situation. He kept himself from bitterness and depression. Here was beginning to form, dear reader, the heart of an "Overcomer." What's an "Overcomer?" Simply put, "One who, has learned to live above disadvantages, trials, and unfairness, so consistently, that they no longer trouble his thoughts and feelings. They no longer become obstacles to him, but have become bridges to possibilities." A heart that's so forged by the scorching fires of trials that the steel of true courage and grit had entered into it. It's a truth universally accepted, and one easily proven, that a soft life can only lead to a soft spine.

THE GORGE OF TEARS AND PAIN

It was on that darkest of nights, that Mongkut took a wrong turning, entering into a boiling, pouring, rushing, gushing, roaring cauldron. This was a frightful night baptism, he could never forget. His species was made for the tranquility of still waters. He tried to push ahead, but he was pushed back. Rebuffed as many times as he attempted. Half-drowned, after repeated failures, he decided to rest by the banks, and to reassess his strategy in the morning. Through this, he learned the principle of resting as an alternative to giving up, along the journey of mastering a daunting challenge.

As soon, as dawn came, he saw fishes springing into the air with the agility of flying spears. He couldn't identify the species. He never saw them before. But they were spears sailing in the air. He wished he could do the same. But these were equipped with fins which could turn into gliders.

This is where Mongkut was essentially different. He didn't tell himself "I can't." Didn't give up without trying. Many of his species, coveted greatness and talents, without any willingness to pay the cost or sacrifice to get them. And demanded to have them overnight.

Mongkut had attained an understanding of the wise and mature. He understood how the laws of the universe operated; and knew how he must bend to them to succeed and achieve; He saw problems as challenges to be conquered in order to advance. One thing he learnt quickly from the new species: their courage and calmness in facing the onslaught of the angry torrents. He saw them pacing themselves, building up their energy reserves; and holding their ground, and focusing before launching themselves into the air, with a devil take you attitude. The principle of holding the ground, Mongkut discovered was also a critical key to advancement.

By focusing everything at one point their energy force was multiplied. Through this Mongkut learned the important lessons of timing, patience and focus. He learned the habit of conserving energy for important things, and not dissipating it on insignificance. He was determined to reach the foot of the waterfall.

Then Mongkut spotted an alcove of gentler waters 15 yards ahead. He decided he would at least make his way there first or die trying. Through this he learnt, the principle of gradual ascent. That the mountain can't be ascended by one leap.

When he reached the alcove, it proved to be an ideal training camp: a sequestered oasis, where he could experiment, explore and expand in personal development, uninterruptedly. Here, he gained insight into the principle of isolation for development. He knew he had to have this space for personal growth. Gregarious souls will never understand this need, nor would they be willing to sacrifice social gaiety for personal growth. They judge solitariness basically as an aberrant anti-social behavior. They fail to understand that the journey of the great ones always required solitariness at differing points. That leaders need to walk alone many times. And this must be cultivated preparatory to entering that stature or work.

The rejection and misunderstanding must be embraced by the overcomer, and allowed to transcend and to transfigure. Mongkut came to understand this, as the principle of pearl making. River oysters taught him that one day. Taught him that, pain and wounding can be beatific, if covered with forgiveness and forgetfulness and love. The alcove, crescent in shape, had a space of 90 feet wide, relatively calm and clear, teeming with water life and vegetation. A sun-kissed and shaded oasis it is, at different time of the day. There were plenty of solitude and security too. He could live out his natural life here, undisturbed.

But unlike the others, Mongkut was not attracted to a life of apathetic indolence or languor. He saw challenges as an essential part of life and rest as a brief reward for overcoming. That, challenges make life, life. And uninterrupted serenity doesn't. And rest isn't an ideal or final goal in life, to be seized as Soon as possible, And to be clutched indefinitely. To him, the tests and struggles which so often interrupt our tranquility and regarded as inconvenience, are really for our growth. He found the process as well as the results equally fascinating or important. The difficulties tested and drew out the limits of his potential: while the rest defined and gave meaning or satisfaction to his accomplishments. He soon discovered he learned more from his difficulties than from good times and successes. Stripped of challenges, life, to him, would be stripped of meaning. Would become barren. Sterile.

Pain or no pain, Mongkut re-started his runs. Maybe it was just his stubborn nature, goading him on. He was battered and punished by the waters. Its power and grip confounded the little fish. And it took days before he could try again at times. The results, week after week, were the same. Defeat after defeat took a toll on his courage, if not on his body.

Mongkut, had to learn how to face defeats like a hero. Handling defeats or failures is different from handling victories or successes. And had to be mastered first. Here Mongkut encountered a paradox of greatness: humbling must precede exaltation. This seems to be a principle of heaven qualifying the one that would achieve greatness or power.

Through all these, Mongkut was growing more than he realized. His will was forged as hard as steel. His courage, unbreakable as diamonds. His mind becoming a womb for possibilities, before they happened, and possibilities where there were none.

Then one day, instead of fighting with the white waters, in a split second of a moment, in a flashing disclosure, he just blended with the water, becoming one with it. Water became his friend his ally: not his adversary. No longer was water an opposing force. It became an assisting force.

He learned its qualities and characteristics: learned how to flow with it, when to exert his strength to break through the walls which blocked him: and when to enter through those open doors smoothly. In those last days, he learnt more about water than any other of his species: and became a master of that domain.

His movements in water became effortless. Astonishing! Water became his servant, and would bend to his will. And though he was smaller than most of his species, his armor became unbreakable through constant water compression and stress. His body muscles were leaner, firmer and denser. And although smaller in mass he had incredible power.

Ounce for ounce, he was physically superior to any male of his species. The truth of this only becomes obvious in the proximity of a fight, shattering the outward illusion created by his diminutiveness.

Mongkut was basically still unaware of the extent of his progress. But when he'd some inkling, it was tempered with brokenness. He could never forget the gorge of pain and tears. His feelings of achievements weren't the feelings gotten by direct competition with others, or crushing others. His was the result of self-development and self-competition. He knew how close he was to being completely broken. It gave him a proper historical perspective of himself. As it's said, the half of wisdom is in knowing about oneself. Without that, there can't be any proper growth.

The story of Mongkut could have ended here, had he decided to live out his life here. And it wouldn't have diminished his achievements one bit, if he did. The quality of our lives moves on with us upon death. But temporal things must be left behind or abandoned. "In nakedness we come and in nakedness we go" was not spoken of spiritual or noble deeds and achievements. It was spoken of heavier temporal things which cannot be heaved and lugged into a higher realm.

Fortunately, our White Warrior didn't consider this the end of his personal odyssey. He felt, much more in life was waiting for him outside. That the present gorge and rapids experiences were just one level of experience he had climbed. There were other higher plateaus waiting for him. He didn't climb mountains just because they were out there: but also because they were in his heart. They were conquered in his heart first.

By now Mongkut was a full-sized albino male. And a very remarkable one in appearance. And when he swam, it was as if he was powered, as if he could cut through the water, like a cold-steel knife. He was visually stunning for an undersized fighter fish.

As Mongkut made his way out of the white-water gorge. He felt he was leaving the place of self-discovery. A place of mirrors. One which allowed him to see himself. And doors which opened up to him knowledge known to few. As the mouth of the stream widened, he felt the wide world open up to him again.

Mongkut realized the liberty and freedom he now gained contrasted with the narrow, painful and constricting, experience of the gorge-stream. It became a metaphor for him. A metaphor for growing, learning, or testing. As he saw it, the initiation into a new skill, is always followed by pain. Followed by humbling limitations. This being, part of the essential path of growth. Or the price to be paid. But once mastered, you exited through a wide door of liberty and ability. Compression and expansion, that's it, the narrow gate of entry and the wide door of exit, is the difference between the novice and the savant. You go in the apprentice but you exit as the maestro.

THE TERROR OF CHAO PRAYA

As he swam by new and interesting terrains, he sensed he was meeting up with fewer and fewer males. Mongkut wondered why? He felt as if he had entered into a region of desolation. He put on his sharpest alert, gliding by the embankments. He wondered whether predatory fishes had caused the desolation. He wondered whether it was, the Giant Mekong catfish or the great Snakehead. Which were sworn enemies of his species?

After 15 mi-les downriver, he felt something glide past and grazed him. It was already night, but Mongkut felt its powerful presence. The presence wasn't coming from any large hunters, but one of his own kind. The scent in the water confirmed this. And Mongkut's olfactory organs were accurate instruments. He could identify different kinds of species thriving in the brooks, streams and rivers. The night being stumbling dark, MongKut decided to pull up and rest for the night. The clouds overhead in the sky were looming like a thick forest and the darkness oozing out, like a sinister force.

It was a starless night. Mongkut hid behind river reeds and rushes, and stayed motionless. He felt the presence several times more. Once it passed by so closely, it even stopped to investigate. But Mongkut held his breath and played dead. The presence, having sniffed about, left. Mongkut was curious to find out about the presence. And he trembled with anticipation. Wondering, what new peril he would be facing? He tried sleeping, but it was a very sleepless kind of sleep.

When morning dawned, the river fowls, boomed and called out to one another. The early herons and storks were already spearing the waters for their breakfast. Others dredged mud and filtered ooze. Mongkut swam between the reeds and rushes, embracing the banks. A mile down, nothing! He thought himself free. But just then, he felt a strong turbulence speeding towards him, like a stick shot towards his back. The speed and power were quite astonishing. As it was too late to do a full reverse, to face the onrushing attack, Mongkut expertly just side-stepped; but he felt the heavy, hard and powerful body of his attacker, gash him. Their scales rubbed in friction, in the first contact and contest of strength.

Mongkut's armor was none the worse. He was now looking at the back of the "rushing torpedo." When the torpedo turned, Mongkut was ready with his first combat signals. Such were the rules of engagement. Mongkut turned sideways with a very dignified swerve, and flagged his fins in full flare, displaying them in all its glory, like a matador shaking his cape before a charging bull. It meant: "I'm ready to fight if you are. But if you are not, better back off."

But the opponent, Mongkut faced today, wasn't a greenhorn. No! But a battle hardened, battle scarred veteran. A black fighter. That's why; Mongkut couldn't see him in the dark. He was an invisible master of darkness. A grand champion released back to the wild, to enrich the natural stock. To spawn future champions. Here's an all-conquering hero, who never lost a fight in his whole life. And you could see that he suffered no fools.

After a history of impeccable fights, he has now become somewhat rogue. Psychologically disturbed, he was unable to settle down; unable to sublimate his aggression. His glands, filled to excess with the lust for fighting, he cleared the waterways of many great fighters. Daily, he patrolled the river, for that very purpose. To see the backs of his enemies, or their carcasses, carried away as flotsam by the river. He was an angel of death. The terror of Chao Praya. Mongkut knew that the old warrior was sick; knew that imbalance would kill him one day. But today wasn't the day. Mongkut still had to face him, in all his menacing craziness.

The old champion had no respect for Mongkut. Why should he? Mongkut was a mere juvenile to him. He was already thinking of a quick coup de grace. Again he charged, spurning Mongkut's warnings, like an adult impatiently wanting to brush away childish toys. And again, just before actual contact, Mongkut dodged. Several embarrassing misses later, the old gladiator, went berserk. Misses? Impossible! Unacceptable! Shrewdly, Mongkut started his zigzagging run here. Not to run away. But to submerge into the depths of the river. Discerning correctly, that the old bully would soon run out of breath. Deeper and deeper they dove, and still the old fighter was on his tail. But no matter how fast the latter sped, he could not match Mongkut's pace, kept at even knots, just ahead. And the old general comple-tely failed to realize the ploy.

But he went deeper than Mongkut had anticipated and won his admi-ration. Then, he faltered. Stopped dead in his tracks. Oxygen depleted and oxygen deprived. His body shut-down and cramped. And he almost pa-ssed out, becoming motionless. And only by slow flotation, could he rise, to where he could breathe again.

Mongkut could have finished the old warrior off here. But he had a deep respect for life (and fights only when cornered). In this, he was the polar opposite of the old champion. Mongkut approached near enough to peer in-to his attacker's eyes. As much as a gesture of peace as it was brave.

When the eyes of the two great champions met, everything else just seemed to stop. Time itself seemed to stop, as they plumbed the depths of each other's soul. The old champion had recovered by now to acknowledge the extraordinary quality of the young fighter before him. He had never done this before, nor did he need to do again. Mongkut's shield of serenity seemed to envelop the old fighter. Something he badly needed. That "Inner rest which many coveted," entered the old general. What Mongkut had received in turn, was hard to define. Maybe it was just that aura of invinci-bility, stemming from countless victories which are a tangible force in it-self.

Then Mongkut turned, and in a flash, was gone, leaving the old cham-pion to ponder about the significance of their encounter. That was the starting point of the latter's inner healing and balance. And he mellowed, continuing on to a ripe old, satisfying age.

REFLECTING ON WISDOM

Reflections make great lives greater. Through reflections, Mongkut surpassed his ordinary plane of existence. With it he drew from the deep well of wisdom. Mongkut's primary objective was Wisdom. Cleverness he felt had been overestimated and often substituted for wisdom. Mongkut knew about that by watching others.

Mongkut experienced the healing powers of holistic wisdom on his life. Cleverness he knew had little to offer. Its early promises of successes can be likened to a pretty piece of fabric, stitched with dark threads of self-destruction.

Mongkut discovered Wisdom, could only be entered into by quietness and reflection. Just as only, when the surface of water is mirror calm, can reflections be seen and sustained. Mongkut experienced that by only a few moments of withdrawals, each day, by bartering a few minutes of time, he was able to enter into the portal of Wisdom. And bathe in Wisdom's effulgence.

CHAPTER 2

(TURNING A NEW PAGE)

Mongkut's story now runs in the direction of a young Siamese couple. Sawadee and Ratana. The couple met three years ago, panning along the streams, feeding into the mighty but muddy Chao Praya River. A year after, they got betroth, having fallen in love. Sawadee, is a wiry young man, darkened by being under the sun excessively. Ratana is on the other hand a petite and olive-skinned, dimpled, beauty of the village.

Lately, Sawadee had been obsessed with catching a great albino fighter fish. He sighed, thinking about the impossibility of it. With the catch, pictures of supreme happiness would pop out from his mind; dangling, dancing and skipping before his imagination. Visions of screaming children happily playing, with pretty dresses and bright clothing. Then, the appearance of an imposing wooden teak-house, with many rooms, on strong stilts, and eaves curving upwards like elephant tusks, set on a good spread of land. And rounding off, an unbearably charming vision of Ratana in a figure-hu-gging Siamese sarong called the "Pa Toong." "A dream worth dying for," Sawadee muttered to himself. But the geckos on the wall, however, crying out then, with a human-like voice, seemed scornful of his dreams.

HOW LEGENDS ARE MADE

Capturing a great White Warrior (Nak Su Kao) is hard. Oral traditions warned, only a handful has been caught so far. The inherent weaknesses of the albino genes, made success improbable. But the catchers' enthusiasm in pursuing their" holy grail," hadn't been killed off altogether. Their motivation being fed by an authentic love for the ancient sport of combat in any form. In this case by Creation's perfectly designed flashing swimming jewels.

We mustn't forget that the Siamese people sprung from the loins of great warrior races, and are still passionately enamored with fighting skills and courage in any form. And they recognized in the fighter fish, a species embodying the virtues of the ideal warrior.

Catchers universally agree, a great fighter fish isn't just a product of chance, but of great adversities, if nothing else. Great hearts, great heroes, great legends, great fighters, by necessity must all emerge from such a womb. But they alone can't produce greatness: for without proper responses to their mentoring, without proper submission, one can hardly be whipped into the shape of greatness. Mentored ones, go on, becoming the greatest fighters − and live on as immortal "legends," in the folklores and memories of the people.

Heaven has so preordained, that hearts must be tested and humbled, before they can be promoted. Else, greatness in untested hands, like manna, will become worms. The first prerequisite for greatness is lowliness of heart then, which alone has the power to stop power becoming a monster in our heart. Difficulties train and fit us for the management of greatness.

GETTING ON THE TRAIL

One night, the couple was having their usual after dinner chat. They were in Ratana's living room, a Spartan affair, with a few rickety rattan chairs and straw floor mats. When the wind blew, the oil-lamps would flicker, casting caricatures on the walls.

As the couple, chatted hither and thither, midnight gained hard upon them. In drowsiness, they witnessed a bizarre phenomenon. An ancient epigram on Ratana's wall, her grandpa's legacy, started flashing. It says, "FROM THE GREATEST OF NOTHING WILL COME THE GREATEST OF SOMETHING." Usually, the scroll was an inert artistic piece of ink calligraphy, but tonight it had transfigured into a "flashing neon sign."

The epigram's a form of proverb common in ancient Siam. These logic defying oxymorons thrive like common herbs in the land. They dominate the thinking of people, like the many shut-eyed, sitting stone Buddhas, domina-te the landscape. By mere preponderance. But thankfully, in Sawadee's work, there weren't too many oxymorons to taunt their intelligence. For they were simple fishing folks.

The calligraphy throbbed and pulsated, and made them question: "What can we do?"" Their consciousness was pulled in every direction, sucked, as if, into an altered state, a parallel dimension, of a surreal world. Wisdom was speaking and continued quickening their understanding because of responsiveness.

The first law of Wisdom then is: "Hearing you will hear." Without ears we can never hear. Wisdom speaks only to those who cares and responds. Those with ears but fail to hear can never receive. Just as those accustomed only to city blare are unable to discern the subtle nuances of the jungles. They mistake the outward clatter and fail to taste the marrow of true existence.

A vision was given to Sawadee and Ratana. When the "ecstasy" ended, they seemed to understand the vision verbally. It said: "Only likeness will a-ttract likeness in the higher realms." This they understood as the "Law of Kindredness." Some religious folks call this the voice of the human spirit. But call it what you like, Wisdom always operates on a higher plane. And the differences between them and cognitive functions are the difference between the heavens and the earth.

CHASING THE VISION

Sawadee and Ratana received the full vision of an albino female. And intuitively understood, great males do not mate indiscriminately. They choose their females. The next day, the couple started visiting the markets in Songkla, talking to every fighter fish-vendor. Frankly, their inquiries drew blank or puzzled looks.

Females are low priority items; albino females, even lower. Why ask for them? Their hands came away empty on the first day. They expanded their search to other villages. The first was Trang, a medium sized fishing village. Few people there were into fighter fishes.

Next, they checked Chiang Nai, and found a vendor with a batch of females: but none were albinos. They were now getting desperate, and despe-ration is a signature of the impending birth of a vision. Just as birth-pangs must precede and climax before actual birth itself.

In Praket, a bustling commercial village, they finally ran into a vendor with a special mission for promoting this neglected breed. Sawadee and Ra-tana were so happy, they could almost die.

They selected several females without physical defects (costing a month's wages), and dropping them into a bamboo container, they shut it tight.

To celebrate, they sat at the roadside to relish durians; a unique thorny fruit, about the size of a coconut. To eat, you've to get past its protective thorns. Chambered inside are a number of yellow-fleshed seeds, the texture of dough or softer, with a heavenly smell or a hellish stench, depending on what your nose tells you."

Many such fruit stalls commonly lined the roadside in ancient Siam to refresh travelers. There's also coconut-water to sip. It's a highly refreshing drink, since it's a natural tonic for our body. They bagged mangosteens and lychees for their relatives and friends too. And that's Siamese hospitality for you. Few cultures are as generous.

They saw life as bountiful and found reasons to share it with everyone. They weren't takers but partakers of the fullness of the earth. It took five hours, trekking back to Songkla, and it was midnight when they arrived, tired but in a good spirit. The albino females were kept in the storage room.

Next few days, they studied the females leisurely. The couple had, perhaps, only one chance to trap these warriors, who are great escape artistes. They settled, at last, on a very dainty female, with a very expressive personality. She'd a lively manner, swimming about, blowing bubbles, and entertaining herself. Too many females, clam up in fear, and wither in a corner, in captivity.

Sawadee started designing a trap. He'd never done this before. Previously, he caught all his fighters using the traditional method of basket-panning: a simpler affair requiring only skills of dexterity with straw-baskets.

They planted the trap in a very remote part of the northern jungles, at a confluence of four streams, where their flow slowed to a walking pace. One exit stream, carried the all the superabundant water away. The trap had three trap doors, which once entered into has no return. The female bait was interned in the innermost chamber after the last door.

Sawadee and Ratana were prepared to camp for an extended period to achieve their mission. Having sprung the trap, they went about collecting dry wood for campfire. They knew night would fall very quickly and very densely in the equator, unless the heavens switched on its billions of stars. So they worked fast and were well ahead of sundown.

When dusk approached, hundreds of pesky mosquitoes, hurried to partake of their free meal, flying together like a droning black cloud. Human blood, a rare commodity in the jungles, can easily be smelt, seen and felt by the horde. But the couple was prepared. They jerked out a container of crushed jungle herbs and leaves and rubbed it all over their body. The concoction had an evil medicinal stench. After this, the blood-suckers, fled in te-rror, to their amusement, like vampires from a crucifix.

Every self-respecting catcher must know how to prepare this folk liniment, ironically called, "Mosquito Perfume." It's difficult to find a stench e-qual to it in God's wide world.

Consumed judiciously, the couple's stock of provisions, should last. Sawadee, an experienced jungle trekker, had no problems setting up camp, with the safety measures in place. Ratana felt excited, felt being included in his life; felt safe, assured of success, knowing she was in expert company. And most of all because Sawadee was her man. And she'd implicit confidence in him.

Sometime ago, Sawadee had caught several whopping bull-frogs, and had them skinned and disemboweled. Frogs were considered a greater delicacy than chicken in this region. And Ratana could easily whip up a smacking meal. She was no mean cook. A dash of spices on the gravy, some strips of ginger and voila, perfection! For a vegetable accompaniment, they plucked water-convolvulus, growing in wild abandonment, from the nearby stream. They ate their dinner with gusto around the fireplace.

So they spent their first night, with heightened expectations, near a clump of hills, called Five Grey Elephants. So named, because they were fi-ve hilly humps which looked like grey elephants. It was also the location of an elephant graveyard. Younger elephants would pilgrimage to the clearing intermittently to perform memorials. Their acts of mourning expressed tenderly with their long proboscis, is a poignant model of filial piety. Local folks are afraid therefore to venture out there, not wanting to face a stampe-ding herd.

Superstitious and fearful, they also don't want to piss on the wrong tree, and unwittingly desecrate one, provoking vengeful spirits to bring retribution on them. Or even, just to run into a prowling tiger in the night and be eaten alive.

As the ashen embers started dying out in the blueness of the morning's coldness, the couple had a quick peek at the trap. But they had lucked out the first night. The female fighter however, was in good spirit. Breakfast was spare, consisting of hard-boiled eggs, eaten with soya-sauce, and washed down with plain tea.

After washing up, they propped against some trees, and passed time with simple chit-chat. They went over topics they had talked before, but ne-ver seemed to tire of. Couples have this wonderful facility for small talk, as you know.

When lunch hour arrived, Sawadee chopped bamboo stems and shoots for Ratana, who washed them in a clear running stream farther up. She filled the bamboo stems (cut crosswise near the sections) with soaked rice-grains and bamboo shoots. And capping them, burned the bamboo over a voracious fire. The rice and bamboo released a very wonderful smoky aroma, when burning over the fire. The couple ate lunch to their fill, served with pieces of chilled saltfish and gravy.

THE DISAPPOINTING SUCCESS

Mongkut meanwhile had arrived on the morning of the fifth day. He pa-ssed by the contraption. And approached to examine the device. Curiosity, was the one weak chink in his armor. Swimming outside, his eyes fell upon the female inside. It reminded him of his sibling sisters, and her personality intrigued her.

Here she was, swimming up and down, building a bubble-raft by herself, a deed rarely performed by a female. Mongkut was fascinated by this anomaly. He decided to check it out. Mongkut's guardedness evaporated from that moment of discovery, and all he cared for, was to join the enchanting fe-male. And to spend time with her.(Alas! it's hard indeed even for a great he-ro to overcome the allurement of beauty).

When the bell in the trap rang, and the ante-chambers closed, the couple jumped and raced to the trap. Through the reeds, they could see a strange display of synchronized dancing. But upon their focus clearing, their expectations dampened somewhat. Yes, the male intruder was indeed an albino. But...!(Sawadee uttered an oath here),he doesn't have the dimensions of a top fighter.

In the world of the fighter fish, girth is the first rough indicator of potential. It looked unlikely that the albino could take them to the top of the championship. Sawadee scooped them into a bamboo container listlessly, and closed the lid. Then, used another female for bait. In totality, they harvested five other gladiators of different colors and potential; ones which gave them greater hope than the little albino. But hope as they would, they weren't able to catch another better albino at Five Grey Elephants this time.

Their training equipment consisted of several glass containers and ancient mirrors, which are metal plates, polished to the point of reflectivity. With these, they conducted training without risking injuries to the specimens in real fights; and to gauge with precision the potential of each candidate.

THE INTERVENTION OF FATE

After careful testing, they found two that were above the rest in prow ess. One was Steel Black and the other Orange.

They didn't trouble themselves to test the little albino, having decided, that it was pointless.

But they did embark on the ambitious plan of building up his bulk: feeding him with a high protein diet of first grade meat and live diet. Through rapid feeding, they hope his girth would thicken in time. Say, for the great international "rumble championship" at Rangoon, the capitol of Burma, next year. His chances of winning would then increase double fold.

Their dismissive plans for Mongkut would have been carried out, except for the intervention of fate again, even if it came only in the form of a playful house cat, Puteh. Puteh, a cute Siamese tabby, with blue eyes and brown tipped ears, was "sparring" excitedly with a toy ball, claws all drawn, when she accidentally knocked away, during a tumble, the separator, shielding Mongkut from his Orange neighbor. Immediately, both in their own glass containers, started engaging. The Orange neighbor especially, all in a frenzy, going for the kill. Body thrashing, and eyes glaring, head down, wanting to gore Mongkut to death. His gill-flaps, protruding sideways from the head, following Mongkut's every move. His ferocity only held back by his own glass container which "pinged" with each stinging bite.

This extravagant display of aggression, was very impressive, but normal. What wasn't normal was Mongkut's quiescence. He was mostly nonchalant. When Sawadee, passed by, with a bucket of water, he stopped dead in his tracks, and squatted down to watch, calling out to Ratana simultaneously. The passive behavior of Mongkut was of a great concern to them. His conduct, was either that of a weakling or an unflappable hero.

But they couldn't decide which. To say he was craven, didn't add up altogether. Spooked fighters would lose all glow and color, and be cowering in a corner. Mongkut displayed no such tell-tale symptoms. But yet, he exhibited none of the spleen worthy of a great champion. After all, flamboyance was essential for a great show. The entertainment factor being a desired crowd puller.

They called in Precha, a more experienced elder in the industry, to compare notes. Precha had 25 years of experience in the circuit under his belt. When he came, he didn't speak at all. For a full 30 minutes, he merely chewed on his betel nut and leaves, spiked with white lime. And spitting it out whenever his facial pouches became filled with a reddened mash and salivary juices.

When he had finished observing, he offered his hands and shook Sawadee's, slapping him on his back. All, he said, was "You lucky devil!" and left smiling, like a monkey who had furtively eaten a great mango. The couple looked at each other nonplussed. After all, Precha had been known for wry humor at times, and was not beneath playing a trick or two. Can he be trusted?

Ratana finally asked, "Well?" as if resuming a previous conversation, "Why don't we just call the little albino, 'Mongkut' then? Come what may. After all he could be our "crowning" achievement. (Mongkut means "Crown"). And don't forget, we caught him because of a vision." Sawadee, not too articulate a fellow, scratched his head, and acquiesced, by nodding.

TOURNAMENT PREPARATIONS

It was a good name anyway. Short. Symbolic. Grand. Days passed quickly. And time put on wings. Sawadee had all his tournament candidates, including Mongkut, periodically taken back to Five Grey Elephants. There he was re-submerged into the streams. The escape-proof net, allowed Mongkut plenty of room to exercise and move around. This simulated natural conditions as closely as possibly can for peak conditioning. He was also given his female companion. This way, they helped him and the others reach and maintain their best form.

Such days were the happiest for Mongkut in captivity. In his net, he could swim against the currents and to continue building up strength, stamina and form. He could even feed on premium food, swimming past. Natu-re invigorated him in every way.

THE TOURNAMENT AT AYUDIA

A carnival atmosphere filled every street and corner of the ancient capital of Ayudia, on the first day of competition. Pretty decorations fluttered briskly in the breeze. Intriguing booths displayed their novelty wears and services, and traditional performances for different entertainments were rendered. Siamese songs, to the accompaniment of ancient instruments and dancing girls, with long curvy fingernails, and measured feet stomping, added to the atmosphere of the day.

The crowd was massing up early in the arena with excited anticipations. The fighting pit, encircled by a huge seating stadium, had a mounted jumbo sized combat glass tank in the center, strangely, looking very much like a transparent bull elephant, filled with water. My, the Siamese people do love their elephants, don't they? The combat glass arena, created specially by a great master artisan, magnified the participants somewhat once inside, making viewing better.

The seating for the VIPS were regally marked out: gold-plated chairs for the royal guests of honor and lesser ones for the ruling nobility, high military ranks, and judges of great distinctions.

Participating owners, seated together, had access to stools in the inner ring itself, to personally handle their fighters. Several days were declared public holidays in all of ancient Siam. Many bets were placed up to the last minute. Not only for the winners: bets were also placed for losers. There was nothing that wouldn't tickle their fancy.

The rules were direct and simple. You have to field three fighters in the first round against three fighters of a competing owner, local or international. You could only progress into the next round if you'd at least one winner in each round. The last fish standing, would be declared the grand champion of the international championship at Ayudia, the most prestigious in the whole region.

For each individual round, winners and losers would be decided on the following grounds:

1. The combatant ran or yielded.
2. The combatant stopped or refused to engage.
3. The combatant suffered injuries, which prevented continue once.
4. The owner threw in the towel.
5. The combatant was killed.
6. A combatant won by overwhelming superior skills

These few ground-rules were wide enough to help judges regulate the tournament and award decisions. And the chief judge would flag results in the direction of the owners. A red flag for victory; a white one for defeat; and a black flag for death or incapacitating injuries; and a golden flag for superlative victory.

Sawadee and Ratana, weren't expected to reach the finals. Just squeezing into the second round would be a considerable achievement for greenhorns. In a way, this was less pressuring. They had short-listed five good fighters (from which to choose): which they felt would have a slim chance in progressing.

Sawadee and Ratana named their stable, the "House of SawaRata". They were scheduled last. And everyone considered them fodder for others: small fries which shouldn't be in a big fish competition. Such impressions were conveyed by the dismissive looks of the other owners.

All through the morning and afternoon, the contests see-sawed back and forth.

Sometimes, there were serious commotions, and owners also brawled alongside their fishes. Other times, a very contemplative atmosphere prevailed, as a serious sport should.

At last, time for the House of SawaRata to show what they're capable of, arrived. The audience had become fidgety, and wasn't expecting very much. The day had been long and proceedings very tiring; some were already making their way to the exit points.

The first fighter SawaRata fielded was "Kla"(meaning "Brave"). He was the Orange fighter mentioned earlier. After the required warm up was done, they were both poured into the combat arena at the same time.

Immediately, Kla went in for the body kill. He was a body-attacker. And he wasted no time tearing away at fins, knowing it was harmless and energy-sapping. The other contender was a wilier fighter, constantly using his back to push Kla back. And simultaneously, shielding his own vital points and blocking Kla's view. So, Kla was basically denied the view, positioning, space, and distance to mount any attacks. His opponent's strategy was rather like that of a clinging boxer using a "Rope a Dope" trick.

In the end, Kla was exhausted trying to get away, to get space, to get going for an attack. But try as he would, the other contender wouldn't allow Kla to get into his usual rhythm of fighting. After that it went badly for Kla: and all his bravery couldn't compensate for the loss in strategy.

This was a bad start for SawaRata. Nothing could be more discouraging for the young couple. Sawadee's vision of happiness dimmed considerably after this. But they still clung to hope, and prayed fortune would smile on them next. People on the benches, shook their heads, as if saying to them, "We knew." "We told you so."

For the next match, they fielded their best fighter, in an attempt to turn fortune around. Their next fighter "KriangSak" or "Powerful," steel black in color, was a more complete fighter, and knew how to pace himself. His blows were very strong and accurate, as his name suggested. Although both were pretty even in targeting, Kriangsak's hits were stronger and wore the opposition down. To the unspeakable joy of his owners, who both leapt up, and hugged each other profusely, the decision was given to Kriangsak by the chief judge. It was unanimous. Now it was Sawadee and Ratana's turn to shake their heads at the benches: as if saying, "We knew. We told you so."

Now that their passage was booked, it didn't matter, if they lost their last match. "So why not try, Mongkut?". Ratana had a feminine intuition about this kind of thing. And since masculine logic could only plod heavily, whereas feminine intuition had wings, Sawadee decided to meekly follow Ratana's cue. So they brought out the White Warrior. The crowd gasped loudly at the unveiling of this rarity for the contest. Those leaving hurried back to their seats, on the strength of that gasp.

This was the first White Warrior that had been seen in an Ayudia competition for a long, long time. But after sizing him up more clearly, the spectators were mutedly disappointed at Mongkut's lack of stature. There were a lot of hushed murmuring, significant glances and even cynical smiles.

Those who returned regretted they did. And once again was tempted to get up. During the pre-warming up session; again Mongkut didn't impress with his lack of zeal. People being people, were apt to judge externally. Most weren't hopeful about this puny White Warrior. So the bets were decidedly one sided in favor of the opponent.

Meanwhile, the phlegmatic Mongkut, was studying his opponent, sizing him up. He was analyzing him for strengths and weaknesses, favorite moves, blind spots, sequencing of moves, strategies and tactics. Anything that would help. And all the aggressive displays by his opponent, were so helpfully revealing to Mongkut.

Mongkut could see that, this was no mean combatant. He was certainly bigger and more aggressive.

When Mongkut was ready, he swam around the bottle several times, blowing bubbles, as if gargling and clearing his air passage. Then he did a little signature jig, remotely like a Muay Thai ritual.

Mongkut was then jointly poured into the central combat tank. Immediately, upon surfacing for air, the opponent went for the kill, gill flaps all aflare like a mini tyrannosaurus. He rushed headlong in great speed at Mongkut. Mongkut, with eyes closed and treading water, could feel the ferocious vibrations hurtling towards him, and could sense how far or near the attack was. At the very last second, he just sidestepped, and launched a reverse attack, of such venom and speed, no one actually saw what happened.

It was just a flash! The blinking of an eye. In that nanno second, Monkut, had launched a counterattack of his own, as his opponent sailed past him. The other contender was dispatched all the way to the end of the container, and stayed there motionless before tipping one side; then a significant blotch appeared in the water, enlarging like an ink-drop.

After much scrutiny, a frowning chief judge, dramatically pointed the red and golden flag at the House of SawaRata and the black and white at the opposite camp. For this win, Mongkut was awarded special prize money for the quickest knockout or kill.

At first, silence fell over the whole arena like they seen a ghost. People tried to make sense of what had happened. "What? Why? How?" They were thrown into confusion. People would have liked a replay or to see the kill in slow motion. Then pandemonium broke out, and things were thrown into the air, as if the whole city of Ayudia had come alive and exploded into a violent riot. But they were merely welcoming, the emergence of a new phenomenon in aquatic combat. Mongkut! Mongkut! Nak Su Kao! Nak Su Kao! They shouted in adulation repeatedly. Waves after waves of adoration swept around the stadium.

Sawadee and Ratana, still glued to their seats, just sat in utter silence, unable and afraid to comprehend the whole incident. "Are we dreaming? "Did we see what we see?" Precha, then walked to them, stretched out his hand again, and smiled with that monkey like expression. He was a man of few words. None in fact this time. It was too important an occasion to blather. He just shook his head, as if saying, "I knew. I told you so."Then he encouraged the couple to move. So they scooped up their champion preciously, and sto-red him away before, a great crowd congested around and gawked.

That first night of the contest, nobody could stop talking about Mongkut. Nobody even wanted to sleep. For with just one blow, the diminutive warrior had become an instant sensation, a celebrity in the great city of Ayudia. In the process, he also lifted up his owners from obscurity to fame, from poverty to potential wealth.

Sawadee's visions now truly burned brighter. And his excitement, like a moth, was fluttering around a flaming torch, called Mongkut. That night, s-prawled upon his and her beds, with the lamps still burning, the couple kept replaying the events of the day.

But were still too afraid to believe, lest it should melt away like morning dreams or mist. They were thus preoccupied, until exhaustion took over, and sleep swept over them. And when they opened eyes next, the sky was already bright but the sun, not yet a burning fireball.

The sleep, though short, was surprisingly refreshing. They rushed to the special container, where they now kept Mongkut. The little chap was entertaining himself and was in a positive mood.

Ratana quickly prepared a meal of chopped animal heart for Mongkut, which he relished. He seemed to be self-aware as a fish, and showed recognition of his owners, and even attempted to communicate, by swimming back and forth excitedly.

Sawadee and Ratana were wonderstruck at this little critter. But they didn't share with anyone about Mongkut's behavior, lest it generated crowd curiosity and superstition, which would result in fan pressure.

As they neared the tournament ground, on the second day of competition, Sawadee and Ratana, had hard decisions to make. They could either field both the same fighters or rested one of them. To go on to the final rounds, all they had to do was to get one win in. "What should they do?" Four stables had qualified for this round, and they were all established stables with glowing reputations, except for the House of SawaRata.

The house to watch out for, in particular, was the "House of Win," the champion stable from Burma. They had two grand-champions before and their training methods and care, guarded secrets, passed down from one generation to another. In the first round, all of their three fighters had won their bouts. Many betted on Win, but some bets now have shifted to SawaRata tentatively. Mongkut was like a welterweight fighting in the ranks of the super heavy-weights. The history of aquatic combat had never wintessed such a thing.

The odds were massively stacked against him. But he was a new wonder on stage, and many wanted to know how far he could go. Many wished he would go all the way, but others still doubted, and considered the result of the first day, a freak accident. They weren't even far from thinking Mongkut himself, a freak, and asking the results to be declared null and void.

Upon arrival and checking the "jousting" schedule, it wasn't comforting to find themselves pitted against the House of Win. A heavy sense of having hit the end of the road sat on their hearts. In the end, SawaRata decided to use the same fighters. Kriangsak was first, matched against Kovit the "Expert." Win's candidate. Both had already fought one round and were slightly ragged but none the worse physically. As they entered the common tank, there was a lot of preliminary razzle-dazzle by both parties, to impress or psych the other. The crowd liked it. Wowing with each swerve.

But as the match progressed it became increasingly desperate and the crowd increasingly silent. Obviously, both were evenly matched in every department. The blow by one was returned in kind by the other. The swerve by one was countered by the same. Tail flicks executed by one were countered with tail flicks by the other.

In the end, a draw had to be declared, because a long drawn-out stalemate was unavoidable and bad for the show. This was considered half a point win, and if the next bout was another draw, this could make a full point, and the entry of one fighter of the owner's choice to the next round.

Now SawaRata had only one fighter left and only half a point to their credit. Everything now rested on the undersized "Mongkut". Their dreams , hung in the balance, upon the little fella's shoulders, and they could all go up in smoke in no time. All Mongkut needed to do was to hold on to a draw. That's the best the couple could hope for. Win on the other hand, had two more good fighters, ensuring passage into the next round.

Win now fielded his best fighter next, in order to force the issue. Nothing less than a famous win would do. They put up RomRan: the "Warrior." A humongous fellow, who never lost any fights before. He had an impeccable record. So it would be a David and Goliath kind of a fight. And everybody felt fearful for "David." The conclusion to them was a foregone one.

After observing RomRan in the warming up bottles, Mongkut determined to have a contest of strength with his bigger opponent. He wanted to win where the adversary was strongest. But his true weapon was the element of surprise.

As they entered the common tank, and before RomRan could surface for air, quick as bullet, Mongkut was at his side, and had succeeded in chomping on the former's gill-flap. Then he started to jerk, ramming RmRan down.

People could visibly see the incredible strength of the twirp. With each jerk, he visibly jarred the giant. The startled RomRan, infuriated to no small measure, thrashed about, like someone trying to shake a terrier loose from his leg.

Mongkut just hung on limply, and allowed RomRan to exhaust himself. And when he sensed, RomRan weakening, he pressed his advantage home, yanking the hapless RomRan all the way to the bottom and pinning him there.

As the giant ran out of oxygen, his color faded, and he started to show the death-color. Win quickly threw the white towel down. And at the same time, Mongkut, also released his ghastly looking opponent, who floated to the surface and slumped motionless. This time, the whole arena witnessed the event clearly. This was no fluke.

A riot broke out again. The spectators marveled at the skill, intelligence and courage of the little critter. They adored Mongkut. It confirmed in their hearts, that they were in the presence of a supreme albino fighter fish. One who fought not with blind aggression but with intelligence and skill wedded to courage.

The whole city was buzzing to no end with the latest exploits of the White Warrior. Runners were sent throughout Siam with news of this new Nak Su Kao. The ancient capital was electrified. A strong sense of national pride swept over the whole country.

An interval of two days rest, allowed Sawadee and Ratana time off. They toured the spectacular city of Ayudia; intimately holding hands and tripping along the magnificent hanging gardens and parks, visiting the marvelous trade bazaars, or visiting fabulous food stalls. People recognized, and waved to them as celebrities. The magnificent bungalow which, Sawadee often dreamt of, had a few more rooms and better furnishings added to it by now. And he was almost ready to move in.

As the final two contenders squared out in the warm-up containers on the final day, Mongkut was now facing a breed he had never encountered before: a great champion from Cambodia: a short finned species that had thicker girths, shorter body length; and Were quicker in speed and responses, and generally, hardier fighters.

Their fins were shorter and rounded, and did not get in the way of their vision or movements. And they were more streamlined, attacking in faster spurts, hitting more directly, in a straight line, and from shorter distances. A parallel from the world of Chinese martial arts, would be to say that he was like a Wing Chun master. Exponents, in the art of close-fighting. A punch administered by a Wing Chun master, from the distance of a finger length, would send a boxer flying and crashing.

As Siamese rituals were played out with a lot of musical fanfare and invocation of spirits, reminiscent of our modern day Muay Thai, only much grander, Mongkut put on his final preparations for the match.

He closed his eyes, and slipped into an oneness of consciousness: like a warrior putting on his invincible armor. Only in this case, it was invisible, and he took on the flexible qualities of water, wind or cloud. It was a state of being where, his conscious mind was kept in abeyance, or locked out, and his responses animated by pure instincts or subconscious flow.

There were no pre-thinking or ritualized steps, only reflexes. Ritualized steps would be too slow and limited for such an occasion. The development he displayed here was the highest possible attainable for any exponent.

And Mongkut had attained it from the many lonely nights of vigil, self-examinations, and practice. Nights, with no one there. His only companions; pain and loneliness. Every move was light, easy, masterful, and ahead of time.

He had arrived at a stage of "prescience", or knowingness, before something happens; as if he had tapped into his opponent's thinking, and hearing him think aloud. It was as if Pich the "Diamond" fighter, his opponent, was a completely open book for Mongkut to know. So on that day, whatever Pich threw at him, Mongkut parried easily.

Every disguised feint was recognized for what it was, and before Pich arrived at the intended spot, he was met, and every tactic was nullified as effortlessly as wind. Whichever path, Pich took, Mongkut knew and was there ahead of him.

It was exactly like a Latin dance, a samba or a tango, where the partner just knew what the lead dancer was going to do ahead of time: swerving, bending, pirouetting, hand gesturing, forward, sideward, backward.

Mongkut's responses were like an image on the mirror following those of the owner's. Rather, it was Pich, who was the image following Mongkut. In the end, fear seized Pich's heart, with a force so paralyzing, that it drained him of all will to continue.

Mongkut had won. And won with the widest margin, and on the highest plane possible. And in the most amazing manner. That's, to win without striking even a blow, as only the greatest warriors could.

The audience there, that day, rubbed their eyes in astonishment. People didn't even know how to begin to describe it. Such stories can't be reported without feeling oneself far-fetched or stupid. Such things aren't possible in a normal world.

Dogmatic folks would never accept it. "No way!" Detractors and skeptics will deny it. But there were thousands of other spectators who witnessed it. The most qualified international judges were there, the dignitaries of the nations were there. There was only one legitimate decision   possible. And it was the one given to Mongkut. Especially, after Pich pitched to one side in fearful confusion and refused to continue.

The award ceremony was a grand finish with cultural presentations and dances. Then the Queen, representing his Majesty the King, was invited to present the prizes. In their proper standing: RomRan the "Giant" was third, Pich, the short finned "Diamond" fighter, second, and the Grand Champion of champions of the premier international tournament, Mongkut, the Great White Warrior. Mongkut, the Crown.

The purse was a very princely, giddy, sum, with an additional ten percent from all winning bets. SawaRata was set for life. And for bringing honor to Siam, an honorary title was conferred upon them.

Owners of all grand champions, had to make a short speech as part of the prize-giving ceremony. When ushered on stage, Sawadee and Ratana were tongue-tied and wobbly. They had never made a public speech before, let alone address such an august body.

They talked incoherently about wisdom. But the refined city –folks, the detractors, thought it rather mystical and overly embroidered. A little coloring, they can accept. But this...? "Peasants!" "What mystical hogwash!" So they refused to hear.

Nevertheless, they had no choice but put on a face, and to congratulate the couple. To argue otherwise, would mark them out as detractors and trouble-makers. And no amount of argument could prevail against something, witnessed and endorsed by the Queen, hog-wash not withstanding!

© 2011-5-16

Natalie Grigson
Austin, TX, USA

Natalie Grigson grew up in Austin, Texas, where she recently obtained a Bachelor's degree in Creative Writing. She is currently working as the Director of Marketing and PR for a local company; frantically planning a move across the country, made just a bit complicated by a very large and slightly restless dog; and of course, trying to solve that whole problem of world peace. In her free time, though, she enjoys reading, writing, and spending time outdoors with aforementioned large dog.

Like a Dot on a Page
By Natalie Grigson

She stared at the black and white picture pretending to be thinking very hard about its true meaning. Really, though, she was wondering about the doctor whose pink fingertips she could see curled around the edges of the picture. She moved her eyes onto his face for just a moment, then back onto the black and white card. Dr. Sable had thick brown hair, a short neatly trimmed beard, and red cheeks like he had just walked in from the cold. He reminded her of a lumberjack in looks but he treated her like she imagined a lawyer might treat a client. When she came in he shook her hand like an adult. She thought he pretended just like she did, but he was pretending to respect her. When he spoke to her though, she was once again a naïve 11 year old in his office. The inconsistencies of his actions made her nervous, like he was an unpredictable animal.

"I think in this one, that man in the corner there? I think he is trying to escape from the woman in the middle. That's why that window is opened, see?"

"I see," the doctor replied as his pen danced across the page. "Fear of abandonment... Trust issues with male authority figures... Possible history of verbal abuse...Questionable case of Attention Deficit Disorder," he muttered just loud enough for her to hear.

She sat in the chair watching the man utter and scribble but when he looked up, she acted as though she didn't hear him.

Finally, as she could invent no more meanings for the pictures of people scattered over the desk, Dr. Sable rose from his leather armchair and filed the pictures away.

"A very good session today, Ms. Jessica. Now run and get your mom from the waiting area and she and I are going to have a little talk," he smiled broadly.

"Okay," the girl replied as she slung her backpack over one shoulder. She shuffled into the waiting room counting her steps and taking a small pleasure in how her tennis shoes dragged on the carpet.

She watched her mother for a moment before saying anything. Her mother was named Jan and the very idea that anyone called her anything other than "mom," made Jessica laugh. Her mother had long brown hair which was pulled back into a ponytail today and the same blue eyes as Jessica. She was reading *Elle* magazine and chewing absentmindedly on the tip of her in-dex finger.

"Jan, Dr. Sable will see you now," Jessica said in her best nurse's voice. She laughed as her mother walked by and ruffled her hair. A large chunk of it was missing by her temple.

"Well thank you, miss." Her mother's eyes darted on to the small bald patch and then back to Jessica's face. She smiled but she still looked worried.

Jessica sat in Doctor Sable's waiting room for fifteen minutes before her mother returned from his office. Through the door she could hear muffled voices but no distinct words, which made her think of the scientist from the Muppets. Every now and then her mother's indistinct voice would raise, which was always followed by Dr. Sable's low hum of a response. As she listened to the rise and fall of sound behind the door, she imagined a line graph moving up and down, up and down, like mountains. Soon the image faded into nothing and Jessica's mind was blank.

When she opened her eyes again she felt very light, lighter than air, and found herself standing in her kitchen. Her step father, Kevin was sitting at the counter before her, completely unaware of her sudden appearance. She walked over to where he sat and pulled up a chair. Still, he took no notice. Kevin stood up and walked to the refrigerator, and as he opened the door a carton of milk fell off the shelf and burst onto the floor.

"Shit," he said. Jessica clapped her hand over her mouth and laughed in delight at having caught him cursing. Then she felt a pressure on her shoulder and the kitchen slowly dissolved. She felt solid in her body once again.

"Jess, let's go home." Her mother was squeezing her shoulder, worry etched into the very wrinkles of her face. "Were you asleep?"

"No, I was just dreaming. Can we go by the store on the way home, Mom? We just ran out of milk."

Her mother opened the door and Jessica walked through, under her outstretched arm.

Her mother opened her mouth, perhaps to ask how she knew; perhaps to explain that hadn't really happened and that she was confusing daydreams with real life, but instead climbed into the silver 4 Runner and drove to the store for the milk.

"Mom what did you and Dr. Sable talk about today? I could hear you talking really loud."

"You couldn't hear what we were saying though, right?" She looked even more worried.

"No I couldn't. You sounded like Muppets."

"We were just talking about your dazes, Jess, and why you might have them. He thinks you haven't dealt with... Well, he thinks you may have some bad memories in your head about your dad. Anyway, it's not normal to be able to see things like you do, and Dr. Sable is just trying to figure out what to do."

"Okay," she said as the pulled into the driveway. She wasn't sure what her mother meant but she didn't want to press the issue. Her mother got worried so easily lately.

"Buddy! Buddy! Buddy! Buddilus Floppidus!" the small eleven year-old squealed as she burst through the front door, a blur of brown hair and bright clothing. She flung her backpack from her arms and bent down to embrace a large and rather fat brown and white floppy eared rabbit. As she walked into the kitchen with the rabbit in her arms, she wavered slightly under his weight and arched her back forward like she was pregnant. Her step father, Kevin, sat at the table with a mug of coffee and several legal pads full of small, indistinct writing scattered before him.

"Hey kiddo. How was the big first day of fifth grade?"

"It was gooood." Jessica was crouched before the refrigerator getting out Buddy's dinner: carrots, cucumbers, and plain oats. Her shoes stuck to the tile where the milk had spilled.

"Hey, Jan," he said as Jessica's mother walked into the room. Her cheeks were flushed and in the bright light of the kitchen Jess thought the lines around her mouth looked like rivers on a map.

"Hey, Kev. I got some more milk for the morning," she bent down and kissed him lightly on the mouth, and Jessica rolled her eyes at Buddy. "Jess thought we might be out..." They looked at each other with the same expression Dr. Sable sometimes wore when she told him about her dazes. They changed the subject to adult matters that Jessica found dull so she went upstairs to her bedroom and put out the bowl for Buddy's dinner.

Jessica was very different from most girls her age. When she was seven her father, David Lovette was killed in a car accident and since then she'd been seeing a psychotherapist once a week to treat her "dazes." The general opinion of her doctors over the years was that she *used daydreaming as an escape from reality* and *would continue doing so until she dealt with the death of her father.* She sat on the floor of her room wondering about this, and as each italicized word scrolled through her mind, she became more and more confused. She didn't know how to *deal* with her father's death; she didn't even know what that meant. She liked thinking about her dad. She could still re-member his laugh and the way his nose wrinkled when he smiled, but she was starting to lose the sound of his voice and she could barely remember the way he walked or moved. She didn't want to let go and if that is what she had to do to "deal with it," she simply wouldn't. She closed her eyes and tried hard to imagine her father's face as she knew him – round, clean shaven, always smiling. She pushed back the image of her first daze. It happened right before her father died and every time she focused on his face too long, it crept back into her mind. Blood on the pavement. Glassy eyes. She closed her eyes hard and shook her head. She'd never told anyone about her first daze and as she shook the image away, she tried to pretend that it wasn't her fault.

She watched the rabbit's body move up and down as he dug his face into the food bowl. He was a gift for her ninth birthday. His full name was Buddilus Floppidus, but over the years had been shortened to Buddy in most cases. When he was done eating, Jess laid back onto the soft carpet and he climbed onto her chest and fell asleep. Feeling safe, she closed her eyes and focused hard on the red nothingness of the insides of her eyelids. She shifted her blind eyes out of focus and let her thoughts drift away. Then she opened her eyes, eager to see where her mind had taken her tonight.

She found herself in a very crowded room with high ceilings. Buddy was still pressed close into her chest, but she was now standing and cradling him like a baby. Once again her whole body felt light as air and if she couldn't look down and see herself, she might not have noticed that she had any form at all. She looked around the large space, her ears filled with the murmur of hundreds of people speaking at once and somewhere far away, a low thunderous rumble. She had been here before with her dad. It was Grand Central Station in New York. When she had visited this place before it was almost dusk on Christmas Eve, and there were no lines and very few people standing around.

She and her parents had been in New York to spend Christmas with her Uncle Rick and his family. The whole week it had been snowing and by Christmas Eve the city looked like it was covered in thick white frosting.

"You wanna go see the trains?" Her dad asked.

"No John. It is freezing out there. None of the trains will be running in this weather." Her mother crossed her arms in front of her chest and looked down at her husband, sitting on the couch.

He looked at his daughter pleadingly.

"Yeah I want to go!" She would take his side no matter what. She didn't really care about the trains.

"Well, the girl wants to go, Jan. We're just going to have a look. She's never seen a real train."

Her mother looked defeated as her father set a drink down on the coffee table, and got up to get his coat. Jess watched the beads of water form a glistening ring on the table like the halo of an angel before she got up, not daring to look back at her mother.

"You're half an hour late," someone nearby said, jerking Jessica back into the present. A man with a thick New York accent was talking to her. She'd never seen this man before and as she opened her mouth to respond, she realized he was talking to someone beside her.

"I know. Ma just dropped me outside. She said she's not coming. She said she's not going to be home when we get back... She said she's leaving."

The man looked away, pressing his fingers together in front of his mouth like he was praying. He blinked hard and shook his head.

"Alright, kiddo. Well, c'mon. We don't need ma to have a good time in Boston do we?"

They walked toward the stairs leading below where Jess remembered the trains boarded. She looked around the emptying terminal and couldn't see any other reason she was there, so she followed them onto the train to Boston.

At this point Jess was sure that the people around her could not see her or Buddy, which was always the case in a daze, unless it was about her own life. So she sat down next to the man. Her empty mind was soon swarming with thoughts, but they were not her own. They were the man's. She saw what he saw and felt what he felt, though she was still vaguely aware of her own presence. It was as though she were reading a book written by the man Paul, all about his life with his son, Nick. She was completely in his mind, but was still aware, however distantly, that she was also there. He was forty two and his son was thirteen. She didn't know if she should be witnessing this; she felt slightly nosey, but she let their thoughts wash over her.

Paul watched his son over the top of a newspaper. He wanted to say something about Linda leaving; tell him that they were better off; that everything would work itself out soon, but he'd never lied to his son before, so he focused again on the newspaper. He remembered when Nick would sit on his knee and let him wrap his arms around him. *Can't get away, kiddo. I'm not gonna let you go 'til you turn 25, and if you wanna go to college or anything, you're just gonna have to bring me with you.* And Nick laughed and pretended to hate the idea, not knowing anything about things like college. Linda would come up and wrap her arms around them both, kissing Paul on the cheek and they would laugh. They laughed so much then.

And now she was leaving them for some asshole coworker; he was sure of it. He felt a sudden urge to pull his son onto his lap and wrap his arms around him, and held out a hand for a moment over his son's, but embarrassed by the gesture, he bent over instead to pick up a book.

Jess stroked Buddy's ears, flattening them onto his back, white on brown, as she her own thoughts slowly returned. She wondered if Paul would curse out loud in front of his son. She remembered how earlier that day Kevin had sworn and had felt a guilty pleasure at having heard it. It was very odd remembering another daze while she sat next to Paul and Nick, in a completely separate one. Like an infinite mirror. She realized then that she was all alone; most of her memories were not hers at all; they were the thoughts of strangers or moments that she hadn't really been a part of. She began to feel very sorry for herself, sitting on the train visible to others only as air, when a loud noise like fireworks shook her into the present. The compartment a-round her shook, bags fell from the overhead bins, and a collective gasp of shock resounded in the car. A brief image of a cartoon bomb flashed through her mind before the next explosion. This was louder and closer; the compartment filled with smoke and was dark. The bombs detonated at once, but she heard each explosion individually, each closer than the one before, like a long string of firecrackers.

She tried to focus all of her energy on her bedroom at home — the pink walls, the soft carpet, Buddy sleeping on her chest. She kept telling herself this was a daze, it wasn't real; but it suddenly felt more real than anything she knew before. She wanted out but her mind became fuzzy and once again she was reliving a memory that was not her own.

It was the Fourth of July. Paul and Nick were laughing, chasing each other with sparklers. Running down a long hill that seemed to stretch forever. Down down down…

She was on the floor of the car, it was dark but she saw bursts of light from beneath her eyelids. Her body became suddenly heavy and ached as though she'd fallen a great distance. Glass in her hands. Something sticky covered her hair. She felt the floor shudder for the final time before she heard a noise like a gunshot close to her face. Her mind was blank and then she was floating lightly in Paul's thoughts. She felt like her own presence had merely moved across the broken car and settled into Paul's head, showing her his last jumbled memories.

"That was the biggest firework I've ever seen, Dad!" Paul held Nick tight against his chest, their hearts beating rapidly together in silent song, as reds, yellows, and blues rained from the sky. Warm happiness spread over him and he smiled up at the sky.

Then a flash of white and Paul and Nick were no more, the memories of their lives like the floating embers of a firework. Jessica was once again aware of her body, her deep breath, her pounding heart, a tingling in her hands and feet. She laid on the floor of her bedroom, eyes closed and feeling the life course through her veins, knowing that the people on the train were now no more than dust flying through space. Lifeless.

She held her hand over her heart, scared that at any moment she might realize she should have blown up with the train that it was not just a daze, and then her heart would stop. When it did not, she opened her eyes and took in the pink bedroom. It was okay. She was safe. As she pushed herself up to sit her skin felt raw against the carpet and she had to choke back the burning acid rising in her throat. She walked around the room, stepping lightly heel to toe, heel to toe. An image of Paul and Nick holding hands silently before they were ripped apart. Paul and Nick on the fourth of July. Gone. She forced herself back into the present, once again taking in the details of her room. Bed. Desk. Clock. 9:30 p.m.

Her heart slowly stopped pumping so hard and she started to calm down, focusing on the small nick-knacks around her room. A picture of her mother and Kevin, a small white radio on her dresser, and next to it, a picture of her father, still young, still alive, always smiling.

Then she saw it, an image of her father's body sprawled out over the pa-vement. His legs were bent beneath him like a broken puppet, and halo of blood spread beneath his head. His eyes were white and staring like fish eggs.

Jess shook her head violently; the image retreated back into her memory like a cornered predator. The shaking made her dizzy and a moment later she ran into the bathroom and heaved over and over into the toilet.

The image of her dead father crept up on Jess when she slept and sometimes after a daze when her mind was already weak. She hovered by the toilet remembering the first time she had seen this image, one week before his death. She didn't tell anyone because she thought it had been a strange daydream, an image inspired by a horror movie. The thought of her father ever leaving her was unimaginable then.

She laid down on the cold tile floor, warm tears dripping down her cheeks into her hair, hating herself for keeping quiet. Hating herself for thinking these thoughts. Whether or not she caused the events or just saw them, if she kept quiet she as good as killed them. She wondered now if the train had already exploded, if Nick and Paul were already dead.

She crept downstairs determined to tell her mother about the train. She was feeling slightly more hopeful now that she had made up her mind to tell someone, though she still didn't know if it had already happened. She kept telling herself that it could be stopped, if she just told someone it could be stopped. Really, though, she didn't know. She pushed this out of her mind and focused on her new mission.

Jess found her mother curled up on the worn leather couch in the living room. She was half covered by a blanket and a book was opened across her side, tucked under her arm; Buddy was asleep at her feet. Jess lowered herself onto the rug next to her mother listening to the sound of her breathing. She thought of Paul and Nick, living breathing, their hearts beating in unison while fireworks blossomed over head. She thought of her father and how he once held her hand to his heart and told her it was hers. In her mind she reached up and nudged her mother awake and told her about the train. In her mind they had all been saved. In her mind. But Jess fell asleep.

She woke to an unfamiliar voice and the first intrusive beams of the sunrise.

"Tom, the latest reports show the death toll at over 300. There are no confirmed details on the nature of this attack, but insiders are calling it an act of terrorism, as devastating as the attacks of nine eleven, just over five years a-go. No confirmation on whether the attacks are related, Tom…"

Jess blinked hard and held her eyes closed, willing the woman's voice to be part of a dream. She opened her eyes and saw her mother and Kevin on the couch beside her; her mother's legs folded into her chest, one hand laid on the couch holding Kevin's tightly, the other traced absently around her lips like she wanted a cigarette. For a moment she remembered telling her mother all about the train and that somehow they had stopped the explosion; saved the passengers. Her head was fuzzy with memories, which ones were her own, and which had truly happened, she could no longer tell. She was scared.

"Mom did I wake you last night?"

"What? No, honey. Be quiet."

Jess tried to listen to the reporter but was utterly confused that something she remembered so clearly didn't happen. The reporter continued to speak and Jess listened to her, nervously pulling out long strands of hair near her temple. She wondered if this was happening, if it was just a memory, or if she was yet again watching this life as an observer. She couldn't place it, though, and listened to the news, pulling, pulling out her hair.

"If you're just tuning in, a tragedy has stricken America. The nine o'clock p.m. train from New York to Boston was bombed last night — apparently detonated by timers — leaving no survivors. The act is being called a terrorist attack…"

When Kevin left for work at 7:50, Jess followed her mother into the kitchen. She continued to pull at her hair, just trying to feel something, clinging to the hope that she had found reality. Nick and Paul were dead. Her father was dead. It was her fault. She told her mother she was feeling too sick to go to school.

"I understand. After hearing about that train I don't feel too well myself. Maybe you need to eat. You don't look good," her mother said. She poured a glass of milk and handed Jess a plate of waffles not looking at her daughter.

"Mom, I need to tell you something."

She didn't respond but winced like she'd been slapped. She stared out the window.

"Last night I had another bad dream; or day dream, kind of."

"A daze?"

"Yeah, a daze. I couldn't help it. I saw what happened on the train and I'm sorry." The words tumbled out of her mouth and before she could stop them, tears were streaming down her face. She felt sick again and watched her mother, unmoving. Jess began breathing very hard, too hard. She was lightheaded and the kitchen swam around her and just before she fainted she wondered if any of this was currently happening. When she came to a moment later her mother had her cradled against her chest, her body laid over her mother's kneeling knees.

"We'll fix this, Jess. We'll fix this," she said over and over. They sat silently for a while, and then her mother went into the study to make some phone calls. She set up a movie in the living room for Jessica.

She sat in deep thought and about an hour into *Aladdin* she decided what she had to do. She needed to stop the dazes and she was determined that the only way this could be done would be to enter one willingly, and then prevent it from actually happening. She knew her mother would be scared if she knew her plan, and Jess didn't want to worry her. She listened for the sound of her mother's voice. She was talking quietly into the phone down the hall; she was busy and wouldn't come back for a while. She looked once around the room, as though searching for surveillance, before closing her e-yes and allowing herself to fall into the last daze she would ever have.

She was in a small waiting area, white carpet, white walls, and white wooden end tables. She felt dirty and out of place in the room. She found that she was sitting in a hard, gray armchair and her mother was sitting next to her reading a magazine. She was tracing her fingers around her lips absently, and Jess wondered why she was nervous.

"It will be okay, mom." The words escaped her mouth before she thought about saying them, they were beyond her control. She watched the scene — her mother smile weakly, a woman open a large white door into the room, and say something without sound — out of her own eyes, but she was detached. She was still vaguely aware that this was a daze, that in fact her body was still laying lazily on a couch in another time, another place; but as she sunk further and further into the daze, she began to forget.

"Jessica Leavitt," the woman said again from the opened door. She wore jeans and a sweater and carried a clipboard under her arm.

Jesses wrenched open her eyes, breathing heavily. She was in the living room, Aladdin was fighting Jafar and Buddy was asleep. She couldn't remember what she had just seen, who's memory she had fallen into, but she told herself that was because she hadn't let herself sink into the daze. Her mother's voice trailed into the room as low indistinct noise. It was safe and she closed her eyes again, determined more than ever to surrender to the thoughts, whatever they had been, and when she came to again, prevent them from becoming real.

Her eyes remained closed as the sounds of Aladdin were replaced with the low hum of a computer and the soft whir of machines. A small turn of her head told her that small metal clips with wires were attached beneath her hair like alien barrettes.

The memory of her living room faded away as though it had happened a long time ago, or had not happened yet at all. She was only aware that she had thought of a plan somewhere, sometime in a living room. Then it was gone. Dust flying through space.

"Now Jessica, tell me about this latest daze. Your mother told me that is what you have been calling them with Dr. Sable." A man's voice from far a-way, but when she opened her eyes he was sitting next to her on a small stool. He was too close.

"It was *here*. I came here because Mom was worried after the bomb... I remember I saw the waiting room and the lady with the clipboard, and then I came in here and waited for you to come in and you put these clips on me."

"Jessica that is just what happened *today*. You're just relaying a memory to me." He shifted in his chair and touched something on the computer. With each movement his face was etched into the air and an outline hung there so she couldn't tell what the man looked like, but heard his voice like an echo.

She tried to concentrate but was becoming more and more confused. The room was spinning and shifting in and out of being and she didn't know why. She closed her eyes hard and felt white, snowy static fill her mind. She pulled hard on her hair nervously. There was something more that she needed to remember; something important. An image of *Aladdin* flashed in her mind.

She opened her eyes and found herself laying down on a long, hard surface, completely still. She couldn't remember getting onto the surface or into this new room. A large machine circled around her head, humming softly in her ears. It was a CAT scan machine. She watched as bright lights pulsed above her rhythmically. She watched from somewhere far away, or deep within herself. She couldn't tell.

A blurred movement like a memory struggling to surface, more static, and she was in the doctor's office again, with metal clips attached to her head. She batted at the wires like flies and something nearby beeped like an alarm clock.

Static, loud like the roaring of a train.

Paul and Nick sitting in the train to Boston...

Paul and Nick holding hands, melting like toy soldiers...

Her father laughing as they walked through the snow. Then broken and surrounded by blood.

When she opened her eyes again she was running down a hall. People were opening doors because someone was screaming. She was screaming. Her legs hit the ground and with each step she felt how her shoes sunk into the carpet, felt the vibrations running up her legs, but could hear her steps. Heel to toe. Heel to toe. She ran until she was surrounded by blinding, white light, somewhere outside and then there was a loud noise — a car horn — pain, and then silence.

When Jess opened her eyes again she found herself on the living room couch, cowering like she'd been beaten, with her arms folded behind her head and a small trickle of blood running from her nose into her mouth. *Aladdin* was over and static filled the room.

"Jess," her mother's voice made her jump. "Listen, I'm worried about... what's going on with you. I've been talking to some psychologists and I found a specialist who'd like to meet with you tomorrow morning. His name's Ted Rubin." She didn't look at her daughter but fidgeted nervously with her hands and stared out the window. A moment later she walked out of the room and left Jess on the couch alone.

"Okay."

Jess hugged her knees into her chest and felt her heart racing, but she didn't know why. She had never come out of a daze not remembering before and it terrified her. She knew she had to stop it from coming true if she was ever going to stop the dazes completely, but how could she prevent something if she didn't know what it was?

"You look awful," Jess said to her mother. It was 7:30 a.m. and she sat at the counter, fully dressed, sipping coffee, ready to take Jess to Dr. Rubin's.

"I didn't sleep. How are you? Are you okay? Are you ready?" She forced a smile that left lines around her mouth.

Jess ate breakfast in silence then sat in the car waiting for her mother. She pushed buttons on the radio to fill the silence but didn't register the sounds.

When they arrived at Dr. Rubin's office Jess thought the place looked familiar. It was a plain, square, office building; two stories, with large, reflective windows covering most of the front. Inside the waiting room it was white—the floors, the walls, and the end tables were all white and sterile—and the furniture was grey and uncomfortable. Her mother sat down next to her with a magazine and traced her lips nervously. "It will be okay," Jess said mechanically.

"Jessica Leavitt," the woman in the doorway had been calling her name for a while and looked irritated. Her mother gave her a fleeting smile as she got up and walked through the door. The walls in the hallway were close together, the ceiling was low and made of loose tiles covered in small, black dots, and the floor was white carpet. There were several closed doors on either side and at the end of the hall was a door marked EMER-GENCY EXIT. They turned in to the third room on the left.

"Okay, Jessica. I am just going to take your blood pressure and do some basic measurements on you here, and then Dr. Rubin will come in and talk to you."

She sat down on the edge of a long, cushioned table as the woman buzzed around her, taking her pulse, blood pressure, and writing things down. Jess noticed that her handwriting was small and scratchy just like Kevin's.

When Dr. Rubin came in she thought he looked like a doctor from a movie. He wore a long, white lab coat, had a small line of a mustache, wore glasses, and was bald. She felt like she had seen this man before. When he spoke she his voice as if from a dream. He motioned for her to sit in the chair by a computer. She did.

"Jessica, I'm Dr. Rubin. Do you know why you are here today?" He wasn't looking at her, but was picking up several small metal instruments from a table.

"Yes."

"Well then let me explain what we will be doing, okay?" He held the small metal instruments out in his hands like an offering. "These clips are connected to this computer by wires." He motioned to the monitor on the table as though there were more than one large computer right in front of her. "I am going to put the metal ends onto your head with a glue-like substance, and they will record your brain activity. It will show up on the computer as a sort of graph, and I will ask you different questions and see how they record."

The doctor combed through her hair gently before attaching each clip to her head. When they were all attached he turned away and rummaged through a small blue kit. When he turned around he had a syringe in his hand.

"Now, Jessica. I am going to give you a little shot. It won't hurt, don't worry. What this does, is it will go into your blood and when the blood pumps into your brain, this will temporarily impair the connection between the hemispheres, so we can get a better idea of what's going on. It is going to activate some memories, either from early on or even small things that you may have repressed for some reason that may have happened more recently." He spoke slowly and clearly but was already moving toward her with the syringe. She made a small noise of protest, but didn't pull away as he sunk the needle into her forearm. Her mother was worried about her and she would have to cooperate. He watched her for a few moments before turning to the computer to start a program. Little lines appeared on the screen moving up and down.

"Now Jessica, tell me about this latest daze. Your mother told me that is what you have been calling them with Dr. Sable." His voice echoed from far away now. She struggled to focus on one thing—the computer, his face, the room, anything—but her thoughts were becoming detached.

She relayed the daze from the day before—how she was sent to his office because her mother was worried; how she sat in the waiting area, and then in this room… As she spoke she had no idea where the words were coming from. Her mouth moved mechanically and she was only distantly aware that her heart was beating violently. The faster her heart raced the farther re-moved she felt. She could almost hear the drug pulls behind her temples.

"Jessica that is just what happened *today*. You're just relaying a memory to me." As he shifted the imprint of his shape was left hanging in the air, hundreds of outlines of the doctor like a hand of cards. An image of *Aladdin* flashed across her mind and she reached up as though to catch it. When she missed she pulled out several strands of hair.

"Why don't you tell me about what you saw before the bombing in the train, Jessica?" He was so far away and she saw each word like a different color. "Bombing" was yellow.

She told him how she laid down with Buddy that night, closed her eyes, and was on the train. She spoke flatly and was hardly aware that she was speaking at all. All she heard was someone breathing, perhaps the machines, and small beeps from the computer. She imagined the doctor's voice like a computer and smiled slightly, unaware that she did so.

"Jessica, it seems as though you are having trouble differentiating between reality and imagination. I know you told me that you saw the attack before it happened, but perhaps you just *imagined* that you saw it, after you saw the newscast? What do you understand about the concept of time, Jessica?"

She held up her hand and made an imaginary dot in the air with her forefinger. "It's like a dot on page."

"Okay. If you understand time like a dot on a page, the past, the present, and the future would all be happening right now, wouldn't they Jessica? Now that wouldn't work very well, because then you'd have all the things that happened when you were little and all the things that will happen when you are older all happening at once." He began speaking to her more slowly and carefully as he watched the monitor.

Her father sat on the couch, her mother stood behind him, her hands on her hips. They had been arguing about whether or not Jessica could get a pet for Christmas. Perhaps when they got back from New York, her mother had said. Her father ran his fingers through his hair and then down onto his face. He held them over his eyes and for a moment Jessica thought he would move them and shout "Peekaboo!" but when he lowered his hands he looked tired and old. "Perhaps," he had said. Then he winked at his daughter and went into the kitchen.

The beeping and hum of the rooms crept back into Jessica's ears, like someone had just turned up the volume on the world.

"It does."

"Pardon?"

"Everything is happening at once. There are so many possibilities for the future but they are all happening right now; it's just a matter of which one you think into being. It's... like a dot..." She thought of Paul and Nick and how she must have thought their fate into reality. It happened the very moment she believed in it; the very moment they thought it and felt the first explosion, it was real. She began to laugh quietly at the simplicity of it all. She wasn't aware of whether or not she said the words, but each one raced through her head in brilliant colors, and she knew it was the Truth. A moment later the thoughts were gone and her head swam with magnificent co-lors.

"Jessica, we're going to take you into another room now to do a CAT scan." Dr. Rubin said watching her smile fade into a look of hard concentration.

"Wait..." A brief memory of a CAT scan flitted across her mind's eye.

Cat scan, hallway, Aladdin.

Aladdin, hallway, father.

Nick, Paul, red on the concrete.

Where words once filled her head to make sense of these things, colors, bright, beautiful, and new, replaced them. She watched from outside of herself as her senses dulled and her thoughts made less and less sense. She felt the burden of her body become a mere idea, a word, now a color, and she felt for a moment very free.

"Okay," she mouthed. She walked into the other room hardly feeling her steps.

In the next room, the last thing she remembered was sitting in a room with clips attached to her head, and before that, the white, white waiting room. Then there was a gap. And now she was on a long, hard surface surrounded by a low humming noise.

When the CAT scan finished, Dr. Rubin walked behind Jessica to the third room on the left. He watched her apprehensively as she stopped occasionally to look at a certain spot in the hall or a certain detail of the floor. She stood for a while before entering the room.

"I just can't remember. I can't remember," she kept saying. She was pulling out large clumps of hair and holding handfuls of it against her chest.

He placed a hand on her shoulder and guided her in and left it there as she sat down in the chair again.

"That's okay, Jessica. The medicine is just wearing off. Your brain might feel a little confused right now but it be back to normal soon." His face was close to hers as he spoke in a voice that sounded very much like her father's. Father was red. He turned away and a shadow lingered where he had been like a ghost.

As he stuck the metal clips to her head she could vaguely remember being in this room before, but she couldn't decide when. Broken images tumbled through her head.

Waiting room, chair, clips, machine, chair, clips, hallway…

Nick, Paul, explosion.

Father.

Father was red.

Father was dead.

"Dr. Rubin I have to leave soon, *Aladdin* is almost over and mom will worry. She worries so much you know.

I have to tell you something, though. Call my father and tell him to be careful because he might get hurt. Tell him to be careful and then we can see the trains…"

She opened her eyes and saw Dr. Rubin staring at her, he looked worried. He put his hand on hers to stop her from pulling at her hair. His hand felt warm and her body was beginning to feel solid again.

"Jessica, your father is dead. He died four years ago, you know that."

"I should have told you, Dr. Sable. I saw it and then it happened, but it might not have happened yet, so you should tell him. To stop these dazes, you know. I have to go, mom worries so much." She could feel her body, her head throbbed and it felt like it might split at any moment, but her thoughts were still running into and over each other. They were mud brown.

"Jessica, you didn't see your father's death before it happened and we can't tell him anything because he is already dead." Dr. Rubin sounded stern now. "Isn't it possible that after your father's death you created a memory of a daze? Perhaps because you felt like you should have seen it coming?"

She didn't understand. This man seemed to be calling her a liar. *Who was this man? His voice sounded familiar.*

"After all, your father's death was due to a drinking and driving accident. Your mother tells me that your father was an alcoholic. Perhaps you felt that you should have predicted it and you created a memory."

The computer buzzed now like a swarm of insects closing in on her. She batted at the air for flies and found that they felt like wires.

"An a l c o h o l l I c..." The word came slowly from her lips and each letter blurred with the next as it scrolled through her mind. She didn't understand. This voice was lying, had to be lying. The walls closed in and the beep and hum of the machines pressed in as the room got smaller.

Her father walked into the living room and put a drink onto the table. Her mother swept by and picked up the drink and said something Jess couldn't hear. Couldn't remember. She heard the drink being poured into the kitchen sink.

"Fuck you, Jan. I was going to drink that."

Jess didn't laugh at the word then.

He picked up his car keys and left the room without another word.

The living room dissolved and there was the woman with the clipboard in a room that looked blurry and white, like the colors had been drained. Nick and Paul held hands on the train, fireworks bursting all around them and they laughed. And now she was back in the room with the man who was telling her father was an alcoholic, that he was dead.

Liar.

This man whose voice was God's was lying and Jess could see his words in black.

"Jessica, are you alright?"

But she did not answer. She was out the door, wires swinging heavily with her hair and she ran down the hall screaming. People on either side of the hall stepped out of the rooms to stop the screaming child, but she ran un-til she reached the last door in the hall, EMERGENCY EXIT. She was still screaming as she raced through the parking lot, the sun blinding her. Dr. Rubin and her mother ran after her out the door and screamed her name in horror as she ran into the intersection. She did not hear a sound until a car came up on her left and honked as the driver pressed on the breaks and it screamed and screamed like the voice in her head. There was a bright light, and then silence.

"What did you think of those trains, Jess? Pretty big right?"

"Yeah, they were good. Maybe I'll get to ride in one someday."

"Maybe so." Their steps left footprints in the snow.

And she fell to the pavement, a halo of blood surrounding her head.

Jess opened her eyes and found that she was lying on her bed; Buddy was fast asleep on a pillow next to her.

"Jess, what are you doing back in bed?" Her mother was standing in the doorway. "It's the first day of fifth grade! You don't want to be late. Oh and don't forget, you've got an appointment with Dr. Sable this afternoon."

She left the room, presumably to wait outside and sneak a cigarette if Kevin was already gone. Jess sat quite still for a long time, trying hard to re-member what she had just seen. She traced her fingers nervously over her lips like she had seen her mother do, and she was scared that she could not remember. She listened to the clock, each second passing into the present, then into the past. She laid there completely still holding onto this thought, trying to carry it with her as the clock ticked away, when her mother honked the car horn outside.

A blur of tangled images.

Car horn, bright light, silence.

But even before the clock ticked again, it was gone.

Moments later she walked out of the house and climbed into her mother's car. She smelled like smoke, gum, and strong perfume.

"Did you get everything?" Her mom asked as she backed out of the driveway.

"Yes," she said, but she couldn't help feeling like she had forgotten something.

Nebeolisa Okwudili
Kaduna, Nigeria

Nebeolisa Okwudili is a chemical engineering student of Federal University of Technology, Minna, a citizen of Nigeria. He graduated from Federal Government College, Malali, Kaduna. He writes poems that could be found at:
poetrysoup.com.

An Afternoon in a Cave
By Nebeolisa Okwudili

It was a thing close to a cave; crescent opening, gray and old – perhaps living for the past two millennia – and had little life to boast of at the entrance. At first it was scary for as knowledge was to go by, bats were expected to exist in this cavern, but they were bent on having fun. And it was a long way here, for as it had seemed in this hallucination, their legs seemed worn out by an unmemorable trek, trying to overcome the jagged, limestone relief to get to this fissure. The place was dead; no closeness to a tree, no movement to be heard, not a sign or relic of drifting of colour or smoke. The place was unbelievably clear. They were seven to be reckoned, the oldest being in his earliest teens.

"What are we waiting for?" asked the first boy, ahead of this grouped boys, slim that he was given Slimy. "Let's get in and see if there's anything, perhaps gypsum salt." He wore a black shirt that had been torn, perhaps by his effort in overcoming this elevation.

"Me I hate bats, and something may be living inside," suggested another, he was averagely sized and wore a blue face cap, brown short-sleeved shirt, jean trousers and brown small *timberland* boots that gave him the air of those engineers that worked on the new road somewhere in this story bound pla-ce. But though he had contemplated on that, he was thoughtful of his asthma and his anxiety in there.

"Then why did you follow us, you could as well go back please," the first, Slimy, said, annoyed.

"Please, please, let's not be too high with this," another of them countered in, sensing an imminent bicker. Emma, he was tall and appeared the oldest of this heptad. He used his hand to shield himself from the light that flickered from the mirror of water it got from the sun. Everywhere was bright, the inside of the cave seemed to.

Now and then the water came with a little milky sand and deposited it on their legs and some into the mouth of the cave, providing a landing site. Dripping sounds came from inside and outside the cave in an apparently rhythmic style with the flies around that hovered for the next dead body or decomposing thing. So agreed, they got in, seven in all into the hollow, careful not to go against any stone and ware of the tiniest sound produced. Slimy led the group, albeit he was not the eldest but his social emphasis on his ideas into the minds of this little group had made him important of the group. He walked without any dread, his old shoes making the chief sounds in this cavity for the cellulous sole had worn out and the metal sounded against the stone, quite hard.

"You see, nothing to fear for, Mark," he said, his eyes about this under-ground chamber, admiring the icicles that tore from the roof of the cave and pointed down and those that sprung from the floor and pointed the roof. The flowstones from where water came was beautiful, the tiny, tiny deposits that had dried up too. That managed to dry, Slimy thought as he tried to get the tiny height of a scar-like feature, driving right of him and the rest follo-wed. The opening curved in unevenly with the darkness and heat was getting evident, only what in the hollow gave light of its own. The boys looked around like tourist, jumping ecstatically to the next capti-vating like a translucent icicle or gem, blue and red and green.

"This one looks like an egg, a witch's egg," said Fry, that was the nick-name they gave him because he was like a fish and behaved like them, jellylike. It was gemstones that lay in a colony on the floor and created a near circle of light from the torch one of them held, at the roof, jaggedly. Mark picked one of the stones and tucked it in his jeans trouser pocket.

"That will give birth to you, I think," added Emma and the rest laughed except Slimy; he was afore a pillar that seemed to have the face of a beard-ed man, like it had been carved carelessly. "You'll be fair and colourless and all your organs I can see when you're born."

The rest came and joined Slimy and held the grooves of the white pillar, one of them held a piece like a protrusion and broke it in the process. Slimy left them and went further, near a ditch that had water in it. The water dripped from the roof as he looked atop that seemed very high, at-rophied with cobwebs and fungi. A further look told of the fine stones that were in it like it was the remnants of an archaeologist's pit. He felt like jumping in, it was like the proposed well his father had told him where merchants dug gemstones and sold to traders. But it was yawning, the depth almost as the height from the floor to the roof. He went through the thin side around the ditch and went further, it was getting adventurous.

"Here's this ditch, guys, see," said Marvy, pointing to the ditch. The rest joined in the jumping manner following Marvy to the ditch.

A luminous insect came with much speed from the darkness, towards Slimy and he had quickly run into hiding but he had been sure the rest had not noticed his fright. He loved to have his pride justifiable and his impor-tance not prejudiced. By the time he was sure the insect had gone – be-cause it had followed him into the board of stones he had hidden into – he appeared, wiping the sweat from his temple.

"Slimy, where did you run to?" asked Mark the one who had at first had doubts of getting in. "We heard sounds like run."

"Me... I didn't run. I was imagining something."

"Did you see that big bug that is shining light?"

Gaining his courage, he spoke, brandishing his knowledge. "O a lightning bug you mean."

"It is firefly," Emma corrected.

"Yes I know about that. Let's see what's there. Today we're explorers."

"And surveyors," one of them, Christian, said. He held a small electric torch and its light was enough.

They continued to get into the cave, the width of the way getting ampler and the light was not penetrating well into the region. The space was sufficient to line with the breadth. Slimy got the wrong foot afore and had gotten a stalagmite, it got broken and it hurt him but he had made an effort to bury any countenances emanating. But even though, they had doled their apologies like it had been their fault. He picked the icicle and led the group like a returning commander. It seemed like the features appearing before them were no longer interesting, only thick, unfriendly and coarse walls that shut them from outside totally; a few pillars that were almost plain or craggy, white mixed with black and brown; a roof that were grooved undulated, iterating like contours in a big farm. It was no longer getting funny to feel, Slimy got ahead faster and faster, wanting to be the first to see it all, the icicle swinging with his hands like a prodding stick. He loved as he held it; it gave him the headship air he desired, like it was a staff he held.

A near circle depression dug deep into the wall aback a thick pillar that cast a shadow at the dip and Slimy rushed to it, poking his icicle to the dent. He felt he heard some noise so he drew closer to discern what was producing it.

"What did you see?" Emma asked Slimy, he was with the group, aback Slimy.

"I'm coming, the explorer is on his way, Emma."

"Just be careful, we don't know this place." Then the group separated into where they thought was of interest in this park in a cave, but Emma stayed aback Slimy.

"You're not the one to tell me this, you know." He kept on prodding. The dip seemed deeper than his thought or how the darkness was posing it to be. Or that his thoughts had felt that it was only the pillar's shade making it penetrating; or that he did not feel that Emma's ideas was not anything to go by.

"But what do you think will be inside, do you find anything?" Emma asked; he was a few paces away as he had his eyes about the gloomy opening, where the rest had divided into.

"Nothing, bros. Just wait and see. He drew closer and the dip was before his face, a few inches. Since he was close he had more room with his hands and he poked into it till he heard flapping sounds. "Something's living here, bros."

"Like what? Be careful, Slimy."

"I think I'm getting it," proud triumph depicted in his voice. "Perhaps a weak bird."

"What kind of bird could be living here?" He fastened the distance to enjoy in the discovery. Slimy struck hard against the sides and the flapping turned to a crying voice. "That sounds babyish, Slimy."

Scampering reached their sides from the others' division; they were all waving their hands over and over their heads and necks. Slimy turned to them angrily like he had been woken from slumber by their scuttling, his hands still waving the length of the dark dip. He had not noticed the dust that fell from the mouth of the dip for he was still with the others, his attention. On turning the creature darted from the hole and descended on Slimy, using its claws to thrash at his face, grazing and grazing as one of its legs were attached to his cloth. He shouted for help, the icicle had fallen in the process of security. It was Emma who hurried to him and dragged the creature that looked close to a bat, off. Without looking at the rest Slimy hurried to where his mind told him the mouth of the cave was. The creature withdrew to its hole and in just that second it came again with its fellows, reinforced. They descended on the boys, each on one like it had been decided and shared. Emma could not believe this number could appear from the dip, they reckoned about ten to twelve. They took to their heels, Emma being the athlete of them, evident that he was the oldest of them. Mark's shout could be heard, a bit aback, gasping.

But Slimy had not been too far when the rest joined him and it was thin to overcome the space of the well where the water stood inside and a few gem stones that he was not certain whether to follow the thin line around the it or jump. He slipped in quickly and the water splashed coldly at his fa-ce. The rest were careful to jump the underground opening, Emma being the touchstone in the long-jump. Mark was careful even when the creatures we-re so close, now trying to grip or tear at his collar at the most possible means. But he fell on getting to the other side, injuring on the knees as the jean there had torn. It had been a rough and careless landing, it was his *timberland* boots that had helped to shrink the effect of the fall. He quickly made to the opening.

Slimy called on Mark but he had not heard for he was sure he would wait and offer albeit the least to rescue. The flapping and quick chirruping and the cries had been able to shut his words. Then they stopped on noticing Mark was way gone and descended to the well that Slimy began to cry. They were much to barricade, he tried his best to secure what he felt was essential: his eyes, nose, ears, and his face in all. The dialogue outside was surprisingly within his earshot.

"Slimy's gotten himself into that hole with water," Emma said to the heaving and dirty group, dusting his trousers.

"With those wicked birds in there?" Mark asked, openly dreadful.

"But we can't leave him there to the birds, guys. We should do something quick." He could discern it, T.Y .

"Please help me, the birds will eat me!" Slimy shouted but it came up almost silent words out of the cave.

"Let's go to the rescue side," suggested Marvy. "We against the birds are good army. Quick!" and it sounded like a war cry. They hurried into the cave again and towards the hole, careless of the relief. Slimy heaved deeply but the sight of his helplessness and that he was left to this group of *younger* ones was unbearable and the whole fantasy vanished like ether with the sweet smell with it. But it was not like those which he would have forgotten with its termination. He was glad it was so, he was happy he was only on a counterpane over a good flat cushion with the light very bright before his e-yes as he reached for the socket. It was a good adventure, explorers, he thought.

....

The end

Steven Ruben Strickland
Roseburg, OR,

Steven Strickland is a junior at Harvard University. He was born and raised in the only Puerto Rican household in Roseburg, Oregon. He is currently a landscaper.

Open Pores and Open Hearts
By Steven Ruben Strickland

*D*efinitely should have used deodorant, this always happens. Fucking sweat. The brown paper towels are shredding your armpits and the sweat is *still* gushing out all over your dress shirt. Fuck, your armpits hurt. It would definitely be better to bleed than to be sweaty though. The stain would be smaller and you could totally pass it off as a sports injury. If you put your jacket back on, you could cover up the stains, but that would mean opening up the floodgates on your face and you really don't want to want to walk around with sauna-face all night.

Your best friend walks in and wonders why your bitch ass has been in the bathroom for five fucking hours and reminds you that the dance doesn't last all goddamn night. You tell him to fuck off and pretend you have diarrhea so he leaves you alone. He says he'll meet you outside once your period is over. Bastard. Shit, why didn't you think of going outside where it was cooler? Whatever, you dab at your armpits one last time and head out to where you belong.

Peering up at the disco ball in the middle of the dance floor, you think of all the other dances where you've gotten nervous as shit and ended up in the bathroom or sitting with the guys outside. You hate dances. Your heartbeat catches up to the beat of the flashing lights and thumping music and you hurry outside. Hey, at least you haven't thrown up this time. Small victories.

The over decorated gym looks just like all the ugly girls who have too much make up on. You can see your douche bag principal hitting on your chaperone aunt whose presence eliminates any libido you possessed and leads you to determine that you are ready to go home. It's 9:30. You aren't sure if this is an excuse or the truth, but you really wish you were watching shitty Saturday night TV shows with your mom and dad, even if you *do* hate them. At least you wouldn't be sweating at home.

You find your friends sitting outside, wagons circled to avoid female intrusion. They are debating who they should ask to dance even though they all know there is no way they will get the courage up to ask any of the girls they fantasize about.

Schools of semi- to un- attractive girls flit around your table like frightened fish. While their behavior seems spontaneous, even you know that their dance around each table of men has been carefully prepared for, planned, and rehearsed at least a hundred times. You wonder if dances were this uncomfortable back when everybody waltzed and shit.

Dissolving into the group, you rate girls for about a half an hour until it dawns on you that your jaw is sore and you realize you've already gone through your whole pack of gum and most of a box of orange Tic Tacs. You sweat trying to get the last two Tic Tacs unstuck from the bottom of the box.

As you walk home you remember how much you hate your parents. Oh aren't you jumping for joy at the thought of being just like them, doing chores all day and looking forward to getting the mail. Thank god you're still young. You wish you were twenty-five though. In your prime. You'd have a girlfriend then and your own place and be able to do what you wanted all day long. What the fuck was the principal doing with your aunt? Fucking jerk-off.

Entering your house, you walk past your parents without saying hello. Your mom asks you why you didn't dance with anyone. Of course she already heard from your aunt, it always happens that way. You lay in your bed and exhale. As you lie still you continue to hear the fateful thump of the music and the flashing noise of your friends chatter. Screams of disappointment hail the release of every flavor of pain. You cry and you cry and you cry. You stop sweating.

Justyn L. Hardy
Wyoming, United States

A Stranger
By Justyn L. Hardy

I awoke late last night to the chilly draft of the moonlit air tickling my dulled senses. Oh drat, I thought to myself as I rose to close the clattering shutters. My covers, all tangled in a bunch, attempted to further ensnare me but I persevered and slid forth out of the bunk. As I fastened the cloth cord around the wooden shutters, my eyes scanned the gentle town beneath. The soft glow of candlelight illuminated the living rooms of numerous households, all resting in peaceful unison. Silhouettes of nocturnal rodents scuttled across the cobblestone streets like tiny ghosts pre-paring for a scare. Although the moon shone from behind clouds its opaque beams remained clear. There was no haze or lack of clarity it the cool air.

I finished fastening the shutters and climbed back into the warm comfort of my matted bed. Rolling to the shoulder I most often sleep on I found myself in a great surprise! For there at the side of my bed knelt an elderly gentleman in prayer, a man whom I'd never seen the likes of before, a stranger in all facets of the word. Yet, I felt no fear from this man only curiosity. His full beard hung low to his chest and had obviously not been tended to in so-me time. His tunic was torn and ratted with bits of leaf stuck here and there and his pants looked like they had been fashioned from the very earth. Of course, I felt the urge to ask just who he was, but I found my voice caught in my throat. His head remained bowed and his lips moving in slow but steady pattern. The wrinkled skin of his tan leathery face caused me to wonder if he spent much time outside or perhaps had been a heavy smoker at an earlier age.

I shied back toward the headboard causing the bed to squeak in awkward unwanted noise. My teeth clenched. Who was this man who had mysteriously broken into my apartment to pray by my bedside? Maybe had he been younger and more intimidating in physical presence I would have been more frightened but alas I still only felt rampant curiosity. Suddenly the quiet whispers of his pursed lips abruptly stopped and the thin arms came unfolded. My eyes first caught scars in his forearms from needle puncture. A slight fear vibrated up my spine. Was he just an old druggy from the rougher side of town? His eyes opened revealing tired but brilliant blue pupils beneath sagging eyelids.

I slid off the back side of my bed and onto my feet using the bed to create some separation between the two of us. My voice returned to me.

"Why are you in my house sir?"

The man shook his head as if he didn't understand the question.

"Sir, I have half the mind to call the authorities. You have broken into my apartment and I demand you speak now?"

The tired blue eyes gazed up in didactic trance and scanned me as if he were looking for something.

"Sir, now!" I shouted.

The man raised his hand to silence my voice.

"You asked me to come", the man spoke in a deep shaking voice like the beat of drum in an old folk song.

I rolled my eyes fearing now he was some delusional old bat escaped from the old folks home a few street corners away.

"I did no such thing. I've never seen you before in my life."

The stranger smiled revealing two rows of crooked yellow teeth followed by a strong whiff of a foul scent. I steadily moved further away for fear of this man was carrying some new plague.

"No that is true my son. You have never seen me before; you see, no one has. I tend to be a bit of a recluse I'm afraid."

My curiosity was quickly being ebbed away be fear of what this man might be. Was he psychotic? Was he violent? He was obviously deranged.

"Does my appearance frighten you my child?"

I bit my lip before answering, "Yes, and considering the present situation I think any appearance would frighten me."

The old man sadly shook his head and stepped back from the bed. He looked into my eyes and the brilliance of his blue pupils struck me peculiar.

"What is your name", I asked?

"You already know, Roy", he replied.

"Is this a dream?"

"In this world most people live in dreams, or more like trances I suppose. You see dreams are meant to bring us joy and joy is not what most people have found. So to answer your question no this is not a dream but a trance."

I felt a warm tingle in the depths of my heart. My fear left and was repla-ced with agonizing pain I as remembered the events of the previous day. Warm hot tears raced down my cheeks like fire to the furnace. The emotions came in an onslaught tearing my being from the foundations of my soul. I looked up to the man who was now standing right before me. Tears streamed down his lowly eyes to fall in unison with mine.

"Ask me anything my son", he spoke through broken sobs.

I tried to steady my vocal cords but they shook in divine hurt for an irreplaceable loss. Finally I found a break in the pain and uttered forth an audible sentence.

"Why did you take her from me?"

The old man shook his head as the tears began falling harder. He tried to speak; to answer my question, to even look at me, but he could not for his pain somehow was equal to mine. My heart raged with the torrential rain of Noah's great storm at the pain encircling the room. Together we sobbed, and whimpered, and felt the pangs of loss so deep that not even death could bring solace. My resolve broke for I could take it no more. My hands reached out and embraced the old man. His arms opened and ensnared me back. His feeble body shook against my chest as my stronger arms attempted to squeeze the agony out of his frame. After what seemed both an eternity but only a few moments his deep voice cracked.

"I am so sorry my son."

My heart opened up to the fullest extent of its hinges and welcomed the sorry with love both deep and divine. The hurt remained but the fury was gone. The sadness lingered but the doubt was absent. In his bright blue eyes I found understanding not of my own pain, but of his. Another stream of warm water ran down my face onto his matted beard and in quakes of his shaking body I found the courage.

"It's okay father."

Rina Jiménez Vargas
Montreal, Canada

Born in Costa Rica and raised in a small village near the Pacific Ocean by a family of artists, bohemians, and politicians while attending a religious boarding school, she learned to see life from a critical yet romantic point of view. Her passion for books was born the minute she learned to read and write. Ever since, she writes stories that help add spice to the life of friends and acquaintances by giving them a glorious end, often very different from reality.

The stories are based on experience, some vivid, many borrowed, which seek to portray the greatness of the human heart regardless of the adversities that it is exposed to and at the same time it proposes a criticism of the problems that wear on Costa Rican society.

She studied engineering by necessity; however she never ceased to love art, especially writing and painting. This passion has led her to be self-taught and has sold many paintings and has currently written two novels, a series of stories for adults and a series of stories for children, all unpublished.

A rose for Jazmin
By Rina Jimenez Vargas

*M*any love stories have been told, each one has something different that make it special, but this is not just another love story, it is the story of a love so infinite as it is unique.

At eight years of age, I lived with my grandmother in a little house (if a pale of cardboard boxes, metal roof and trash bags put together can be called a house) in the slums in south San Jose, Costa Rica.

My mother left the house one morning shortly after I was born to go in search of a better future and nobody ever heard about her again.

Where is my father, you ask? Neither my grandmother nor I nor my father knew who he was. Grandma used to say, when I asked about him, that she was sure that I had been conceived by the Holy Spirit because I was almost like baby Jesus. The truth is that I wasn't, but I truly loved the poor old lady who gave me all that she had to see me happy, so I tried the best I could to compensate both her love and sacrifice.

At that time, I had a stable job selling wrapped roses with messages on the streets of the city. It was a little hard, but it was going well as I never lacked customers who would purchase a rose out of pity. In terms of occupational safety and health, I had the best of all policies as my grandmother had entrusted to me every saint she could think of before I left to go out to work. She would wait up for me until past two in the morning sitting on a wood stool with a prayer to the Divine Child Jesus and a rosary in her hand while a lit candle maintained the vigil in front of the pictures of Archangel Gabriel, San Martín de Porras and the miraculous Doctor Moreno Canas, who by lack of publicity never became a saint, but gossip tells he has the title by honors made up by the beliefs of people in thousands of miracles as they note. With so many bodyguards so well qualified, it was almost impossible to suffer even a scratch. Each night upon my return, seeing me walk on the narrow streets of the penniless place, my grandmother cried while she thanked heaven and then pleaded with Him that it wasn't fair that I had to work. "I know that one day God will give us a miracle, you will see," she would say. But until that happened, without my work we would not eat. What my viejita earned by ironing and washing for other people was barely enough to pay the rent of the ranchito, electricity, and water, because don't think that in these places there aren't any hierarchies and landlords that watched over our pile of trash that we called home. In addition, the Government is extremely responsible and equitable, so it must collect their tributes in time and their taxes from all alike.

As if all that poverty is was not enough, my grandmother was ill, some horrible venous insufficiency ulcers tormented her and rheumatism was driving her insane to the point that sometimes she could not sleep. Even so, she did what she could to give me shelter and food. Despite all ills and hardship that we were facing, what worried me the most was not having enough to go to school.

We all have a reason to fight; otherwise life would have no meaning. My reason for school was to become a doctor to help my viejita who was suffering so much. As well, I knew so many people in the streets, many of them children, who I'd often see die from infected wounds without any relief, drowned in their own blood by a hemorrhage or suffocated by pneumonia from so much water and cold. I knew that, given the chance, I could ease the pain from these miseries that others chose to ignore.

Although a better future had already stolen my mother from me, I was not going to let fate take me as well. Because of this, I worked tirelessly to help my grandmother so that I could go to school.

Life always compensates what it takes from you. Even though I was robbed of a normal childhood, I was repaid by Samaritans of the streets as the most feared thieves were my friends, the whores were my allies, and drug addicts my protectors. Along with these co-workers, we made up the department of social affairs of the city, night shift. San Jose was the safest work place I might have without hypocrisy or back-stabbers. Nobody was working on a plot to take my job from me as everyone was doing their own job and all one had to do was to respect each other's territory.

In one of so many nights, I decided to take a tour of some of the streets that I never travelled. It was hostile territory but that day was the Festival of Lights. While everyone was occupied in the main streets earning their living as best as they knew how, I was in search of mariachis that were playing in a bar around the area. The old fellows were good friends and we had made a good business: we offered a song including a rose, and it was almost always a success.

At a street corner I found the most beautiful flower that would adorn the huge market of varieties that are the streets of "San Jose at night." She was so beautiful that it seemed like the Virgin of the Immaculate. Since that moment I fell in love with her, and I loved her with the most pure and faithful love of a child.

Without thinking, I approached her and looked among my roses to find a message that spoke for me. There I found one that said, "My heart is yours." Yes, that was it. That woman had stolen my heart forever.

Others who accompanied her surrounded me while saying who knows what things, but the whole world had stopped and I was trying to make the words that I had stuck in my throat come out. Suddenly I could articulate a sentence that I had heard in a soap opera or on the radio or who knows where. I told her: "Miss, you are the most beautiful woman that I have ever seen. Here is a rose for the most beautiful flower."

The others clapped and whistled, she smiled, reached down and said with a voice a little thick coming from a woman so beautiful: Thank you, you're a gentleman, but I am not any flower, you should say: "a rose for Jazmin", that is my name.

She gently took the rose and kissed me on the forehead.

I can't explain with words what I felt. It must be the same feeling a child experiences when at Christmas he receives a gift that has been so desired, I suppose, I had never received one. I felt so happy that without saying anything I ran laughing and jumping in the dark streets. It had been a bad day. It was almost ten 'o clock and I had only sold perhaps five roses, I still had so much to do, but it didn't matter. I could spend the whole night awake because I was as happy as I had been in a long time, perhaps more than I'd ever been.

I got home at almost four in the morning. My grandmother was crying inconsolably at the door of the ranchito. If the Saints were to materialize, I would have seen them all sitting around here and there, on the roof, on the street, ground floor, in the rickety table in the doorway, waiting at the entrance of the precario, or anywhere they could find a place to sit, my viejita had brought them all down from the sky even in their pajamas.

When she saw me come running and with a happy face she first greeted me pulling hard on my ears accompanied by, "Where were you? Do you know what time it is", and then she gave me a hug filled with endless gratitude to every saint who had protected and kept me away from harm.

Inside the house she told me, "Oh my son, I do not know what I would do if something happens to you....they better rip the life from me before you get hurt.

Yes, I loved her, but now it was not just her, I was in love with Jazmin.

What was left of the day was spent thinking about her and I was anxious for it to be six o'clock to go to work.

I wanted to sell all my flowers early so I would have time to go see and talk to her.

At ten at night, I was already ready. Truth is, all we need is a reason to achieve the impossible. I had sold all the roses, except of course, the one for Jazmin, the one saying "I love you."

I came running, almost out of air. I just had time to see her open the door of a luxurious black car to go inside of it. I knew that, from the other women that protected me, their job consisted of accompanying gentlemen. That was my vision of prostitution. My innocence was not to think about the details of that company that was always on promotion in the streets of San Jose. Even exposed to so much misery, corruption and neglect, my grandmother had managed to keep me from many truths of life and on the other hand I have always just needed very few words to feel satisfied, even if it is the truth that in the absence of explanations I invented.

"Jazmin!," I shouted with all my strength before she got in the car. She stopped and turned around to look at me. She smiled and looked at me as if she was the Holy Mary, looking down from the top of the world smashing the head of a snake with her foot.

I ran faster and managed to make it. "I came to give you a rose," I told her, as she looked at me with a big smile. She did not say anything but took the rose, got into the car, shut the door and went away. I stood there, watching her go feeling that I should run after her.

A big and heavy hand layed on my shoulder.

"You like Jazmin, right?" I nodded without looking at her. "She is very beautiful," she added. "But be careful, what you see is only a mirage."

I did not understand what she said; I didn't want to think about it. I pushed her hand off my shoulder and started walking, dragging my feet, watching the ground until I got back to the ranchito. I thought that if I had a car like that, it would be me who would pick her up every night and would take her to McDonald's to eat fries and burgers or ice cream at the ice cream shop with those enormous cones that looked so delicious. Not by selling a million roses could I afford to buy that car as I could not even drive and I was just eight years old.

As always my grandmother received me with her blessings, this day as ever, because I had arrived home early. As a reward for my hard work, she went to the Chinese's store on the corner and bought milk and made me a glass of hot chocolate.

Perhaps because of the chocolate or the disappointment, or both things, I spent the whole night dreaming about her. I dreamed that we danced in the middle of a white dance floor, surrounded by thousands of roses of all colors, a ballroom filled with light, and then all of the sudden the car arrived. A man came out of it and pushed me hard and took my place while Jazmin looked at me with her sweet look and smiled the smile of a fair Virgin.

At school I could not concentrate for a minute. I use to participated in class and spoke with everyone, but that day, I only opened my mouth to ask 'what is a mirage?' When they explained to me that it was something that seemed real but that was only a deception of the mind it made me even more sad. What was Jazmin then and why did that woman with the hoarse voice and strong hands like a man tell me that it was not real?

Later in the evening, without having sold a single one of my roses, I went to wait for her at six o'clock.

I sat in the corner, and with the roses on my knees I devoted myself to wait for her. There were many who felt pity for my sad figure and in the course of my agony, I sold several roses. There was even a young lady that bought one and paid for two.

At ten o'clock, the group of girls that had that corner as an office began to arrive. I got up and waited eagerly for my beautiful Jazmin.

Before she arrived, the women with manly hands approached me and told me:

-Jazmin is undoubtedly beautiful, but is not what she seems as she is only a mirage.

-Why do you say that? What is a mirage? Jazmin is the most beautiful woman that I have ever seen.

-All the beautiful damsels that you see in this corner, including your Jazmin, are men by nature. Transvestites as they are often called.

Then I learned the significance of two new words, mirage and transvestite and the reason why they say that the street is the best school.

Of course I couldn't believe it. It was impossible for a man to look like that. Then I looked at the others and I realized that in fact they have something strange-the hands, face, excess makeup, something. But my Jazmin was so beautiful…

Soon she appeared at the corner, and when she saw me with my frightened face she asked what did those "witches filled with envy" had told me.

I looked at her in astonishment. It could not be true, that voice so subtle, although a bit harsh, could not be man.

Without a second thought, I asked the question that was oppressing my chest........ Is it true that you are a man?

Jazmin touched my face, dried my tears, took my hand and began to walk. -Come on...I will treat you to dinner-, she told me smiling.

She took me to a Chinese restaurant, and as we walked in, I was able to see how the stares and whispers that resounded in the middle of the silence.

We sat down and she ordered Cantonese rice for me and a beer for her.

When we were alone, she took my hands and said: -Tell me, what do you see?

With the ease with which I always answered I said "I see a beautiful woman who looks like the Virgin at church."

She smiled, stroked my head and her eyes filled with tears. She kept a long silence as she took a napkin to clean herself and prevent a black river from staining her cheeks. Then she spoke.

-I am not a monster, I am a human being like any other. I was not born a woman, but I do not look like a man. You are what you are, what you want to be, and not what others see or say you are. I want to be a woman, you see me as one, then, that I am. Do you know what color is the sky?

I shook my head no.

-The sky has no color as it's only a reflection of the light of the sun. Still, this doesn't stop it to give us a gift each day of the wonderful spectacle of a blue sky or the complete symphony of colors in a sunset. The sky is so beautiful that it always captive us, although in reality, it is not as we see it.

I could not help feel that my heart broke. Whatever color (or sex) that she was, I still saw, before my eyes, the most beautiful woman in the world.

As guessing what I was thinking, Jazmin asked me, -Do you like me?

-Yes-, I replied.

-And what do you want me for?

-To give you flowers, to go for a walk, to dance with you, to go to eat dinner, to be with me and love me…..to be my girlfriend.

-Well, the only thing that I can't be is your girlfriend, due to age, as you are just a child and I am not going to jail. But for everything else, I am available. It would be a pleasure and there is nothing that can stop us, right?

I smiled, took the bouquet of roses and gave her one. This time I did not noticed the message. But to my surprise, it was the first thing she looked for. She read it and smiled. The message said "Friends forever". She took it and saved it in her purse along with the other two that I had given her. She took another drink of beer from the bottle as she always did, and with her beautiful smile she told me to talk about myself. We talked for a long time. I told her my story, about my grandmother, my absent father, my run away mother, of my work and my school.

When we finished dinner, Jazmin said goodbye and gave me a kiss on the cheek. "Don't forget my rose," she said when she walked away to go to her corner. "No, I answered while running toward downtown to sell my flowers.

I did not need a million roses to have the opportunity to go to eat at McDonald's or sit and enjoy an ice cream cone. We saw each other every day without missing one, I gave her a rose and she gave me her time and affection. We agreed to meet a little bit early so neither will be up too late.

We went to the movies, I accompanied her shopping on her days off, she helped me with my homework, and bought medicine for my grandmother.

That immense love that I felt when I first saw her grew more each day.

Every night, after our meeting, I walked her to her corner, she gave me a kiss on the cheek and I gave her my rose. "Here comes the groom," shouted the other ones, jealous.

It had been a little over a year when one day after work I found my viejita lying on the floor. She could not get up as it seemed that an elephant was pressing her chest.

I ran to the end of the street to find a pay phone to call the Red Cross and they arrived but did not come into the neighborhood scared they might be assaulted. A few neighbors helped me take her to them and thank God my grandmother survived, although now she could not work anymore for her right hand and part of her face fell asleep forever. Without her work we could not pay for our ranchito. I did not go to sell flowers for three days and in the afternoon of the fourth day, while I waited for the visit line to sneak in with an adult, I saw Jazmin dressed as a great lady, Then and there, I felt protected as never before. When she saw me she took me by the hand and said, "Why didn't you call? I went to your house looking for you...Oh, my poor boy, I didn't know...you will not go back to that place."

We did not go back to the slums, but instead, moved in with Jazmin to a small but comfortable, clean, organized and good smelling house with a bright floor and hot clean water. We never even went back to get the few rags or pots and pans darkened by fire, we never again went back that way.

My grandmother was around for ten more years thanks to the care of Jazmin. I kept selling flowers until shortly before eleven years old. Although Jazmin and my grandmother insisted constantly for me to quit, I had my pride and, after all, I was the man of the house and did not want to be a burden.

Unfortunately, the overwhelming concern of a good neighbor about my future forced me to leave my job. This woman was so concerned about the influence that Jazmin might have in my life that, for reasons of morality and decency, she called social services. To make matters worse, selling flowers at night was the proof needed to blame my two women of abuse and exploitation. People could only see what was happening from outside the door: a child who sells flowers, an old woman who looks at everything and keeps quiet, a transvestite who, every morning lovingly kisses a child, when coming back to the house.

I was about to go to an orphanage, but we managed to convinced a lot of people that the reality fell far short of the details mentioned. My grandmother had fought furiously, alleging that she preferred to die before taking us apart. Jazmin said that she would leave the house and give us everything that cost her so much misery and humiliation, all that she had earned with the blood of her work, because in that profession sweat is not enough. Luckily other neighbors, my teacher, and the school director gave their testimonies. With the help of some influential friends of my beloved protector from both government and private enterprises, soon there was an agreement- a visit to the social worker twice a week and no work for me. Government and neighbor harassment lasted a few more days until Jazmin, with a few of her friends armed with sharp nails and a little glamorous but daunting vocabulary, shouted out to the entire neighborhood that it didn't matter how many people they had against us, she and her friends would silence them if they tried to separate us. Even the social worker assigned to me was there protesting that my dysfunctional family cared more for me than many "normal" families care for their own.

As soon as I could, I got a job in the farmers market to at least help pay for my books, I also had good friends there because of my connections from the roses supplier who always helped me, such as giving me a few extra roses or used apparel and shoes of his children.

But just the same way it was done when I sold roses, I still walked Jazmin to her corner, she gave me a kiss and I gave her my flower, then I walked home.

At five in the morning, when Jazmin arrived from work, my grandmother with half of her body working, would prepared breakfast while I prepared to go to school. Between happiness and harmony of a beautiful family we would sit down to eat to talk about our day and the life we knew.

In this house full of peace, no one ever complained nor fought. There were no questions, they were not needed. My viejita, who was devoutly religious, never broached the subject of Jazmin's work or her real sex. Only once did my grandmother say that sanctitude is in the heart of those who are good. "It doesn't matter what she is or not is, her heart is the heart of a saint."

By the end of the first year we lived together, I finally knew what a birthday was and what it was like to receive Christmas gifts. There were never many kids in my house as mothers thought that it was a bad example for their children to see our way of life, but Jazmin and I had so many friends from the streets that I never longed for anyone extra to accompany us to blow out the candles of my cake and eat ice cream.

I never had hunger or fear, and was finally never cold at night. I had time to play and study with enough love to make me happy.

I never cared about my classmates joke, the parent's disgust, or the criticisms of some teachers.

I felt proud that in every triumph, in the presentations of the typical dances, parades of Independence Day, in the works of theatre, and when I looked at the audience, I always found my grandmother and Jazmin happy and tearful.

Of course, there was the time when I came home with a split mouth and broken nose from stifling criticism about the noblest woman I had ever met. I did not care that I lost a "friend" which didn't like my situation.

I never felt intimidated for who I was, where I came from and how I made it here. This is what life has given me and I am extremely thankful for being the lucky one to receive all this.

During my high school days I had the opportunity to understand the meaning of romantic love. I learned what it was like to fall in love with another person in a very different way than my love affair for Jazmin. I realized then that I loved her with the purest and the greatest love of all, a love that knows no gender, no criticism, no limitations. I was proud to love her with the greatest love of a child for his mother.

I finished school as the Valedictorian. At least my viejita could see me graduate from high school. That joy was enough for her to pass and to continue to worship the Saints even more closely in the same Kingdom.

I went college, graduated there with honors, and had the opportunity to study abroad, in medicine, of course. When I returned from abroad, I found out that the man in the black and luxurious car that often visited us before, now lived in our house. Jazmin did not want to be alone and had finally agreed to the pleas of his eternal love. The man is now a respectable father to me.

Jazmin has long left the corners and now has her own business growing and exporting the most beautiful flowers. I devote myself to serving patients in the hospital and raising funds to help the children from the streets. Even though our lives have changed so much, every day when I finish my job, I buy a red rose at a booth in the farmers market to take it to the most wonderful woman in the world, my mother; and while I am alive, there will always be a rose for Jazmin.

Non Fiction

Natalie Grigson
Austin, Texas, United States

Natalie Grigson grew up in Austin, Texas, where she recently obtained a Bachelor's degree in Creative Writing. She is currently working as the Director of Marketing and PR for a local company; frantically planning a move across the country, made just a bit complicated by a very large and slightly restless dog; and of course, trying to solve that whole problem of world peace. In her free time, though, she enjoys reading, writing, and spending time outdoors with aforementioned large dog.

Finding Culture in Barcelona
By Natalie Grigson

*M*y friend Margeaux and I sat across the table from each other, glaring in opposite directions, speaking only to fill the silence and the hunger that seemed to press down on us.

Neither of us had eaten since our very crowded and very screaming-baby-filled plane from New York to Barcelona was somewhere in the middle of the Atlantic, about six hours previously. Aside from the fact that we were in a restaurant in Barcelona on the verge of eating our napkins, another change had occurred since the beginning of our trip. On the flight we were excited, we were ready to see the world and screaming babies or not, we we-re going to Barcelona!

Mind you, we were pretty well caffeinated and we had in-flight movies to keep our spirits up. Who wants to sulk about screaming children when you can watch The Bourne Supremacy in five different languages? It just doesn't happen.

Once we landed in Barcelona, the high of an all-around successful flight had begun to wear off, and with our growing hunger the little "bumps" in the road started to feel more like six foot tall curbs. Our bags took about half a day to arrive and maybe twice that just to lug through the airport. When we got outside we were greeted by a long line of Spaniards and European tourists of every make and model, all squished together and waiting for cabs. When we finally reached the front of the line, the four-door taxi proved to be too small for our luggage and we had to wait for a van. Finally we we-re charged almost double what we expected to pay for the ride, only to be dropped off about two blocks from the hotel with all of our bags. Like I said, six foot tall curbs.

By the time we checked in the optimism from the flight seemed a far off memory. We threw our luggage unceremoniously onto the floor. This was a feat in itself as our bags probably weighed more than the two of us combi-ned, but at the time it only seemed appropriate to take the frustrations of our travels so far out on the heavy, inanimate objects. I may have even kicked my suitcase once or twice just for good measure.

After a few well rehearsed Spanish swear words and a bit of general storming around, we both changed into something a little bit less wrinkled and travel-worn, and left the hotel in search of food.

The dingy and cramped corner restaurant we settled on was only about a block from the hotel. We sat down, exhausted, at a table near the entrance.

And then we waited.

As we continued to wait for somebody to take our order, Margeaux seemed to regain a bit of her energy from the flight and gave optimism one more shot.

"When in Barcelona!"

"What?" I snapped.

"You know, like 'When in Rome, do as the Romans do…'"

"But we're not in Rome. That's not the saying."

"Yeah, but I think it applies to wherever."

And the conversation went on like this for a few minutes. I had no idea what Margeaux was talking about; there was nothing for us to *do* like the Barcelonans would do, unless she wanted us to wait like the locals, which I'm pretty sure they didn't even have to do. The silent treatment seemed to be especially for the tourists.

The small space would have been welcoming, maybe even cute, had we not been so irritable (after about ten minutes Margeaux had given up on op-timistic and was looking downright irritated.) The walls around us were white stone and the small wooden tables were scattered around the place with mismatching chairs. It had the feel of a hundred year old res-taurant, in-to which someone had moved in an odd assortment of hand-me-down furniture, placed it in random places throughout the room, and then forgot to organize it later. Looking back, the place was eclectic and cozy, but Margeaux and I felt like we were skirting the line of starvation at the time, so to us it was dingy and cramped.

As the minutes passed we watched the servers walk around lazily, sometimes stopping to tuck in a chair or straighten the menus, but mostly they just strolled by, as though unaware that we had been sitting there following them with our eyes for the past fifteen minutes. That was our first glimpse at the Spanish restaurant mentality — which apparently ap-plies to most other things as well.

Finally after about twenty or thirty minutes a very dark and Spanish looking waiter walked slowly over to our table. He had olive complexion, shoulder-length dark hair bordering on black, and stood with his hand on his hip like Ricky Ricardo.

"Hello," he said in a thick accent. "What can I get you?" He tapped his foot impatiently even as the words left his mouth. He looked back and forth between the two American girls with a look of bored disgust behind his bright blue eyes. These were not the Antonio Bandares eyes I'd been expecting and their cold contrast to his skin was almost as unwelcome as the look he gave us. He watched us like we were snails—a mildly interesting creature but on closer inspection, just a slimy slug with a fancy shell. As soon as I thought this, a waiter walked by with a plate of the little creatures.

"We want to try something new!" Margeaux said confidently to the waiter in her best (and loudest) Spanish. We had been trying to practice our Spanish since we left Austin and we were a bit offended that this waiter had automatically assumed we were American. Looking back on it, it is no wonder that he did. We were two of the only people in the restaurant so early (it was nearly eight p.m.; a mere snack time for Spaniards), we were toting a-round our American designed purses (walking advertisements for Coach and Guess), and we were wearing sneakers. *Sneakers* at dinner. After about a week in Spain we learned that almost any shoe was appropriate at dinner ti-me, except bedroom slippers and, of course, sneakers. This was a big mista-ke. And so, apparently, was ordering our meal in Spanish.

"You want to try something new? Okay." He responded this time in Spanish.

With that Señor Blue Eyes turned on his heel and was off to the kitchen to prepare our order.

The only thing Barcelonans hate more than two naïve American girls is two naïve American girls trying to speak Spanish in a city where Catalan is the norm. I didn't know it then, but Catalan is the language of northern Spain, not Spanish; and to anyone who was raised speaking it, it is the *only* language of Spain. It sounds like a combination of French, Spanish, and a pinch of Gibberish; and as we sat in the restaurant listening to the waiters we realized we couldn't understand a lick of it. Of course Barcelonans have a handle on both the languages so he understood *us* perfectly and even responded clearly enough in Spanish (though his accent sounded like a comedian's impression of a gay hairdresser), but the people of Barcelona are a peculiar breed of Spaniard. They are proud; they are cultured; they have light eyes and dark skin; and dammit they don't have to speak Spanish in Spain if they don't want to! They also seem to have no qualms about teaching two American girls a lesson.

Don't ask a Barcelonan waiter for "something new" off of a menu in a language you can't read. Lesson learned.

After the waiter stalked away to have the chef prepare whatever it was we would be enjoying that evening, Margeaux and I began to relax a bit. Just the thought that some kind of Spanish food was on its way to our table really brightened our spirits. We were laughing, drinking local beers, and practicing our Spanish and clear, loud voices, as if to shout, "We're not Americans! We can fit in!" We may as well have painted targets on our foreheads.

Several minutes later the waiter returned with a large plate of what at first looked like pasta. "Enjoy," he said as he placed our entrée on the table. We looked at our delicious meal hungrily, forks in hand, mouths watering, ready to shovel the food gluttonously to our faces, when we realized this was not a plate of pasta at all. What we took to be thick noodles were the thick, stubby tentacles of at least twenty miniature octopi. You could fit a-bout three of them in a fist; they were purple and were covered in beads of hot water like steamed cabbage, and their little alien heads looked *hard,* like they had some kind of bone structure. It was a mess of maroon suckers, heads like the villains from *Independence Day,* and beady, ink black eyes.

We stared at the plate for a while. It stared back.

"When in Barcelona…"

I responded with one of those mechanical, nervous laughs and bit my lip when I realized the unpleasant sound was coming from me. I looked at the little creatures, very aware that the waiter was still hovering close by watching, challenging us with his bright blue eyes. Maybe it was our pride; maybe it was our hunger; or maybe it was the combination of the very unwelcome welcomes we had so far received, but after a momentary stare down with our meal, we decided to dig in. Besides, it was a twenty euro entrée. We speared their crunchy heads with forks like small tridents and raised them up as though preparing to make a toast.

"Cheers," we said, and we each bit into one small tentacle.

I looked at the waiter as I chewed (and chewed, and chewed…) the tiny morsel of what may as well have been rubber; and I forced a smile. After he disappeared I quickly pushed the plate away from me and closer to Margeaux, we put a menu over the thing just to avoid the reminder of what was currently squirming down into our stomachs, and drained our water glasses so fast, a small tear trickled out of my eye.

It was probably the single most disgusting thing I have ever eaten. The little tentacle had the consistency of a rubber band and probably tasted about the same. It wasn't the taste, though, that nearly made the little appendage resurface an hour later, but it was the texture. As each little suction went over my tongue an image of it went through my mind like a magnified wart. Needless to say the first bite was our last and the plate remained hidden until we left, but we thought we put forth a valiant effort considering our meal had suction cups. After all, we are Americans. We are stubborn, we speak Spanish at inappropriate times, we have never even heard of Catalan, and dammit we aren't afraid to try new things!

When we left the restaurant we walked into the first McDonald's we saw.

After all, we are Americans.

Don Scheer
Boynton Beach, Florida, United States

Non-Fiction / Memoir Category

Mr. Platnikoff and the Canary: A Love Story
By Don Scheer

fter the batteries of tests, after the interviews, after the
health physicals, I was told I was hired. A week of orientation in Washington at the State Department would be required, and then I would assume the duties of an advisor to
the Indian government at the American Embassy in New Delhi, India.

"Great," I said. "When do I start?"

"After your security clearance is completed," I was told by Harold
Lierly, Assistant Personnel Director of the State Department. "I'll get the
papers off later today to begin the process."

"And how long does it usually take for the security clearance to be
completed?" I asked.

"About six months. It's an FBI full field investigation. They'll be checking your employment application for accuracy, credit background, sexual
preferences, drug use, if any, arrest record if one exists, ability to work well
with others, general moral character – that kind of stuff. Once completed,
if all goes well, you'll be cleared for 'Top Secret.' You'll need to check with
me once a month or so, or sooner, if you change your address."

He held out his hand to me. I shook it, thanked him, and left the building.

While I was deeply disappointed that I'd have to wait another six months – I'd already spent one month going through the interview process – I was determined to begin life as a foreign service officer, see exotic places, breeze through customs with my black diplomatic passport, ride in rickshaws. My reverie stopped abruptly when a taxi just missed me as I walked across the street from the Federal Building in lower Manhattan.

"And I need a temporary job for six months," I told myself. I bought a *New York Times* and sat on a bench eating a Sabrett hot dog, washed down with a Coke™ as I went through the want ads. A big advertisement by the New York Department of Welfare announced permanent and temporary positions as a social case worker. Applicants were required to complete an application and show up at any welfare office with their college diploma.

I went home, located my Bachelor and Master of Arts diplomas and headed for the closest office of the Department of Welfare. One was located at West 23rd Street. I completed the application at their office and had a brief interview with a very bored-looking lady who had one long eyebrow over two tired eyes.

"You can start tomorrow morning at our office on 113th Street and Third Avenue, or next week at this office. Which do you prefer?"

"You mean I'm hired?"

"Right. You're hired," she said.

"There's no security check into my background?" I asked.

"No. Should we be concerned?"

"Well, I thought you'd want to know my credit history, my sexual preferences, my ability to get along well with people, etc."

"Look," she said. "We have 610 vacancies for case workers citywide; the case loads are staggering; the work is tough; the pay is low. You look normal, and you have two diplomas. Whether or not you prefer to have sex with dwarf aborigines, the City of New York doesn't give a hoot."

"You mean I'm hired and I can start work tomorrow?"

"That's what I mean."

"I'll take the 113th Street job."

"Good. Spanish Harlem," she said. "Report to Room 206 at the 113th Street Department of Welfare office tomorrow at 9 a.m. Glad to have you aboard." She never looked up.

I was at the welfare office well before 9 a.m. At least a hundred people were on various lines waiting to see admittance clerks. They looked like the people Emma Lazarus wrote about in her poem on the bronze plaque at the base of the Statue of Liberty: the tired, the poor, the huddled masses. They were at this office along with lots of the wretched. People were shouting at each other, babies were wailing, young children ran about. I sat down and waited.

At 9 a.m. a short bald fellow wearing a suit came over to me and said, "You're wearing a tie. You must be the new guy."

"Right," I said.

"Follow me."

We left the bedlam of the front admittance office and walked through a door to the bedlam of the back office where the caseworkers were seated at their desks. There were no individual offices, just a sea of forty desks with caseworkers on telephones. Everyone was speaking loudly so they could be heard over the din of voices. I was led to an empty desk with a file cabinet next to it.

"I'm your supervisor, Larry Leno," said the bald guy. "This is your desk, and this is your caseload." He tapped the file cabinet. You have 106 cases. Each client has to be visited at least once every ninety days. When you visit, get a current rent receipt, ask them if they've earned any money during the last three months, look for signs of child abuse and signs that the-re is an adult male in the household, which is a no-no since 99 percent of your cases are AFDC and are on welfare because there's no child sup-port co-ming from the fathers."

"The money we're providing is for the mother and her kids, not to support some guy, so look for signs of adult men, like big shoes under the bed, male clothes in the closets, like that. Men shouldn't be there. Make certain everyone is healthy and if not, make sure they get health care. If your Spanish isn't good, ask your client to get a neighbor who speaks Eng-lish, you know, an amigo to help. If you need assistance, everyone here will help you, including me. Any questions?"

"Yes. When will I go through orientation?"

"You've just been oriented. I suggest you spend this morning looking over your files, set up a schedule of visits and just take the plunge. In Three days you'll be a pro. Look, I'm not being flipped here. I'm busy as hell. The job isn't complicated. It's a bitch, but it's not complicated. The clients are poor people who need assistance. Sometimes they're frauds work-ing a scam, but that's rare."

"To summarize, these people are just making it *with* our help. Wel-come to Spanish Harlem. If you need me, I'm at the desk in front of the room."

Before Larry Leno left, he said, "That's Margie at the next desk." He pointed to a young woman who was on the phone next to me. She was writing furiously on a yellow pad but looked up and smiled at me and ga-ve me a little wave. I opened the file cabinet. It was jammed with case fi-les, each one thick with information. I saw a master sheet of client names. Of the 106 cases, al-most half were named Rodriquez or Sanchez. The other 50 or so were na-med Romero, Jimenez, Santiago, Guerra and Figueroa.

One name stood out – Ivan Platnikoff, age 89, old age assistance recipi-ent. I read his file quickly. He was born in 1896 in Saint Petersburg, Rus-sia, was a stage actor in Moscow, and came to the United States in 1916.

He worked as an actor in silent films when he was 20 but was incapacitated in 1918 in a car accident and then came down with polio. Currently suffers from emphysema, Parkinson's disease, high blood pressure, diabetes, and rheumatoid arthritis. Lives alone and has no living relatives. Has lived at the same apartment since 1934.

I decided that Mr. Platnikoff would be the first client I would visit since he lived right across the street from the welfare office. And because of his age and health condition, I thought I'd better get to him before the day was out. Also, he had a telephone, so I called him and introduced myself. "I'd like to come by in the next fifteen minutes or so, if that is convenient."

"Well," Mr. Platnikoff said in a voice that was deep and robust. "I'm scheduled to deliver an address at the United Nations later today, but I can work you in if you get here promptly." And he laughed loudly into the pho-ne.

"I'll see you in fifteen minutes, Mr. Platnikoff."

I told Larry Leno, "I'm off to see Mr. Platnikoff across the street as my first visit."

"Good choice. Interesting guy," he said. "Say hello to Roskolnikov," he smiled.

I wondered who Leno was talking about but didn't ask. I quickly read the rest of Mr. Platnikoff's file and then walked across the street to meet him.

His building was a four-story walk-up with Mr. Platnikoff living on the third floor. Loud music with a Latin beat blared from several apartments as I walked up the stairs. The hallway smelled pleasantly like El Faro's Spanish restaurant in Greenwich Village, one of my favorite haunts.

I was expecting Mr. Platnikoff to be a little old man bent over with pain or perhaps in a wheelchair. I was wrong. Ivan Platnikoff was at least six foot two inches tall, had a large shock of curly white hair and an elaborate handlebar mustache. He shook my hand vigorously and looked at me carefully with large, deep-set brown eyes.

He motioned for me to sit down in a big upholstered chair in his small, neat living room while he sat nearby on the couch.

"Mr. Leno, my supervisor, told me to say hello to Roskolnikov for him. What did he mean?"

Mr. Platnikoff laughed. "Roskolnikov is my canary and best buddy." He got up from the couch and walked to a large bird cage in the corner of the living room, opened the cage door, held out his hand and a small pale yellow canary jumped onto his middle finger. Mr. Platnikoff then returned to the couch smiling at the bird, which started to sing in a loud voice.

"Ah, he's happy to see you. He's in good voice this morning. This wonderful, happy little creature who sings to me all the time is Roskolnikov. He hasn't a worry in the world. He has plenty of canary seed and water to drink, a clean cage and a big bowl in which he bathes. He's one contented fellow."

"And yet you named him 'Roskolnikov,'" I said, "probably the most complicated, conflicted character in literary history? Dostoyevsky's Roskolnikov never sang in the morning, Mr. Platnikoff." The old man looked at me for several seconds without speaking. Then he asked incredulously, "You've read *Crime and Punishment* by Dostoyevsky?"

"Oh, yes, I've read all of his works and Tolstoy's and Turgenev's and on and on. I majored in Russian literature in college."

"You've read these authors in English or in Russian?"

"Sorry to say, only in English translation. Learning Russian is my hope some day when time permits."

"I cannot believe that God has sent me a caseworker who knows Russian literature. It's a miracle. But to answer your question about why I named him Roskolnikov, it's because he is exactly the opposite of the literary character. It's a joke name, like the name 'Tiny' for a Great Dane."

"Ah," I said. "Sorry, I didn't understand."

"I know you are busy," he said, "and didn't come to talk to me about Russian literature, but I must ask you one question."

"Please do."

"Have you read Pushkin?" Mr. Platnikoff held his breath until I answered.

"Of course. One cannot major in Russian literature without reading Pushkin. It would be like an English literature major not reading Shakespeare."

"Yes. Quite right, but Shakespeare compared to Pushkin is not right either. Compared to Pushkin, Shakespeare writes like Mickey Spillane."

"I think you've gone too far, Mr. Platnikoff."

"You say that because you haven't read Pushkin in Russian. You cannot know the real Pushkin in English," Mr. Platnikoff said excitedly. He got up from the couch still holding the singing Roskolnikov on his finger, went to a bookcase and pulled out an old book. I could see by its cover that it was printed in Russian.

Mr. Platnikoff pointed to the coffee table and said, "My rent receipt is in front of you. I haven't worked in the last three months, nor have I earned any money from a lottery or from my secret life as a gigolo. I know the information you need, but you must indulge an old man. You must listen to Pushkin in Russian read by an ancient Russian actor. I'll only read you a short passage, but you must listen. Believe me, it's the best thing you'll hear all day long, all week long, all your life long."

"Okay, Mr. Platnikoff, what will you read?"

"I'll read you a short piece from Eugene Onegin." He put Roskolnikov back into his cage.

"Will it be Tatyana's confession to Onegan?" I asked.

Mr. Platnikoff shook his head and placed his hands on his cheeks. "I will say it again. I cannot believe what I'm hearing. God has sent you to this apartment on East 113th Street so an old man can receive a bit of joy in his life."

"Mr. Platnikoff found the paragraph he was looking for and started to read in a quiet voice in Russian. Almost instantly this tall white-haired courtly gentleman with the Wild Bill Hickock mustache transformed himself into a young woman named Tatyana who painfully and tenderly disclosed her love for the aristocratic Eugene Onegin. After three or four sentences, his voice cracked. He stopped reading. Tears dripped from his eyes. "Sorry," he said. "It is too beautiful to continue. I cannot. I am sorry." He put the book back in the bookcase.

Roskolnikov, who had stopped singing when Platnikoff began to read, started to sing a different, more soulful song as Mr. Platnikoff wiped away his tears with a large red handkerchief. Then he started to laugh. "There is no fool like an old fool, right? Just like a Russian, we're always crying or laughing, sometimes at the same time. We are a strange people."

"No, no. I thank you. It was a beautiful reading, but I still don't think Shakespeare writes like Mickey Spillane."

"Perhaps you are right." He shrugged.

I picked up the rent receipt in front of me and made a note of it on my pad. When I put the receipt back on the coffee table, I noticed a framed faded photograph of two young men seated at an outdoor café holding their glasses high in the air as though they were toasting each other.

"Is one of these fellows you?" I asked.

"Yes, this is me," said Mr. Platnikoff, pointing to a young man in the photograph. "I was nineteen, already well known in acting circles, having a glass of tea with my good friend, Gorky."

"Is that *Maxim* Gorky in the photo?"

"Yes, it is. We were in Saint Petersburg. It was July of 1916 and unusually hot. We had just come through a wicked rainy season and the mosquitoes were relentless. I'll always remember what Gorky said as we sat at that table drinking glasses of tea and swatting mosquitoes. He said, 'The mosquitoes are so big and nasty they could rape a chicken.' Not a bad line, no? It's sixty-nine years since he said it, but the line is still fresh."

When I said goodbye, shook his hand and walked down the worn staircase to the street level below, I could hear Roskolnikov singing a lively, upbeat tune.

Larry Leno was right. In three days I felt comfortable in my new job. I was getting the hang of it. During the first week I visited all twenty-three of the Mrs. Rodriguezes, checked every one of their rent receipts, played with more than one hundred children, looked for big shoes under beds and found three pairs, but each Mrs. Rodriguez with the suspicious shoes assured me that the shoes had been left by their former husbands when they disappeared and were currently not being worn by anyone. They were kept because they simply could not bring themselves to throw the shoes away and, who knows, maybe some day the husbands would return and wear their shoes again.

I helped one Mrs. Rodriguez get an appointment with an orthopedic specialist who accepted Medicaid patients so that her youngest son could be fitted with orthopedic shoes to help correct the child's right foot from turning inward when he walked. And I got a wheelchair for one of the teenage daughters who had a recurring spinal condition. I was impressed with the variety of support services provided by the Department of Welfare for assisting welfare clients with problems ranging from counseling to physical therapy.

I liked the job. I felt I was doing something important. I liked all the Mrs. Rodríguezes and looked forward to the next week when I would meet all of the Mrs. Sanchezes. But most of all I liked Mr. Platnikoff and decided I would visit him again soon – off duty – so we could talk more about Russian literature and his old days in Saint Petersburg.

A couple of days later I was eating dinner with some friends at the Second Avenue Delicatessen when I saw a sign on the wall advertising a special of borscht with home-made sour cream, boiled potatoes and a half loaf of Russian black bread. I called Mr. Platnikoff.

"It's your caseworker, "I said."How'd you like some borscht, sour cream, potatoes and black bread? I can be at your place in twenty minutes."

"Good," he said. "I'll be here. And don't forget the caviar. I prefer Beluga." And he laughed his deep, rich laugh into the phone.

I left my friends and spent a pleasant half hour talking with Mr. Platnikoff about another one of his Russian cronies, Leonid Andreyev, an ardent anti-communist writer who had left Russia at about the same time as Mr. Platnikoff.

Every couple of weeks I visited him in the evenings, bringing along some Russian food – sometimes piroski, sometimes blinis, and once a special Russian herring in wine sauce which I had located it in a small appetizing store on the Lower East Side. To my delight, Mr. Platnikoff proclaimed the herring was the best he'd had since he was a boy in Saint Petersburg.

* * *

One evening, along with the food, I brought a small bottle of Vodka which he savored between bites of his piroski.

"You know," he said, "canaries are by nature not friendly birds. They are loners, happy to sit in their cages all day long. They brood a lot. They are a popular bird in Russia because they are such moody creatures, much like Russians themselves. They sing not because they are filled with joy. They sing to entice females or to scare away other males. They are not like parakeets that are eager to be with people. No sir, canaries are peculiar chaps. They don't like to be handled, either.

"It took months of training to get Roskolnikov to sit on my finger, and now he'll even gently peck seed off of my lips. It looks like he's kissing me. This is no big deal for a parakeet, but for a canary, it's earthshaking. It took all my patience to get him to be the bird he now is, but I had little else to do. I've outlived all my old friends who used to visit me. Now it's just me and Roskolnikov, but how much love can a little canary give? Thank God you have come into my life. I am so grateful. You are like the son I never had."

"You've given *me* a great deal," I said to him. "For years I told people that the greatest short story ever written was *The Abyss* by Lermontov, and then you corrected me and told me *The Abyss* was written by Andreyev. I looked it up and sure enough, you are correct. Now if I'm ever on a quiz show and they ask me who wrote *The Abyss*, I'll correctly say Andreyev, and I'll always have you to thank."

Mr. Platnikoff poured the last drop of vodka into his shot glass and said, "You know, Americans have some decent writers, too. Mark Twain is read by every school child in Russia, and Russians consider Walt Whitman to be a great, great poet. It was Whitman who made me understand what is going on between Roskolnikov and me. Whitman let me know that the moment one zeros in on anything, even if it's as inconsequential as a blade of grass or a canary, that thing can become an indescribably magnificent universe – mysterious and wondrous. It can become an entire life."

"Get some sleep, Mr. Platnikoff. I'll be in touch." As I left his apartment I looked at him sitting at his little kitchen table. His shoulders drooped. He stared at his empty shot glass. He looked like a man who was at least eighty-nine years old.

At Christmas time I decided I'd buy some small gift for Mr. Platnikoff, but couldn't think of what to purchase. After I told a girlfriend about the old Russian actor and his canary, she suggested I buy him a female canary. "Maybe he could get into breeding the birds, make a few bucks on the side, fill his life with something more to do," she said.

Good idea, I thought. I visited a small Pet Shop near my apartment and put a deposit down on a young female canary that was slightly smaller than Roskolnikov but had a deeper yellow color. Three days later on Christmas E-ve I delivered the female in a brown paper sack with air holes poked into it.

"What's in the bag?" he asked as I entered the apartment. "The way you're holding it so carefully it must be caviar. You got me some Beluga, eh?"

"No, something better. I got you a female canary which I have temporarily named Tatyana."

Well, Mr. Platnikoff was all excited. He carefully took the paper bag from me and placed it into Roskolnikov's large cage, gingerly opening the sack. Tatyana walked confidently out of the paper bag onto the floor of the cage. Roskolnikov started to sing.

"We have to be very careful," whispered Mr. Platnikoff. "Sometimes a male will kill a female quite suddenly."

But it was clear very quickly that Roskolnikov's thoughts were very far from violence. He joined Tatyana on the floor of the cage and nuzzled her head with his neck.

We watched the two birds getting to know each other for several minutes. "They look like love birds," said Mr. Platnikoff. "I think we have a match."

The birds were sitting very close on the cage perch rubbing their heads together.

"Merry Christmas, Mr. Platnikoff," I said. "I have to leave."

"Thank you, thank you," he said.

I closed the door. I heard him yell after me, "Merry Christmas." Mr. Platnikoff was happy, and I was filled with the Christmas spirit of giving.

In mid-January I received a call from Mr.Lierly at the State Department. "Congratulations," he said. "You now have a Top Secret security clearance. We need you in Washington on February 1st. Your black passport will be waiting for you."

I was delighted that at long last I'd soon begin my career as a Foreign Service Officer, but I had some remorse, too, about leaving my welfare clients. My caseload had increased by sixteen additional cases. I had four mo-re Rodríguezes and four more Sanchezes, but still only one Platnikoff, whom I would miss most of all.

Later, on the day I learned my security clearance had been approved, I visited him. I hadn't seen him since I'd given him Tatyana on Christmas Eve.

When I knocked on his door, it took a long time for him to open it. He was hunched over as he walked slowly to the couch and sat down, sinking heavily into the cushions.

"Are you okay, Mr. Platnikoff?" I asked. "You don't look so good."

Mr. Platnikoff raised his head and looked directly at me. "It's Roskolnikov," he said.

"What happened, is he sick or worse? What happened?"

"No, he's happy as can be."

"So what is the problem?" I asked.

"He has forgotten me," said Mr. Platnikoff slowly. "He has not sung a song since you came with Tatyana. He won't come near me. He spends all of his time, day and night, with Tatyana who has beguiled him. He has been hypnotized by that female. Roskolnikov has forgotten I exist."

"But Mr. Platnikoff, remember you told me that male canaries sing to attract females. Well, he's attracted one. He has no reason to sing anymore. He's doing what he's supposed to be doing."

Mr. Platnikoff slammed his large fist down loudly on the coffee table. "No, what he's supposed to be doing is paying attention to me. I'm the one who feeds him. I give him fresh water to bathe in and to drink. He should pay attention to me." He slammed his fist once again onto the coffee table, this time so forcibly that the framed photo of him and Gorky fell over on its side.

"I want you to take Tatyana out of here," he yelled. "I still have the paper bag you brought her in." He pulled the sack out of a kitchen cabinet. "You must take her, or I swear on everything that is holy that I will crush her in my fist."

I had never seen Mr. Platnikoff in such a state but knew from the way he looked at me that he would do what he said.

"I'll take her. Please, please calm down."

He walked to the cage and cornered Tatyana with his large hand and forced her into the paper bag which he gave to me.

"I'll return her to the shop where I purchased her," I said. "I'll be in touch."

I left the apartment. I decided then to write Mr. Platnikoff a farewell letter as soon as I arrived in India. I didn't want to upset him further by telling him now that I'd soon be leaving the country.

As I walked downstairs, I could hear Roskolnikov singing in a quiet voice a mournful tune.

Epilogue

I felt terrible about what I had done to Mr. Platnikoff. Despite my good intentions, I had taken away from him the little bit of love that he had in his life. By following his instructions and removing Tatyana from his apartment, I hoped that Roskolnikov would soon resume his singing, hop on Mr.Platnikoff's finger and become his loyal companion once again. But even if things returned to where they were before I had intervened, I thought about how I had disrupted another relationship – that between Roskolnikov and Tatyana, and I hoped that the little female would end up in a good home with an attentive suitor.

I then pushed all thoughts about Mr. Platnikoff and the two canaries out of my mind and thought about my new life coming up in India, where at least a billion people were waiting for my good intentions.

Yves Goddard
Orlando, Florida

My name is Yvi Goddard and I am a sophomore at the University of Central Florida in Orlando, majoring in Social Work. I was born in Illinois and moved to Florida almost four years ago after living in Maryland for ten years. I started my writing experience in the fourth grade when my poem was published in the 2002 edition of the Anthology of Poetry for Young Americans. In my spare time I enjoy writing everything from prose, poetry, and short stories. This summer I am strengthening my artistic skills by playing the piano, writing songs, and entering writing contests

Whispers of Change
By Yves Goddard

"I'll be back," I tell my roommate before leaving the room, not caring to explain where I am going. It would not be an issue clarifying, but I really need some alone time right now. I was completing homework all day and desired to relax at the pond that gave me solace numerous times throughout the year. Closing the front door, I walk down the hall and stare straight ahead with only one thought on my mind: getting to that pond. I press the elevator button to go down, and wait for it to open. Inside, I feel this urgency to get there the quickest way possible and immediately decide to take the stairs instead. I head in the opposite direction of the elevator, continue down, and open the emergency door leading outside.

I feel the stress already subsiding when I see the bright rays of the sun peering through the gazebo surrounding the stairs. Its warmness begins to thaw my skin, which I didn't notice was cold from being inside the air conditioned room. Bolting down the stairs, I enjoy the sky view. There are no clouds and although it feels like eighty five degrees, the accompanying breeze makes it bearable to walk through without sweating before reaching my destination.

Normally I power walk everywhere, but I didn't have the strength to mo-ve my feet faster than necessary. In exactly seven minutes I reach the pond and sit underneath a big tree with a canopy of shade. I am on a hill of grass and not too far below is the famed Reflection Pond on campus. Its simplistic structure brings me peace with its soft, rushing sound as water shoots up into the air from the center, with other spouts coming out but not reaching as high. The grass stops about fifteen feet away from me and in its place are cement steps leading to the pond. Behind, there is a building with tinted windows that, if looking closely, display the reflection of the water. So here I am, observing all of this and gradually forgetting the worries of what I face when I head back. For a minute or two I just listen in silence.

I try channeling out everything going through my mind and just con-tem-plate on reaching a state of peace, knowing the place of serenity is the only way to help me. I whisper to my best friend who speaks in those soft breaths and who knows the struggles I go through before they occur. Through nature His works are seen everywhere and in this moment I see Him as I feel the slight coolness of the air and the light sprinkles of water on my arm from the pond.

Sighing, I say, "Ok, God I've reached this place where I don't feel like doing anything. I have absolutely no motivation to return to what I need to do, even though I should. It's just so easy to get distracted and not care about the billion and one things on my to-do list. I just need some comfort-ing words right now from you to make everything ok."

I have no doubt of the possibilities that could come – just a refreshing energy recharge or a sense of optimism that everything is not as difficult as I perceive. What I need in this moment is to let out everything I am keep-ing inside.

"Why do I do this to myself?" I continue in frustration.

"I always think I have everything under control even when I know things are bothering me. I assume I'm a superwoman who can hold the weight of these burdens, but I don't need to do this alone. And in these moments when I feel like I am dealing with personal problems on my own, I'm really not."

I'm at awe with what I discover about myself when I take the time to just sit and observe. A lot of people are afraid to do so because they fear of what is unearthed, but it's so important. It's scary to ask the question: *Do I know who I am? Do I really know?* Sometimes I don't. Every now and then, who I think I am doesn't match the person I know I should be and who I know God wants me to be.

Why am I inconsistent? I always feel like I'm changing personas, that I'm one way with a group of friends and different my family and people I don't really know. I realize I'm not going to be the same person with a stranger as I would be with someone I've known for a year, but it bothers me sometimes. Why can't I be constant everywhere I go?

The answer to this question comes with the small, inspired thought: *be-cause that's how I was made.* Everyone's personalities come out depending on who they're with. Just like air and water are two different elements, these e-lements have their own distinct characteristics. They can work to-gether to create something new, but they are always meant to be different.

I know that's how I am as well. I have diverse characteristics about me that don't always match, but when I combine them, they still shape me.

Those different traits come at appropriate times, but that doesn't make me unfaithful to myself.

I snap out of my thoughts and look at the peaceful scene in front of me.

"Thanks, God." I whisper in humility at what was revealed. I continue to sit and just stare, this time paying particular attention to the water and the breeze and how they complement each other. The water seems to form a mist as it brushes against my skin, its coolness alleviating the warm effects of the summer day. I didn't notice the sun going down, signaling it was time for me to return to the work ahead.

In the hour I spent rediscovering myself, I had the intention of merely finding strength to complete what I started, and I did receive it to some extent. Learning about myself gave me the courage to do anything I set my mind to—now and in the future. I stand up, glance at the pond once more, and walk away.

Safire Arista Lieurance
Fort Gratiot, MI,USA

The Mundane Condition
By Safire Arista Lieurance

To dwell on what is set in stone seems to be the nature of humans. The things we know we have no hope in changing, things we have no effect on in anyway- they are the things our sad hungry eyes settle on. To live in the moment or to live the happiest this moment will allow is just not an instinct to us mundane creatures. We linger over depressed thoughts our mind seeks, and we do pity ourselves for them. We pity ourselves- for a self-inflicted torture. What madness is this?

To live in fear is a sad life; wasted on staring forlornly at the inevitable. Why linger on what cannot be changed when you can smile in the rain that pours down to wet your cheeks? When you can see with your own two eyes the beauties that hide in every pain? I try to see the best in people and in life- if I only live once am I doing how I would want to? If I died tomorrow would I be pleased with yesterday? Each morning we wake is a miracle, a new day, a new chance for a journey! Yet when we awaken to the screaming alarm and roll out of our crumpled blankets we silently curse the sun for rising. We whine for hours of our poor tired condition, and we mope. We are depressed in nature- humans. The average is very negative, and the sad part? We don't even see this as sad or wrong. It is a norm, a custom even. Please, pity you this.

Ambition and success are qualities stressed more than almost anything else in our society. But are they always the key? Eleanor Roosevelt said, "Since you get more joy out of giving joy to others, you should put a good deal of thought into the happiness that you are able to give." This is just a small step towards happiness- but it is one often overlooked. Do something nice for someone today; not only will you realize YOU feel better in doing so- you have made another person feel better. If only each person said, "Today I will be happy," then the whole world may start to smile again.

Joanna Marie O. delos Santos
Philippines

The "Literary Queen", as they called me. I'm the former Associate Editor-in-Chief 2010-2011 of THE BLAZE, the official publication of Nueva Ecija University of Science and Technology in the Philippines. I'm currently residing at M.S Garcia, Philippines. The middle child among three siblings of Mr. Jovito and Mrs. Marita delos Santos. I finished my Bachelor of Science in Information Technology last April, 2011. As a campus journalist, I've been a competitive person and have the passion in writing different articles like news, opinion, feature and most of all writing poems, short stories and novels. In my college days, I've been busy competing in different places in the Philippines with my forte "Poetry Writing" and "Feature Writing" in English language. Before being the associate editor of THE BLAZE, I started as a simple member of the publication being trained by seminars for competitions.

I won 5th place in Poetry Writing English in Regional Tertiary Press Congress in Region 3 entitled *"Somewhere I Called Paradise"*, and for the next year bagged the 2nd place in the same category, entitled *"O thy Waking Youth"*. Af-ter that year, I also won 10th place in Feature Writing category discussing the drug abusing my fellow youth.

Million Times Rejection
By Joanna Marie delos Santos

I know the feeling of being rejected. Yes, because I've been rejected a thousand times since the night I was born until the years of staying at the academe. I didn't want the feeling of being rejected, it feels like as if I am an idiot, an idiot that for almost two decades of my life, I grew up as if I gained nothing – as if I learned nothing but foolishness. If I have to count the times and to tell all the scenarios I've been through with the people who did nothing but to hurt my feelings by the rejection they made to me, one day was not enough. Why? Because even the small rejection when I was young would have to be counted; the childhood days that even the simplest thing can bring happiness to everyone, the day that we owe nothing to anyone for the mistakes we made, and the time that only candies, chocolates and toys would stop us from crying. This is also the stage of my life when I got my first ever rejection. I remember I said *"Uy! Laro tayo?"*(*"ei, let's play?" in English*) then I would show my Barbie doll to my playmate only to feel the disappointment when she replied *"Ayoko nga! Di tayo bati."*(*"I didn't want to play with you, I didn't like you!" in English*)

A funny scenario way back childhood days. But still, it's a rejection. The only difference was that, it didn't hurt that much. But for as someone who went to school for a decade, I know I have acquired the skills and knowledge that is needed to gain respect and praises from others. This is me. I am a person with dignity and principles to believe in. I will respect people if they will respect me, because this is what I am. I don't care if people will judge me and tell me that I am living in the world with tangled rules. Anyway, I'm not here on earth to please them but I am living because of my pri-de.

For sometimes, I really feel offended when people criticize me for *"being vulnerable"*, and then they will come just to tell me that all people feels rejected too! I just always fake a smile and appreciate their sympathies even if I felt exasperated. I could still remember the time when I was on high school. I took a qualifying exam to be part of a prestigious organization of our school. I took the exam together with my friends, only to find out that I am the only one who did not passed the qualifying exam. My friends and teachers expected me to pass that exam than anyone else, that's why they were even shocked too. I felt deprived at that moment – as if I was numb! The feeling was very destructing to the point that I carried it inside my pocket where ever I go, and it's hard to move on. That had made me wondering if I am really an idiot.

There even came a time when I felt like I needed to double the time for studying my subjects, and to always check and review what is already been done to improve the craft I possess. I am afraid for another big rejection, that's why I obliged myself to leave mundane and alter it with careful living. I thought I would never experience big rejection, that I would never interfere with those people who only know was to hurt my ego and pride. I thought I am matured enough to accept the reality that I am not the only one who suffer from the rejection of others, but I am also that *"person"* who sometimes refuse others, so I would hurt them too. But the worst thing, this is me as I have said. I always give importance to my feelings and unfortunately I was wrong with my thought.

I decided to run as a student council in our university when I was second Year College. That was one big decision I made because *"study"* is what I am talking about here. I must give 50-50% to study and student government. Who told you that campaigning in school was easy? It was like one big political crap that must be done to convince other people – to vote for you. It was a true campaign. I am not pleased with politicians, I don't even have any in-terest in politics of our country – but why did I let myself be part of this freaking politics in school? It's because I'm an active student who always joins extracurricular activities and organizations that I knew from the very start would help me develop the craft I have and to be competitive so it would help me in my future.

In the midst of campaign, I became very busy. My friends helped and supported me. My parents were there too! It was like I became a crack-brained person. I always have to smile to the students around me just to please them. But the whole thing *"effort"* ended up to nothing. The students rejected me and left me like a looser – as if I didn't passed their standards to what they were looking for a leader, another sigh for that.

But I have to admit. The rejection that I had from the students like me made me realized to decide once more. I gave myself the last chance I need. I told myself that I have to try for the last time to join in one of the organizations in school – to take a qualifying exam of the official publication of the university, to be a campus journalist.

Now, I am a member of the publication of our school. I think that the rejection I had from the election happened was totally a gift for me. If ever I won that election, probably, I wouldn't be able to join the publication. Luckily, I'm here now at my true family.

"The stone that the builders rejected has become the cornerstone". <u>Psalm 118:22</u>

Yes, like a rejected stone that has become a cornerstone, anyone could find their worth to other people - anyone could feel that they're important too with the help of God. I didn't say from the start that rejection do goods nothing. I only said that it really hurt one feelings and pride. But what I love about rejection is that it makes people become stronger, it makes us lo-ve our own self pride and give importance to it, we become smart, we tend to look for somebody who would be sitting-up beside us – who would give their sympathies. We just have to bear in our minds that we are stronger e-nough to face everything even if we experience million times of rejection.

New World, New Addiction
By Joanna Marie delos Santos

*W*hy would some people become fanatic of nothing but purely crap online/LAN game? I mean, I am certainly a diehard fanatic of something and got addicted to novels like Twilight and Harry Potter in which I knew at the very start at some point offers me even a "little" bit lesson. Yeah, just a "little" bit in terms of lesson but the word "reading" makes it a good hobby, right?

I have been trying to accept the reality (because I'm an IT student!) that kind of game was a sort of fun thing. Unfortunately, I found out that my youngest brother who happened to have a failing grade in Chemistry, secretly boosted his self of new discovered hobby; by playing the Defense of the Ancients or popularly known as Dota. I am very annoyed on how my horrified mother took several steps just to hinder my brother from becoming a dota addict. My family was very affected here.

I thought dota's appeal and mania of its nerds were slowly fading away. I was wrong. I can't realize how its popularity drowned its own devotees and turned them into addict monsters (monster after 12 continuous hours playing in front of the computer) that became non-stop headache to the poor parents. How ironic that a person playing dota inclined to have a sudden amnesia. You know what I mean. By forgetting the reality and responsibilities (especially studies) with just a blink of an eye when at last, they are in front of the computer playing the favorite game together the playmate addicts.

Don't be bothered! Maybe it's not yet too late to change your hobby. You just have to be sure first of yourself. Below are reality check (I interviewed dotaholics!) to know if you are one of the certified dotaholics. I hope you're not.

INSTANT BESTFRIEND

First-thing-first, "don't talk to strangers", our parents' favorite line when we're still young. But if you are a certified dotaholic, you might re-fuse to follow that. You are old enough to socialize and be known. Yap! Enter the internet shop and you'll find instant friends, and then play your favorite game: DOTA. Look to your right, and then to your left. A stranger isn't it? Strangers who initially don't know each other can easily become friends through dota. After the game, there are plenty of topics to discuss with your new friends! Heroes, weapons, and tactics (even if you ended up a looser or a winner). Then again, the other day you would play with those instant friends of yours and new strangers would come to join the club! The dotaholics club!

RACING BULLET

I'm not talking about any weapons in Dota here, I'm referring to the "intense feeling" you have when you're playing Dota. You are a certified dotaholic if your heart is racing like a bullet when destroying the enemy's "Heroes". You become excited especially when you are getting the highest score, right? Or you have this nice feeling when other says you're an ex-pert in handling Dota because of the craft you possess. "Pare, galing mo kanina. Expert talaga, game ulit bukas!", commendations from other will urge you to play and play all over again – that made you an absolutely dotaholic! Congratulations!

TRASH TALKER

From the word itself, "trash", synonymous with worthless, waste or rubbish, aside from being a loyal player, dotaholic would never be satis-fied playing the game for many times only. The dotaholic seeks for some-thing that would make the game more interesting, more fun, and more intense – and that would make the other player excited – through trash talking. They said that dota game would never be completed without trash talking. Those trash talkers tend to shout words that sound awful against the other player who happened to be an enemy. They trash talk for some reasons like first: They are leading with high scores and they want to insult the opponents by trash talking. Second, the opposite, meaning the looser becomes the trash talker. Warning: **It may lead to a true fight!**

UNDEFEATABLE HOBBY

Are you getting fatter or hairier? You don't sleep, you skip home works and meals, you even spend half your allowance for playing Dota, zero lovelife (because you believe in DOTA vs. GF and mostly, Dota wins!), you have an installer of Dota, or worst you post the pictures that you captured on your game in Facebook!

If you have all of those above, and you finally end-up with the thought that it is the game and you can't control yourself as an addict, this online ga-me became your hobby and unfortunately it ends up undefeatable. So here, you should admit – you are a certified Dotaholic!

Stephanie Weiner
Boca Raton, Florida, USA

I am Stephanie Weiner, a seventeen year old from South Florida. I have always enjoyed writing, as a means of expressing my "teenage angst" and problems which I thought were huge at the time, but in retrospect seem miniscule. I only truly developed my writing this year. I had an amazing English teacher, who restored faith in myself and my a-bility to write. I also participated in a writing workshop a few weeks ago. I am very busy with my multitude of interests, but not enough time to fulfill them. My eighteenth birthday looms ahead, justifying the sense of independence I have tried so hard to emanate for years. I, like many teenagers, enjoy television, Face-book, and hanging out with friends. I would, however, like to also more serious interests like research, writing, and college!

Lucky
By Stephanie Weiner

*W*e monotonously wonder why the "bad" befalls the good. It seems as though some are just not as lucky as others. I used to believe this and always wondered why; why are some blessed with good looks, great intelligence, and affluence and others with poverty and sadness. We pity ourselves and blame failure on bad luck. However, I have come to the conspicuous conclusion that these virtues or vices do not matter. What matters is the way in which they are handled. This seems simple enough, but it took me a long time to truly understand why.

My 19-year old brother, Adam, was diagnosed with autism sixteen years ago. My parents- both intelligent, auspicious people- swelled with pride and hope for their young son, until it was sadly deflated by this news. Of course, my parents did and always will love my brother. However, this could potentially affect him for the rest of his life. And, undoubtedly, it did.

I looked up to my brother. While older siblings act in a peremptory manner, Adam was quite the opposite. We got along perfectly; he was a passive sweetheart, always looking out for others' best interests above his own. I did not see this as the anomaly that it was. To my underdeveloped five-year old brain, he was a normal older brother. I was eventually mature enough to realize something was awry. I observed the bickering and selfishness of other siblings, each striving for their parents' full attention. I understood that we did not interact like that. Furthermore, I knew that the attention was not evenly distributed amongst us and I was angry. I felt incompetent. Why did Adam deserve more attention than I? I no longer wanted to be independent; I craved their undivided attention always. It did not occur to me that there might be a justified reason for it.

Confusion is an odd experience. I was trapped in my closed brain, blocking off all new information. I was in a car during a storm; lightning struck but did not reach me. It was the day my parents explained to me that my brother had a disability. They tried to explain it to me and help me understand, but I did not. They gave me a book to help me understand, but I did not. I refused to accept what I could not grasp. I vividly remember crying later that day. These tears were not out of sadness, but merely of confused chagrin.

I told myself that Adam is normal. Normal? I do not even know the meaning of the word. Adam is not normal. He has "problems"- or so my pa-rents called them.

The years passed and so did my confusion. While I avoided discussing the topic with my parents, I did extensive research. I Googled like you would not believe.

I wanted- needed- to understand what these "problems" were. Over time I began to notice how people interact and the social aspects of school. I saw most people, and then Adam. He was "weird". He barely spoke and when he did, it was awkward and forced. He had a few friends, but they too were "weird". He was picked on and teased. I was consumed by embarrassment and sadness. As terrible as it sounds, I did not want my classmates to know he was my brother. I was ashamed. On the other hand, I was worried: every single day I worried kids would bully him more so than the day before. By this time, I understood that he was "different" and had "problems", but I could not fathom why; why him?

Though I had concern for Adam, I was primarily being selfish. All the pressure was placed on me, yet all the attention given to him. I felt so unimportant. I was angry that my parents babied him instead of me. I was the younger one! I tried so hard to succeed and make my parents proud. I could not understand why Adam did not try. He could not do simple tasks like tying his shoelaces. My parents always helped him! This made me crazy; I just wanted him to try.

I knew if he tried and practiced consistently he could overcome these "problems". And I was right. By the time I entered high school Adam was a senior. I liked to think I was independent and no longer needed any attention or help from my parents- that was reserved for Adam. If I could do everything on my own, so could Adam. Soon enough, he was going off to college. My parents were extremely uneasy. They did not think he would be able to take care of himself on his

own, even though he would be living fifteen minutes away. This vexed me to no end. I knew he would be fine, as long as he tried. What worried me, however, was whom he would talk to. I did not want him to isolate himself. I prayed he would make friends and be happy.

Adam has now been in college for two years. He has lived up to my exceptionally high expectations. He is blossoming and taking advantage of every opportunity. He is involved in a program for students with disabilities. There are group activities to provide a safe environment for the students to socialize.

Adam attends these regularly and I am genuinely proud of him. Previously, he would have avoided these social situations at all costs. Adam is also succeeding in school, with straight A's. He could have simply given up and blamed his inadequacy on his disability. Yet he has handled it with the finest dexterity. To me, Adam is luckier than most fortuitous people. He accepted his bad luck and worked against it. He refused to fail. He is the strongest person I know and I now look up to him, for my opaque understanding of luck has become translucent.

Kristen Wiggins
Johnson City, Tennessee, USA

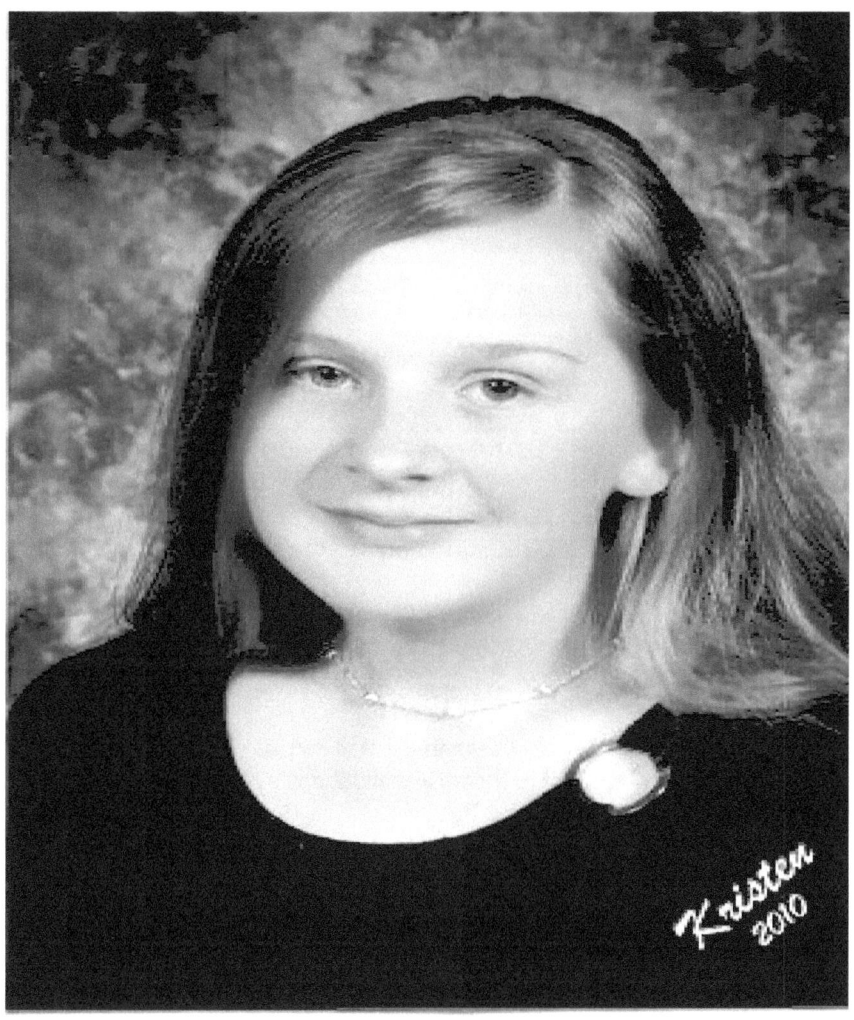

Kristen Wiggins is fifteen and lives with her mother and cat Dusty. She has two brothers and a sister, all are married. These brothers and a brother-in-law are what inspire her love of history and fantasy. She hopes to publish a book that she has been writing along with several other works. Kristen lives in Tennessee, where the mountains and forests also inspire her works. She also hopes to attend college to become a historian and part time author, specializing in ancient history.

Historical

Aegidius
By Kristen Wiggins

*W*hat is the death of a soldier? Our enemies would swear it was justice or revenge. Our mother Rome would say it brought honor and glory to your name and country, but I have learned that there is no glory in having your guts ripped out by the axe of a Gaul barbarian or your head bashed in from the war hammer of a rebel Celt. There is no glory in spilling the blood of a barbarian whom you know was a father and husband. Most of my men thought my brain had been addled from battle I know, but I saw the truth in the bloodshed of Rome. To obtain glory you must live to see your name passed down to history.

Aegidius is my name and I fear that I will not see it live down through ti-me. Some men might set their children on their laps in years to come and my name might be mentioned.

"Did I ever tell you the story of a centurion named Aegidius?"

"Aegidius? No father"

"Aye, Aegidius, it means shield, poor man, he was a good soldier but sadly lived up to his name."

I chuckled from the thought and was instantly brought back to the present. Wracking pain seared through my body as hot, salty blood bubbled up my throat, into my mouth and finally pooled over my parted lips. My story thank the Gods did not begin here but twenty four years ago on a clear and starlit night I am told.

I was born and named Aegidius Octavius Justus, as my father and his father before him. I was born in Rome, as my father was a senator that served our mighty emperor and country. I had grown a robust and head-strong boy but to both of my parents' utter dismay I decided to join Rome's imperial ar-my instead of following in my father's footsteps. I had started as a heavy foot soldier in a legion of the Roman army. It wasn't

easy by any means, I had grown pampered and sheltered my entire life while most of the men a-
round me lives' were the very horror stories that I had been told as a child.

In my first year I did befriend two boys of my age of sixteen. Quintus Fabius Civilis was the son of a rapist who had learned to survive on his own by ten in the world. Servius Vettius Crescens was the son of no one and had learned to depend upon himself since birth. We all served under Legio IV Romanus Draco, The Roman Dragon. Our motto had been the fierce ones. To my dearly beloved parents' even greater horror, I had not joined Mother Rome's army during peace but just as what would be called the Second Punic War began.

Many of my fellow soldiers said that it was a time for greatness of which we would be able to pull upon ourselves as if a simple woolen tunic. Greatness, I had in fact learned, was much more difficult to pull upon one's self and if you did manage it, you also were forced to pull on many horrors.

My first battle had been at Ticinus. News had spread that Hannibal had succeeded in what was thought the impossible; he had successfully crossed the Alps into Italia. General Scipio had rallied many legions to put an abrupt stop to Hannibal and his Carthaginian forces. We were all sadly ignorant for Hannibal had indeed won that victory.

That day something inside of me changed. I fear that after you are forced to see so much bloodshed that it is difficult to return to your previous self. As young and blinded as I was I had not expected such gore and horror. For sure one expects death when a battle comes upon you but I had expected glory and greatness. What I saw was anything but, what I saw brought bile to my mouth and coldness to my heart.

It was during the battle of Ticinus that I ironically stumbled upon the greatness of which I had dreamed of. Carthaginian forces seemed to have been everywhere and it was clear that this battle would not bring victory for our Mother Rome. It had happened as a strike of luck or perchance it could have been fate but it so happened that I was near the great General Scipio when he became injured. It was Quintus and I who pulled the General to safety under the fall of the attack. It took many hours and at several times we became lost or separated from our retreating legions but we dragged the General back to camp.

We were both rewarded for our apparent courage and selflessness with promotions to centurions in a separate legion. It was at camp after the battle that we both learned of the death of our dear friend Vettius. The utter pointlessness of the entire battle turned my heart bitter. The battle of Ticinus was fought only a month ago but now it seems an entire lifetime away.

Because of General Scipio's injuries and the legion's defeat, Scipio's army made to fall back while the General Sempronius marched forward with

an army 40,000 strong. Quintus and I had ridden forth to join Sempronius's army as newly appointed centurions in the imperial army of our Mother Rome. If only my parents could have seen me then, Aegidius Octavius
Justus a centurion, the very thought made me laugh.

So that was where Quintus and I found ourselves, riding the dusty roads of Italia to take our commands. Oh how we must have looked, riding upon tall battle horses, gleaming in silver armor, our scarlet sagums billowing in the wind behind us. On our heads were bronze plumed helmets that according to our ranks was turned sideways as a bloody halo about our heads. On our left sides we now wore our gladius and slung over our horse's backs shown a brilliant, crimson shield. All around me was the color of blood. It was the very color that every Roman soldier prided himself in wearing.

When Quintus and I arrived upon Sempronius's army we were each given a command; Quintus over seventy-four men and myself over eighty-two. Our new legion was called XX Romanus, and our legion's honorary title that had been given by the emperor himself had been Vitrix Vindex, The Victorious Avenger.

Quintus and I learned fast, for we had to. As newly appointed centurions we were required to know battle tactics and maneuvers so that we could command our men perfectly. It was difficult to change yourself from a simple soldier that awaited command to a centurion that your men looked up to for commands. Quintus and I stayed by each other's sides as we trained and marched through Italia for we all knew that a battle was coming.

November passed by slowly and each day grew colder and colder, bringing forth the northern winds. Men began to layer ever article of clothing that they owned and wear their armor all day even when eating and sleeping so to keep in the heat. In the mornings when we woke if you fancied a drink you busted the ice in the buckets to gain access to the water.

Quintus and I rode horses as we marched but I would rather have marched to keep my blood moving, after riding for even a short amount of time I couldn't feel anything below my knees. It was on our tenth or eleventh day of marching that as I rode I glanced up to the grey sky to see snow falling. As soon as the snow started the air somehow grew even colder.

After three days of constant snow General Sempronius finally commanded the army to halt for camp. By now thick blankets of white covered the land. The wind howled with a fierce ferocity and made your very being ache from the bitter cold. Snow was beginning to fall so swift and hard that one could hardly see a hair's breadth in front of you.

I stumbled from my horse as our legion came to a halt to pitch tents and start fires if possible. Quintus caught my arms as I stumbled from my numb legs and feet.

"We best move our legs else we must fear losing them." I handed the reins of my horse to a young man who looked just as miserable as I felt. I clapped my gloved hand onto Quintus's shoulder.

"My friend, I feel as if I already have, how are you walking?" Quintus smiled broadly, revealing briefly his missing tooth that he lost to a Cartha ginian shield that had clipped him in the mouth during Ticinus.

"I marched with the men." I nodded to a soldier who ceased in building his fire to salute us as we stumbled past.

"I was told to stay on my horse so that the men would follow the way easier." We ducked into a tent that had been erected for the centurions of our legion already. Since we were junior to the senior officers we rode at the behind of the legion, but this also meant that camp was usually assembled when we finally arrived.

Inside of the tent was hardly any warmer than outside but it was protection against the raging wind and snow. A table was set in the middle of the tent that was laden with food and drink. Around the table sat our four fellow centurions to our cohort. That evening was spent feasting, drinking much wine and practicing sword play. Outside still raged the bitter weather but inside we all laughed merrily as Quintus and I danced about the tent swinging our swords at one another.

By now December had come and was well under way. The snow only deepened with time so that General Sempronius ordered for the army to keep camp until the snow abated. The snow did stop but when it did Hannibal had made his move. Scouts and watchmen began to disappear, after three days of this an entire patrol of fifty men was found butchered in the forest. I was told that their heads had been severed from their bodies and had been nailed to trees, their hands put in their mouths.

General Sempronius was furious, how dare the barbarians attack our men in such a manner! But the General was wise and would not fight Hannibal yet.

I ducked inside of my tent to see Quintus repairing a strap to his armor. I watched his struggling for a moment before chuckling.

"Here let me, you're only making it worse. "Quintus huffed indignantly before handing the thick needle and strap to me.

"It's hopeless; I've been at this for an hour." Just as he finished his sentence with a sigh I sewed the strap with two simple stitches. I handed it back to Quintus who wore a perplexed look on his face.

"I believe it is you who is hopeless Quintus." Quintus smiled for a moment before staring at his feet.

"Do you think that you will see your family again Aegidius?" I frowned at my hands.

"Sometimes I do, when there is food in my belly and I am lying warm in my bed. But then there are times such as now when a battle is looming close by and there is a fear inside of me like no other." Quintus and I both stared at the ground silently for a moment.

"Do you believe that you will see loved ones again Quintus?"

"I believe that I will see my mother in the next world but I pray to the gods that no matter how much I love and miss her that it will be many years
before I see her." I smiled briefly.

"I never asked, but how did your mother die?" Quintus swallowed thickly.

"After my father was sentenced my mother wasn't the same. I listened to her cry every night; he had been at senate so life had been easy but after my father..." Quintus trailed off." I do not know how many days it was after; it could have been weeks, I'm not very sure, but one morning she didn't wake up." We both sat in silence for a moment. I suddenly stood.

"Well I best be off, Titus will have my head on a spike if I do not send these scrolls to the General." Quintus seemed to gather himself before he smiled.

"I never thought that I would see the day that you would be afraid of Titus." I smiled over my shoulder as I made my way out of the tent.

"I'm hoping to avoid the confrontation."

It was rare that I could ever sleep easily now, so after many hours of trying in vain I was not surprised to see that sleep would not be coming to me this night. Finally, I made my way out of my tent into the biting cold. It was late or very early and the entire camp was silent. Even the wind and snow had abetted after days of complete white. The entire world seemed to be standing still as I glanced up to the clear sky and the pale round moon that hung eerily above the entire camp. This was what my father had called the calm before the storm.

I walked slowly among the tents listening to the silence of the world. My sandaled and cloth wrapped feet crunched through the frozen snow. This was the only sound that broke through the night. After a time of walking through the freezing air I finally made my way back to my tent. After this I soon fell into a restless sleep.

"Aegidius, you must wake." I opened my eyes slowly to see Quintus hovering over me. I blinked.

"What is the matter?" Quintus glanced over his shoulder as I noticed the chaos that was ensuing outside in the camp.

"General Sempronius has given orders for the army to march." My eyes widened as I sat suddenly.

"Under what provocation"

"Numidian cavalry crossed the river this morning and slaughtered many of our outposts; our own Cavalry our fighting now against the forces. General Sempronius has ordered for the main army to cross the river and face Hannibal." By now I was out of my bed and pulling on clothes and shoes.

"How long ago were the attacks?"

"Several hours, the General is raging." As quickly as I could I strapped on my armor and gathered my gladius and scutum.

I stepped outside of my tent to see soldiers forming in their ranks as orders were yelled through the air. Quintus rubbed his bare shoulders as puffs of breath steamed out of his mouth.

"Jupiter's mercy it is cold out here!" I laughed as I pulled my breastplate over my head.

"You will be praying to all of the Gods when we cross the river."

Quintus and I rode our horses among our centuriae as our legion moved forward. Men shivered in their armor as orders were called. It was slow for the army to march forth amongst the trees towards the river. It was several hours' worth of marching in the bitter cold before we came upon the banks of the river. Quintus and I both stared at the clear running water silently. I turned in my seat to watch the men behind us when I glimpsed a flash of silver and red in the distance riding on a midnight horse. I nodded towards the sight.

"Quintus, is that General Sempronius?" Quintus squinted his eyes up to peer ahead.

"I believe so." We both watched the General for a moment before I turned back to face the Trebia river.

"How cold do you believe it is?" Quintus glared at me from under his helmet.

"Are you trying to make this worse for me Aegidius?" I smiled but said nothing in return.

It was one hour more before the army was ready to move. The General and the senior ranking centurions led way. Our legion was ordered to follow, and was bid to start the crossing of the Trebia River. The moment that our horses splashed into the water and our legs were enveloped in water so cold I felt my heart stop, Quintus let out a string of curses underneath his breath. I would have laughed had my breath not caught in my throat and my heart tightened.

The freezing water rushed around us as our horses battled through the swift currents. After just minutes in the water I could no longer feel my legs. I looked back at my men as they splashed and fought to march forward. Some men were using their shields to keep afloat while others were battling the water all on their own. At a point towards the middle of the frothing white river I noticed one man fall underneath the water and not rise back up. Without a thought I reeled my horse around and swung off of the saddle and dove into the water. I gasped as the cold water surrounded me but I kicked my legs to swim further into what felt like Hades.

Just as my lungs began to burn with an intensity that I could not ignore my hand found the grip of the man's arm and I swam to the surface. As I burst out of the water Quintus had a hold on my armor and with one mighty pull had me in my saddle. The man I had saved was heaving and whiter than a corpse. He spluttered and gasped.

"Thank you sir, thank you!" I nodded before pulling my horse back to wards the opposite bank.

"Move on soldiers, let's not let these frigid waters gain the better over us!" It took hours of agony and anguish for the entire army to cross to the opposite banks. Once Quintus and had gained purchase of solid ground we reorganized our men into ranks for attack.

Just from the banks of the horrid river that we were crossing was a wide and flat plain where we could see Hannibal's forces gathering. Quintus slid off of his horse to wring water from his tunic. It wasn't much; most of the water had frozen making our tunics hard and shell like.

Quintus and I reseated ourselves as The Imperial Roman Army of his majesty the Emperor rode forth to meet the Carthaginians in battle. General Sempronius wanted the army to advance in standard formation and in traditional Roman tactic, slow and in good order. Hannibal's forces were smaller, this we could see from a distance, but we were exhausted and freezing. As our army continued to ride forth, Quintus pulled his horse up beside mine. We rode without speaking. I listened to the sound of the soldiers marching.

"If I do not survive, will you take my helmet to my mother's grave in Rome?"

"Of course, and if I do not will you give my parent's my letter."

"Of course" Quintus and I had done this at the battle of Ticinus also, as had Servius but all he had asked was for our memory to keep him.

When the time came that we were to give orders of our attack I slid off my horse to join the soldiers on foot. I took my place at the front of my centuriae, drew my gladius and gave orders. Quintus, I could see out of the corner of my eye had also forsaken his horse. He gave me a deep bow and I did the same. As we still continued to march I noticed a man shaking as a leaf in the wind, as I looked closer I realized that he was nothing more than a boy. When the boy caught my gaze I saw the utter terror written on his face.

"Do not worry soldier, the Gods are on the side of the stronger." He gave me a shaky nod but said nothing. In honesty I felt the same as him, I only could hide it better. I still remembered every moment of the battle of Ticinus, I remembered the blood and the horrors, to know that I would be facing that again, it took all of my strength not to turn and run.

As we found ourselves closer to the Carthaginian forces I could pick out Gauls at the center, Libyans and Spanish forming the flanks and five thousand Cavalry on each wing. Our forces held 16,000 legionaries in the centre, this was where my men and I stood, 10,000 allied infantry forming each flank and 2,000 cavalry on each wing.

The first clashes began with battle cries and swords clashing. The skirmishes had begun on the flanks I could see as our centre pushed forward. Within minutes I could see that our soldiers were lost. I could hear the anguished sounds of battle. When the centers finally met I gave orders to my men, as did every centurion to charge.

The moment it begun there was blood everywhere, I tore my sword through the barbarians' armor that even as I killed them, reminded me of the Greeks. I pushed a soldier to the ground using my shield before with one quick thrust he lay dead. Another soldier I nearly took his leg off, and while he screamed and blood gushed from his wound I brought my sword through his neck.

It continued like this, the blood, the screams. Eventually we found ourselves breaking through the Gaul lines but not before I heard the pounding of hooves and the yells and screams coming from our own men. I turned to see what could have been 2,000 cavalry soldiers between us and the Trebia River. I could almost feel my heart sinking, Hannibal, curse him, had layed a trap, and we had fallen perfectly for it. Men screamed as they broke formation, diving in whatever direction to escape the hooves or our apposing riders.

I forced myself to turn away from this sight and continue fighting. We were to lose this battle also, now that Hannibal's cavalry had literally squeezed our army between our enemies.

It was at this point in the battle that I, covered in blood and gore, found Quintus being held to the ground by a Gaul barbarian. I rammed my sword into the back of the man's knee and he let out a blood curling scream while trying to twist around to face me. Quintus took advantage of this and with one thrust had his sword through the man's chest. The man fell limp and Quintus rolled to avoid the man falling on him. I pulled him to his feet before we were both thrown back into the battle.

We continued to fight side by side as the battle continued. We watched one another's backs as we picked Gaul barbarians off one by one. The battle still raged about us when we heard the cries of retreat. Quintus paused for a moment to look about and that was when the Gaul came from nowhere swinging an axe and screaming as if Mars himself. Without a second thought I through myself forward and let my shield take the brunt of the axe's force. Quintus whirled about to keep another Gaul from coming up behind. I stood there, pushing my shield forward at the Gaul. Then he drew a gladius that had been picked from a dead Roman soldier to swing at me.

I met his attack with my own sword, having to drop my shield, at this same point the Gaul twisted his gladius and with blinding speed was swinging the sword at my side. I managed to partly block the sword, but not before its tip was in my stomach. Blinding pain seared through my body as hot blood seeped through my frozen tunic. I wrenched the sword from me and screamed as I wedged my sword into the Gaul's neck.

Quintus suddenly held a firm grip on my arm as he drug me through the throng of retreating soldiers.

"Aegidius, stay with me!" I held my side as blood continued to gush from the wound. Retreating soldiers streamed around us as I stumbled through the cold. Some still fought, some simply tried to evade the cavalry that was trampling men down.

The pain in my abdomen had increased to such a blinding pain that my vision swam and my head felt stuffed of wool. Now Quintus was holding me on my feet as we struggled forward. I forced one foot in front of the other to keep myself moving. It felt as if an eternity before Quintus pulled me closer and seemed to quicken our steps. Around us I could hear soldiers and wounded men.

"See Aegidius, the river is close by; I'm going to get you home." I nodded mutely, focusing on not collapsing.

Quintus suddenly lowered me to the ground. I opened my eyes slowly to see men collapsed and dying around us, even though we had made it nearly to the river.

"I'm going for a horse Aegidius, wait for me here." I smiled even as another wave of blinding pain flashed through my body.

"As if I could go anywhere else" The moment that Quintus was out of my site I fell completely to the ground and closed my eyes. I listened to the dying men around me, even as others rushed past to cross the river. Moans and cries filled the air along with the rushing of the river. So this is where I find myself now; dying by the banks of a freezing river.

I open my eyes to stare at the grey sky. White snow falls softly from the sky. Maybe it is the Gods way of cleansing the blood from the battlefield. I can feel the cold around me, just as I feel the pain in my own body. I close my eyes and send a silent prayer to the heavens. As I continue to lay here my thoughts grow foggy and the cold seeps into my very soul so that I can no longer feel it.

Perhaps this was the way that I was meant to go. I see neither glory nor honor in battle but perhaps the Gods do, I have not earned the home of heroes but I know that I have not earned eternal damnation for my actions.

I can feel myself slipping even more as I lay here but then I am being pulled to my feet.

Slowly I open my eyes to see Quintus pulling me towards a horse.

"Come along Aegidius, I cannot lose you yet!" Now Quintus is painfully pulling me into the saddle. Blood dribbles from my mouth but Quintus chooses not to see it.

"I refuse to believe that the Gods are calling your name Aegidius, now brace yourself, we are crossing the river now." As Quintus rides the horse into the freezing water my consciousness begins to ebb away. It is the Gods decision, only the heavens will know of whether the fates choose which road my life takes tonight.

Neha Srivastava
Haryana, India

Neha Srivastava has a blend of 14 years of experience in the advertising and Education industry where she learnt how to communicate to people, understand their psychology. Mudra communication was her birth place and she grew up with Equus, Xansa India and then Inbrit in London, then worked as the Regional Training Coordinator with ICFAI University.

At present, she is working as a Full time Mom and a freelance writer. Worked for CRY, INOX theaters etc. She has her articles published in Times of India and Readers Digest. Her job in advertising entailed of writing copy for print adverts, writing brand names and scripts for commercials, at ICFAI she formulated creative training modules and held soft skill training workshops.

Writing adverts, articles, studying human psychology and bringing about changes in individual lives are things she wishes to be part of.

Short Memoir

Sabina
By Neha Srivastava

ometimes life doesn't give us choices,' I thought, as I saw her white toothy smile that overshadowed her dirty face, torn saree and cracked heels. Was this frail lady going to help us settle in our new house? 'Sabina,' she pointed to herself. With a twinkle in her eye, she said would do all my housework for Rs 1000 per month. I agreed, only after an argument as I had to live up to the Indian haggling protocol – her beam widened. She was employed.

Little did I realize that this was a meager amount to change my vision of life.

Opening and settling our luggage boxes in our new house would have been like a climb to Mount Everest but for Sabina, who arranged everything with effortless dexterity. The temperatures were rising steadily but sultry summer heat was not a deterrent for Sabina as she tirelessly cleaned and scrubbed our house. I lay on my couch with the chilled iced tea and threatened her to do her job properly or else...she only responded with a wide smile. 'This time life hasn't given her a choice', I thought. She has to bear with me. I pay her.

As days passed she grew into an integral part of our lives. The bell would ring at sharp 6 AM, whether I wanted it to or not. Hiding under my pillow only made her press the bell more. Her work was like her prayer. She did it with her soul.

Honesty is something that we don't expect out of domestic help in India, but she was an exception. Be it my earrings left carelessly by me or money left in my husband's trouser pocket, it would be promptly returned to us with a little chiding. We got accustomed to her friendly beam early in the morning. Each time I warned her to work properly, she responded with a smile that somehow made me feel really small. Her calm reminded me of my mother's face when I used to throw a tantrum without reason.

The only time I saw a frown on her face was when the door of our two year old baby, Akshat, got locked from the inside. Like any hysterical mother I was howling and calling up locksmiths. 'This is an emergency, I screamed, 'come right now...my voice trailed as I saw Akshat in front of me. Surprised, I hugged him tightly, 'Shabina safed Aki', he babbled. I looked at her. She had a bruised elbow. As I put medicine on her, she answered the query in my eye - she had jumped from one balcony to the other, then to the other and forced open the balcony door and got out 'Pinku', as she lovingly called our son. The monetary arrogance in me broke. I couldn't pay her for this.

After the incident I wanted to understand the roots of her value system. One day she coyly invited me to her 'home'. Jumping over the water drains and slush, I reached her 'home'. It was a modest shack with a tin roof that was like an 'unidentified flying object', on a windy day. She quickly got a chair that creaked under my weight, 'Didi sit, sit'. Her two children peeped behind a torn curtain, as if catching a glimpse of a Hollywood 'biggi'! Soon she appeared with a bowl full of rice 'kheer', an Indian sweet. 'I've cleaned everything properly like you do,' she specified. I looked deep into the bowl to hide my moist eyes. She was so conscious of her status, when that was the last thing on my mind. For me she was someone I owed a lot. For settling our house, for keeping it sparkling, for saving our son...

As I dug into the pudding, she sat on the ground and narrated that she was from a poor village and had lost her parents at an early age, her uncle who couldn't care less, got her married to a lame man, who could not support her. She was the sole bread winner of a family of four. The more she talked the more I realized how much god had given me, yet why didn't I smile as much as her?

How did she manage to smile all the time? As if reading my mind she said, 'I have two choices Didi, either I cry or I laugh'. Her words struck me like a thunderbolt. The two choices are with all of us.

She introduced me with life's biggest choices. And I have never been able to repay her for it.

Neha Shrivastava

Ellie Rowe
England, UK

About Me: I've never really given much thought to myself as a writer, despite having a strong interest in English a subject. I've always loved to read, and am still quite proud of my little seven year old self having a fifteen point three - I never truly got that either - reading age. Despite my voracious appetite for literature, my words never come out right. Fifteen years old, with a very helpful and flattering English department at my school (a small private one in England, where I currently attend on a healthy scholarship), I decided to take a stab at reliving a memory through black and white words on a page. It was much more difficult than I had imagined, yet I enjoyed myself immensely. In my spare time, I volunteer at Cancer Research UK, am a Corporal in CCF (a sort of mini-military thing, which has helped me do cool stuff like fly a plane over my house and shoot a machine gun), practice Shotokan Karate, and talk to my friends a lot. In the future, I plan to attend Oxford and do either International or Criminal Law, but right now, I'm content to enjoy my life just as it is.

The following is a non-fiction memoir from my childhood.

Some Children Are Lucky
By Ellie Rowe

I was going to die. Probably. This gloomy thought struck me in my serene yet surreal state. The water rushed around me, swept me up, down, around and under, like a tiny ant in a giant hurricane. I tried to take a deep, calming breath, but then I realized this wasn't a good idea. I realized this too late - the waves wormed their way into my lungs, leaving me panicked and choking. It was my own fault. How could I have been so stupid, so blind and naive?

We were on holiday, having a good time. Or meant to be. Unfortunately, our pre-booked boat ride of the surrounding isles had been cancelled due to a storm and the unusually asperous, choppy ocean. So, instead, we had a 'relaxing' day in the brilliantly British summer rainfall at the nearby beach. Odd as it may seem, I didn't feel particularly relaxed as I was tossed like a beach ball from one wave to the next. I couldn't survive much longer - couldn't breathe, shout or even swim to safety.

You see, I was at the measly age of four. My mother was a stone's throw away, looking after my eighteen month old little sister. My elder sister and I had run off, as always. We enjoyed playing silly games with each other; 'jump the wave' and 'fairy sea shells' amongst the best loved. Free from our incessant toddler reins we had dashed away with surprising speed, eluding the watchful eye of our anxious mother. She didn't really mind - it was a remarkably safe beach, with mostly families similar to our own and no dogs. Besides, where could I go? I couldn't swim, and hated salt water (one of the numerous problems of sensitive skin, it makes you itch) and it was purely soft sand. Anyway, there were no obstructions - she could see us wherever we went.

Or so she thought. She had underestimated my power of finding trouble anywhere, despite the extreme amounts of caution exercised. There had been a pier. Normally, I had no interest in these - you couldn't feel the sea properly, and you were separated from the luxurious pleasure of feeling sand trickle through your toes. But because the sea was so rough, I was fascinated. I abandoned my sister, who was happily occupied playing hairstyles with another child, and rushed onto the pier. I loved watching the tide struggle to make up its mind, playing games with the land. It wanted to touch the beach at first, bounding up to it with eager, crashing waves; but then it withdrew them sharply, as if burned. This was how it seemed to me with my impressively childish logic.

At the end of the pier stood a metal pole. Always the audacious one, and dense, it seemed, the notion had struck me to attempt and swing around it, coming back to the high pier straight away, but being directly above the sea for the briefest of moments. Of course, this didn't happen. I plummeted straight down, falling fast like a pebble into the deep, violent and vast pool of water straight below me.

So here I was. I contemplated my demise, while struggling to hold on to my wellies. If I was to be put in a coffin, my beloved Paddington Bear Wellington Boots were definitely coming with me. The water sloshed into them, weighting me so I was dragged downwards towards the crab encrusted bottom.

I heard shouting echoing from the safety of the shore. Finally, my mother had noticed my absence. She called to me, warning me I had better hurry up. When she got scared she got irritated; a rare occasion for her. I wished I could answer her. I desperately opened my mouth but found it clogged with seaweed and saliferous water. By this time I was shivering furiously, and terrified. What would happen to me?

Suddenly, I noticed what appeared to be a giant yellow blob speeding towards me. I glanced up, enthralled by the shiny reflections. It came closer and closer, never ceasing in its seemingly fruitless attempts to beat the current. As it drew near, I realized it was a fisherman of some sort, clad in bright yellow waterproofs, which shielded him from the heavy rain. He picked me up in one swift, strong movement and allowed the powerful waves to let us float back to shore. My mother was delighted. She could not thank him enough. I merely grinned at him as best I could with my teeth chattering so hard I thought my skull would smash into tiny fragments. Lisping a "thank-you" from my numbed and purple lips, I ran off to get a warm blanket and hot chocolate.

I was treated like an invalid for days afterwards. My mum tended to my slightest whim - neither of my sisters dared argue with me. In short, I think they realized how close they came to losing me and were being extra nice to galvanize the fact I was still here. My Dad, back in Somerset, called us up especially to talk to me. True to my usual devious nature and scheming mind, which I foolishly lost with youth, I exploited this fact regularly. Regrettably, this had a negative impact and things soon reverted to normal.

In retrospect, it wasn't as dire as I had first thought. In the big blue ocean for approximately a mere four minutes, it had felt like at least ten times that while being battered by the fierce waves. The manager at the campsite said I was lucky; many children had fallen off in low tide and cracked their heads open on the sharp rocks below. I never forgot the frantic screams of my mother as she saw me pulled from the sea like a drowned rat. Equally, I ne-ver forgot that day or that fisherman. I was lucky. Sure, I had been so cold they had me whisked to the hospital to check I didn't have anything severely damaged, I came down with a nasty cold, and the salt water left a hideous rash on my limbs. But the fact remains. I was lucky.

Cynthia V. Smith
Los Angeles, CA. United States

I have been a para-educator for 30 years, most of which were spent in classrooms where students were just beginning to think for themselves and about themselves. My creative writing commentary on how life often differs between cultures and socioeconomic groups was written for middle-grade students, the time when youth questions everything. Adolescence is starting and many children feel insecure about themselves, their relationships with peers, or even their own families and homelife. These insecurities manifest themselves in various behaviors; some children withdraw into themselves, while some overcompensate for their fears by teasing and bullying others. I have witnessed that when bullying begins, prejudice often follows not far behind. I wrote this piece hoping to illustrate to children that intolerance toward *any* group has no place in our world today. Certainly, with tools such as the internet, Facebook, twitter, etc., the world is becoming smaller in many ways, and thus the impact of such negativity is more greatly felt. We must learn to accept one another and celebrate our differences, rather than let them separate us. I further believe that more must be done to inhibit bullying; not doing so only enables the passing of prejudice from one generation to the next.

The Have and the HAVE NOTS
By Cynthia V. Smith

It is an early Friday morning in a wealthy neighborhood in Southern California. Birds are awakening and begin their duty of chirping to awaken others. The street-sweeper has already come by, cleaning the broad, newly-paved residential avenue and leaving it smelling fresh, clean and as black in color as if it had just rained. It is a proud street, lined on either side with stately oaks, whose stretching limbs and leaves meet to form a canopy at their mid-point. They stand as sentries, guarding the pristine front lawns of the 6,000 square-foot homes, each one with a personality of its own, one more magnificent than the next.

Less than three hundred miles south in a tiny, impoverished, Mexican village the sun also begins its ascent. Here there are very few trees for birds to sleep in. Instead, roosters and chickens belonging to no one in particular casually peck and cheep from one residence to another searching for a grain of food. There are no avenues here--only narrow paths of hard, dust-laden, tan earth. Streets are unnecessary as nobody has a car. Besides, a car could never squeeze through the shack-lined pathways that often slope at 45 degree angles in the hilly parts.

"Girls, hurry up! You'll be late for school," an attractive, well-dressed woman calls upstairs from her $200,000 newly-remodeled kitchen. Two girls, one age seven and one age twelve, descend a long, curling, mahogany stairway. Both have backpacks slung over their warm, jacketed shoulders, and earbuds from iPods hang around their necks, almost touching the waist-lines of their new, designer jeans. They quickly eat their breakfasts of scrambled organic eggs, 17-grain, whole-wheat *toast and currant jam, turkey-bacon slices, and freshly-squeezed orange juice, making sure to finish in time so they can get a ride from their father, instead of having to wait twenty minutes for the school bus.*

Five children, ranging in age from three to fourteen, stay under their thin blankets in their small cots as long as possible. Their three-sided, corrugated, tin-roofed home affords little warmth in the cold, morning hours. "Despertanse, niños!" calls a sun-baked, tired-looking woman from another part of the open room. Here, one room is multi-purpose, serving as a bedroom and kitchen for them all. There is also a father in this family, but he has left hours ago to pick strawberries today. The children dress quickly in a failed attempt to stay warm. How can they? The girls have only thread-bare, sleeve-less dresses; the boys have long ago out-grown the length of their pant-legs, their chests covered merely with thin t-shirts. At least the bowl of avena will warm them for a little while, as they walk the three miles with their mother to meet their father in the fields for work today. By then, the sun will be fully awake, and the pickers already there, bathed in sweat, will be anxious for the moon's cool rays to rescue them.

Don Scheer
Boynton Beach, Florida, USA.

Romance Category

How to Attract Women
DON SCHEER

arry Moskowitz was not a happy man, and he wasn't certain why. Something was gnawing at him. *What is it,* he wondered as he sat on his high-rise corner balcony overlooking both the ocean and the Intracoastal Waterway.

He missed his family and the few friends he still had, and the noise of the buses. He even missed the unique rudeness of the waiters at the Carnegie Deli. He missed New York.

But that's just part of it, he told himself. *It's the women! That's most of the problem. I've struck out big time with the ladies. My grandson, Zachary, told me my new Lincoln Town Car would be a widow magnet. He was wrong. The parking lot here is filled with so many Town Cars I can barely find my own in the morning. And it's the men, too. I need some male buddies. I'm homesick and I'm lonely.*

He was about to go inside his apartment to watch the morning news when the phone rang.

"Dad, how're you doing? It's 20 degrees in New York with a miserable, icy rain falling."

"I'm okay, Jeremy. Just feeling a little down."

"Down? Why down?"

"I'm thinking about returning to New York. I was going to call and ask you to start looking for an apartment for me."

"Dad, that's crazy. You've only been in Pompano Beach for three months. What's wrong?"

"I'm lonely. I miss your mom. She played a dirty trick dying before me.

Who ever heard of a wife dying before a husband? It's not fair!"

"Dad, what about all the women you've been dating? The last time we spoke you told me you were the geriatric Brad Pitt of South Florida. What happened?"

"I'll tell you what happened. I've had some dates, and I don't want to see any of them again."

"What about the nice Italian woman you told me about?"

"Angela. Yeah, she was nice. A widow. I kind of liked her, and I saw her three times, but each time I learned more about her family. Her daughter has a drug problem and is back living with Angela; she is supporting both her and a thirteen-year-old granddaughter."

"And Angela's son has yet to find himself, even though he's 48. She's helping support him, too, *and* his wife *and* three kids. I thought. Who needs such problems? I want peace and quiet. If I get more involved with Angela, I'll be driving the daughter to rehab and supporting her son, so I cut that off quickly."

"Okay, Dad, but there were other women, too. What about them?"

"Yeah, there was Marlene. She was okay. She was intelligent, and she looked good. We were having a good time talking at dinner when she told me, out of the blue, that since her menopause she's lost all her sexual desire which is a big change in her life because she used to love sex. I almost choked on my brisket."

Then she told me that her OB/GYN said if she wants to get sexy again, he'd give her hormone shots, and she'd be back in the saddle as good as new. And then she gave me a wink. I couldn't get the evening over with fast enough. The nerve of that woman! So forward. Took all the excitement out before I even got interested. So good-bye to Marlene."

"You told me you were going to have a date with a woman named 'Lila.' What happened to her?"

"That was 'Leila.' She was supposed to be a perky and sassy blonde in her early sixties. I can't argue with the perky and sassy, but she was well into her seventies. All these women lie about their ages. She looked like a poster girl for osteoporosis."

"Now, Dad, that's mean. It's not like you. I'm sure she was a nice lady."

"Yeah, she was nice. Perky, sassy and nice, but way too old for me. I don't want to date young women. I can't even talk to a woman who doesn't know who Betty Grable and William Bendix were. I'm not a dirty old man, but I have to have a woman with pizzazz, some style. You know, someone like your mother, God rest her soul."

"Dad, maybe you should back off from women for a while. Don't push it. You'll meet someone. Hang out with the guys for a bit."

"Guys? What guys? Guys over 65 are an endangered species down here. I've tried to meet guys. One day I went to the clubhouse in my complex to play poker and I quickly found a game with three gentlemen more or less my age. In twenty minutes these poker buddies were in a deep sleep while I was left holding an inside straight. Guys down here that aren't drooling and being led around by a Jamaican lady they call 'Mommy' are hard to find. This getting older is not for sissies, Jeremy. I'm having a tough time."

"I've struck out with the ladies, I have no male buddies, I'm lonely as hell, and I want to go back to New York. I was told that the odds were good for meeting women in South Florida, but no one told me that the goods were odd."

"Dad, give it another few months. I promise you it'll get better. You're a good-looking man, you still have all your hair, you're only 68 years old, you can still drive at night, and you're in good shape money-wise. Give it a chance. Good things will happen. I'm late for an appointment now, but we'll talk tomorrow. Remember, it's 20 degrees with freezing rain in New York. Bye, Dad."

Moskowitz hung up the phone and went inside his apartment. He turned on "*Regis & Kelly*" but it was a repeat, so he flipped through the channels and found a National Geographic show on birds. *Fascinating photography*, he thought. *Amazing how they get those close-up shots.*

The show was a segment on the breeding habits of the frigate bird. The male, which is dark brown or black, has a red pouch below his bill. To attract females he picks a clear site on land, puts a few twigs down and sits, inflating his pouch like a toy balloon. The pouch becomes very large and bright red.

Moskowitz watched as the male frigate bird sat, inflated his pouch and waited. Soon females came flying in. They couldn't resist that red pouch. It seemed to work every time.

The frigate bird segment was followed by a piece about a baboon troop in Gabon, Africa, which showed how male baboons form alliances to foster their status and increase the number of females in their harems. So as not to provoke a fight and to show their friendly intentions, a male baboon approaches another male very slowly and cautiously, and when they are almost side-by-side, he simply reaches over and gently pulls the male's penis. If the male responds in kind, an alliance is formed, and the two baboons become brothers within the troop.

Long after he turned off his television, Moskowitz couldn't stop thinking about the frigate bird. *A few twigs, a red pouch and that bird gets all the females he needs. Doesn't seem fair.* Then he had an idea. *It could work*, he thought.

He left his apartment, found his Lincoln Town Car, and drove to Kmart where he bought six gigantic red balloons. He spent the rest of the day blowing them up. Under cover of darkness he securely attached all six balloons to his balcony railing so that they fluttered in the ocean breezes. Then he went to sleep.

At 8:00 o'clock the next morning, his phone rang.

"This is Mrs. Anderson of the condo association. Are you the gentleman with the red balloons on his terrace?"

"I am," answered Moskowitz proudly.

"It's against condo regulations, Mr. Moskowitz. I'm afraid the balloons will have to come down."

"I've read the condo regulations, Mrs.Anderson, and there's not a word about balloons."

She laughed. "I'll show you the exact paragraph of the regulations that covers balconies and what you may have on them."

"Okay," said Moskowitz. "I'm ready. When can you come?"

"I'll be there at 9:00."

"Fine. I'll be here."

He showered and shaved, put on his white trousers, blue denim shirt, a red ascot and a red silk smoking jacket that his late wife Ruth used to call his "Ronald Colman jacket." He waited for Mrs. Anderson.

At 9:00 o'clock exactly the doorbell rang. Mrs. Anderson was an attractive brunette in her mid fifties. She was accompanied by two pleasing-looking women from the condo association. They all smiled.

Moskowitz smiled too, invited them in, and asked them to sit down. *It's working*, he thought.

Then he stopped smiling as he realized it was going to be much tougher to find some good male friends.

THE END

Don Scheer
Boynton Beach, Florida, USA

Historical Category

Diplomacy
By Don Scheer

*W*hen we lived in Bangkok, Thailand, my wife Susie and I went to the movies once a week. And once a week we came close to causing an international incident.

Before the main feature is shown, photographs of the Thai King and Queen appear on the screen while the Thai National Anthem is played. Everyone in the theatre stands as a sign of respect. The Thais, although a very tolerant people, have little tolerance for anyone who is disrespectful to their much revered King and Queen.

The first time we went to the movies, Susie and I stood up along with everyone else. The Queen's photograph looked good. Queen Sarit is a beautiful, regal-looking woman, but the King looked a bit nerdy and seemed to be cross-eyed. His looks, the fact that his name was Bommyballs, and the cacophony of the Thai National Anthem which to the Western ear sounds like an inharmonious combination of musical tones that may be likened to the music of Spike Jones struck us as hysterically funny.

Since I was a Foreign Service officer assigned to the American Embassy and an advisor to the Thai Minister of Health who is the equivalent of a Presidential cabinet member in the United States, it wasn't a good idea to be laughing hysterically in public at the King's photo while the Thai National Anthem was playing. My wife also realized that laughing at this moment was a giant no-no and, Lord, we tried to keep our faces straight. We held hands and squeezed each other's fingers while we bit our lips. I kept thinking of my briefing at the State Department in Washington prior to my departure for Thailand, where I was told how sensitive my position would be due to the fact that the United States was drastically reducing financial aid to the Thai Health Ministry after many years of strong support. The State Department's budget had been cut; monies instead were pouring into the Vietnam War.

This was 1968 and Laos was leaning towards communism. Cambodia and Burma had broken off relations with the United States. Thailand alone in Southeast Asia still supported United States policies. I was told not to irritate anyone in the country, not even a cab driver. "Be the most tactful diplomat you can possibly be."

But the National Anthem droned on while tears of laughter dripped down our cheeks. Somehow we got through it, our laughter unnoticed, we hoped. The music ended and the King and Queen's photos disappeared. We were okay until the next movie a week later.

I would whisper to my wife as we entered a theater, "Don't do any laughing." And, of course, as soon as the National Anthem began, she was convulsed with laughter. The King's photo appeared, and all we could see was his cross-eyed stare, and all we could think of was his name, King Bommyballs, while the Spike Jones music played away. Susie's hysterics caused me to laugh also, but with lots of finger squeezing and lip biting all under the cover of a darkened theater, we managed to get through movie after movie. just hoped no one from the Thai government had seen us laughing, and that I wasn't transferred out of the country in disgrace; we both loved Thailand and harbored no disrespect for either the Thai people or the Royal couple.

Even though I was an advisor to the Health Minister of Thailand, I purposely avoided advising him – he was twice my age and had received his degree from Harvard – or advising anyone else until I had a command of the Thai language. This was unusual. Most American advisors began giving counsel as soon as their planes arrived and walked down the gang-plank at the Bangkok Airport.

Despite the fact that I studied Thai for an hour every morning at the Embassy prior to the beginning of my work day, it took me a full six months to become comfortable with the language.The Thai language is tonal. It's easy to learn sufficient words to cope with everyday situations if one can filter out and separate the subtle tones of the language. While my hearing was excellent in those days, I was nevertheless tone deaf and had lots of difficulty sorting out the nuances of sound. Lots of words sounded the same to me but had totally different meanings. Early on when I tried to order a silk shirt, I actually asked for a tiger with French cuffs. Also my Thai was very formal. I addressed everyone as though they were royalty in a stiff, bookish way which resulted in great peals of laughter from taxi drivers and waiters who were used to being addressed all day long in the bluntest manner.

But suddenly after six months, I began to hear the tones. My proficiency with the language became pretty good. I dropped the affectations and began to converse with folks. I was now ready to give some advice when the situation called for it.

One day I attended a session at the Thai Ministry of Health concerning the purchasing of vehicles for use in remote rural areas for the Thai malaria program. The vehicles used for the past 20 years were either U.S. Jeeps or English Land Rovers, neither of which was very good during the long rainy season when the red clay roads washed out and were impassable. In some areas the only methods for delivering vital supplies were the occasional elephant or water buffalo.

New vehicles were paid for by the Thai government, a large expenditure. Some 200 vehicles needed to be phased out, and at five to seven thousand dollars apiece, this was a serious purchase for the Thais, but a necessary one.

In a discussion of the problem, I sat at the large table with a dozen Thais. The Minister of Health, Dr. Samboon, was present along with several of his top aides. In similar meetings in the past I had politely declined to offer any suggestions, but today when it was my turn to speak, I suggested, *in Thai,* that they should consider the initial purchase of 200 motor bikes with heavy duty off-road suspension and mountain tread tires because these vehicles were relatively inexpensive to purchase and maintain and would be able to traverse the washed out roads during the rainy season.

I also mentioned that the cost per unit was approximately five percent of the cost of a Jeep. "Of course," I added, "the bikes would not be able to carry equivalent levels of supplies as the Jeeps, but could provide sufficient levels to keep the malaria program going during the monsoon rains."

There was silence in the room. This was my first piece of advice, and I had presented it in Thai, something I found out later no American had ever done before. After a brief discussion Dr. Samboon said in English, "Let's do it. Let's request bids for 200 motor bikes. It's an excellent idea that sounds worthwhile to pursue. If the bikes work, we'll order another 1,000."

Well, I was feeling pretty good. If the motor bikes were to be purchased, it would save the Thais considerable funds over the purchase of Jeeps or Land Rovers, plus my advice was presented in the Thais language which was well received as a sign of respect to these proud and sensitive people. It was a diplomatic coup, a way to keep our relations with the Thais solid.

Six weeks later we met again, this time in a large auditorium to open the bids which had been submitted. Three submissions were deemed appropriate; they met the given specifications. The three bids were from Vespa of Italy, BMW of Germany, and Suzuki of Japan. The Thais and I were seated on a small stage in the auditorium while the company representatives and delegates from the Italian, German and Japanese Embassies were seated in the auditorium viewing the proceedings.

The bids were analyzed and Vespa exceeded all of the specifications required plus had a much lower price than either BMW or Suzuki. The choice was simple. After a brief discussion among us on the stage, the Thai Minister of Health announced that the winning bid was Vespa of Italy.

The delegate from the Japanese Embassy leapt to his feet. "Excuse me," he bellowed. "I have a question for you."

"Yes," said Dr. Samboon. "I'd be happy to answer any questions."

"Good. Then answer this: Do you know what your country's biggest export item is?"

Dr. Samboon walked to the edge of the stage and smiled at the Japanese delegate. "Yes, sir," he answered hesitantly. "Thailand's biggest export item is bananas."

"That's right!" shouted the Japanese delegate. "And do you know what country buys most of your bananas? "The delegate's voice was low and menacing. He pointed to Dr. Samboon and repeated the question quickly. "Who buys your bananas?"

Dr. Samboon, still smiling politely, said, "The biggest purchaser of Thai bananas is Japan."

"Good," said the Japanese delegate. "Let me tell you, Dr. Samboon. If you don't buy our bloody motor bikes, we don't buy your bloody bananas. Do you *kowjai*?" He used the Thai word for "understand."

Dr. Samboon's smile quickly disappeared. "I think I kowjai, sir. Let me discuss the matter with my colleagues."

Dr. Samboon returned to the table where I was sitting with several of his top aides. In rapid Thai he said, "I will no longer be the Minister of Health if we don't buy the bloody Japanese motor bikes, so we must change the winning bid."

I was not happy. The Vespa was clearly a better bike and I wanted the motor bikes to perform well in the field. I wanted my idea to become a success.

As I left the auditorium, Dr. Samboon, a short, balding man in his late 60s, put his arm around my shoulder and pulled me aside in the hallway. "Not to worry," he said to me. "The Suzukis will do fine, the Japanese will continue to buy our bananas, and my country will continue to support American policies in Southeast Asia. Also, I'd like to add that we appreciate your efforts on our behalf, and your Thai isn't bad either."

"Thank you," I said. "It means a lot to me to hear you say that."

"I only have one suggestion and hope you don't mind me mentioning it."

"No, of course not, Dr. Samboon. What do you have in mind?"

"I suggest when you and your wife go to the movies you hang out at the popcorn counter for a while until the main feature begins. Kowjai?"

I told Dr. Samboon that I kowjaid.

CONTENTS

Non Fiction

www.ingramcontent.com/pod-product-compliance
Lightning Source LLC
Chambersburg PA
CBHW020339180626
46812CB00001B/268